THOMAS A. R. NELSON
OF
EAST TENNESSEE

BY THE SAME AUTHOR:

Political Reconstruction in Tennessee, Nashville, 1950.

A portrait of Thomas A. R. Nelson by Samuel Shaver, owned by Mrs. Charles M. Austin of Washington, D.C., Judge Nelson's granddaughter, and in the possession of her daughter, Mrs. J. W. Johnson, Jr., of Lookout Mountain, Tennessee.

THOMAS A. R. NELSON
of
EAST TENNESSEE

By

THOMAS B. ALEXANDER

Published by

TENNESSEE HISTORICAL COMMISSION

NASHVILLE

TYPOGRAPHY, PRINTING, AND BINDING IN THE U.S.A. BY
BENSON PRINTING COMPANY, NASHVILLE, TENNESSEE

Members of the Tennessee Historical Commission

1956

Daniel M. Robison	Robert H. White	Mrs. John H. DeWitt
Chairman	Vice-Chairman	Acting and Assistant Secretary

EXECUTIVE COMMITTEE

Mrs. Penelope J. Allen Chattanooga	Francis B. Warfield Nashville
Miss Mary U. Rothrock Knoxville	Walter Chandler Memphis
Miss Zella Armstrong Chattanooga	Robert H. White Nashville
Vernon Sharp, Jr. Nashville	Seale B. Johnson Jackson
Roy W. Black Bolivar	Marshall Wingfield Memphis

OTHER MEMBERS

Lois D. Bejach Memphis	Mrs. John Trotwood Moore Nashville
J. P. Lawrence Nashville	John T. Gray Brownsville
Ernest H. Boyd Cookeville	Z. Cartter Patten Chattanooga
Mrs. L. W. McCown Johnson City	Stanley F. Horn Nashville
Gordon Browning Huntingdon	W. Bruce Turner Columbia
Robert A. McGaw Nashville	Robert L. Kincaid Harrogate
Prentice Cooper Shelbyville	William R. Webb Bell Buckle

Ex Officio

FRANK G. CLEMENT, *Governor*

QUILL E. COPE, *Commissioner of Education*

v

To My Mother
Mary Sanders White
and
To the Memory of My Stepfather
Bennie Edward White

Preface

The years from 1824 to 1873 brought to the United States a procession of issues affecting the very life of the nation as well as its self-imposed mission to make democracy a shining example in the world. Tennessee played a role of great significance in these decades, furnishing three Presidents whose administrations came to symbolize vital aspects of the nation's development: Jackson and the triumph of the common man, Polk and manifest destiny, Johnson and the ordeal of the Constitution.

Thomas A. R. Nelson of East Tennessee became a leader and a conservative early in this crucial epoch, and for more than a third of a century his leadership and his conservatism were measured against exacting yardsticks. First, the political upheaval disrupting the Jeffersonian party presented Tennesseans with the necessity of decision without the comfortable signposts of traditional loyalty. Nor was there opportunity to go along with the majority because the voters of Tennessee divided almost equally between the Democratic and Whig parties. Then sectional issues shouldered their way into the forefront and were compounded by expansion to the Pacific. Political nativism, involving basic policies of immigration, naturalization, and religious toleration temporarily rushed into the near-vacuum created by the collapse of the Whig national organization under the impact of rising sectional strife. As a Whig leader, Nelson was necessarily involved in difficult decisions concerning this Know-Nothing successor to the Whig party in Tennessee.

In mid-career Nelson was plunged into one of the fiercest phases of the 1861 conflict between Unionism and Southern separatism to be found anywhere in the nation. And during the ensuing Civil War he was trapped in a bewildering twilight zone that would yield to no scrutiny whether it was sunrise or sunset for the Union. At no time was his passionate search for the conservative course frustrated by such insuperable barriers as in these war years. Victory on the battlefield proved only prelude to the vital struggle over constitutionalism inherent in the Reconstruction controversy, and Nelson was challenged to devote both legal and political talents in support of conservatism and Andrew Johnson's dogged defense of the Constitution.

Nelson's last political act, undertaken in 1872 "with the frank fearlessness of a statesman," was called forth in behalf of conservatism during a period of fluid party lines and talk of new parties not unlike the first political contest in which he had actively participated thirty-six years earlier. Through it all he sought to lead with wisdom and to deserve the confidence of his followers.

Unfortunately, the large collection of Nelson's correspondence has been stripped of personal, family letters. No correspondence between

Nelson and either of his wives or between Nelson and any one of his children remains available except for two childhood letters from a daughter and one from Nelson to his youngest daughter. If any of these letters are extant no clue has been found to their location. It is for this reason that Nelson as a private person fails to emerge as distinctly as might be desired.

The assistance so generously provided by many friends and colleagues is deeply appreciated. My wife, Elise Pritchett Alexander, and my colleague, Professor George A. Rogers, furnished invaluable assistance at the first stage of writing. Miss Lucille Phillips undertook to provide a clean typescript from the reworked first draft, and Miss Tommie Jean Corbett typed the final draft from an extensively revised copy. Numberless corrections and suggestions based on a critical reading of the entire manuscript have been offered by Professor Frank L. Owsley of the University of Alabama, Professor Stanley J. Folmsbee of the University of Tennessee, Professor James W. Patton of the University of North Carolina, Mr. Paul M. Fink of Jonesboro, Tennessee, Miss Martha L. Ellison and Miss Pollyanna Creekmore of the Lawson McGhee Library, Knoxville, Tennessee, Professor Harold Steele of West Georgia College, Professor Roy F. Powell of Georgia Teachers College, Miss Mary McCain of Birmingham, Alabama, Dr. Dan M. Robison, Tennessee State Librarian and Archivist, and Dr. Robert H. White, Tennessee State Historian.

Grateful acknowledgments are made to Miss Hassie M. McElveen, Librarian of Georgia Teachers College, and to her staff and the staffs of the Library of Congress, the Lawson McGhee Library and the University of Tennessee Library, Knoxville, the Tennessee State Library, the Carnegie Library, and the Joint Universities Library, Nashville, and Duke University Library, Durham.

Mr. Joe McCoy of Jonesboro graciously permitted an examination of Nelson's home and its photographing. Portraits of Nelson and members of his family were copied with the kind permission and assistance of Mrs. J. H. Stewart of Knoxville, Mrs. Charles M. Austin of Washington, D. C., Dr. and Mrs. J. W. Johnson, Jr., of Lookout Mountain, Tennessee, Mrs. W. W. Carson of Knoxville, and Mr. Tim Pridgen of Jonesboro.

In addition to reading the manuscript, Miss Creekmore and my wife have assisted with many of the onerous details; and Dr. White has provided all of the technical and editorial skill needed to guide any study through the process of publication.

THOMAS B. ALEXANDER

Georgia Teachers College
December, 1955

CONTENTS

ILLUSTRATIONS

CHAPTER I

The Proud and the Pristine

TOM NELSON WAS BORN ON A Roane County farm a day's ride west of Knoxville in the Tennessee Valley, on March 19, 1812. The nation was wrestling with problems created by the desperate struggle between Napoleon and the British and was already anticipating the war that was officially declared only three months later. The Federalist party was dying, and this added fuel to the fires of New England resentment over the policies of the Jeffersonian Republicans, arousing the first serious secession sentiment in the new nation. The throes of political party realignment and sectional controversy would play a dominant role in Tom Nelson's career; but in 1812 the Whig party had not yet entered the American scene and the Union's first ordeal was as far removed in spirit as in geography from the Tennessee frontier land. Nationalism west of the mountains was fanned to a hot flame by the same War of 1812 that almost drove New England to disunion. David and Phoebe White Nelson could never have dreamed what a half century would bring to their remote valley and to the infant son David left behind when he volunteered in 1812 to fight the British as his father had done in the Revolutionary War.

Tom was not to grow up as a country boy because his family moved to Knoxville when he was so young that his earliest recollections were of the bustling, proud townspeople and his father's prominence among them.[1] David Nelson was a farmer and private agent for land sales. During his military service he was chief of patrollers and, upon moving to Knoxville, became deputy sheriff. The following year he was elected high constable of the town. He bought town and farm property and served as land agent for United States Senator John Williams. As constable he imposed many fines of fifty cents or a dollar upon those who galloped their horses or allowed their Negroes to do so within the town limits. Occasionally he had to impose a severe fine of five dollars for

---

[1] Thomas Amis Rogers Nelson was born on a farm known as Eskridge Farm about thirty miles west of Knoxville, according to an account by William G. Brownlow in the Knoxville *Whig*, December 22, 1859. An obituary in the Knoxville *Chronicle*, August 27, 1873, calls his birthplace the old "Meredith Place," as does Nelson's son in an article in the Knoxville *Sentinel*, July 5, 1923. Nelson was the second son of David Nelson and Phoebe White Nelson. David Nelson was born in Rockbridge County, Virginia, on February 11, 1780, to John and Jane Robinson Nelson. Phoebe White was the daughter of Benjamin and Martha Jobe White, and was living near Knoxville at the time of her marriage to David Nelson. David and Phoebe moved to Knoxville between 1812 and 1814. See the genealogical article by Selden Nelson in the Knoxville *Sentinel*, July 5, 1923.

selling whiskey on Sunday.[2] When Tom was five, his father joined the ranks of the relatively few slaveholders of the community by the purchase of a servant girl for five hundred dollars.[3] When the boy grew old enough to understand, he learned that both of his grandfathers had volunteered for the cause of independence in the Revolutionary War; and he never tired of hearing his grandfather, Benjamin White, relate his experiences in the battles of King's Mountain, Princeton, Brandywine, and other Revolutionary War engagements and fights with Indians.[4] Tom was the second child of David and Phoebe; Carrick was two years older. After the family moved to Knoxville five more children were born about two years apart—James, Mary, Moses, Lydia, and Martha.[5]

Knoxville of the boy's impressionable years was a village of less than a thousand people, yet it was the largest town in East Tennessee and had served as the meeting place of the state legislature from Tennessee's admission to the Union until 1812—except for a session in 1807. When Tom was about seven, the state legislature met again at Knoxville for the session of 1817. The chief economic activity was retail and wholesale distribution to the fertile agricultural valley, and the principal problem was transportation. East Tennessee had only one natural outlet, down the Tennessee River to its ultimate junction with the Ohio after the sweeping bend through Alabama and back through Tennessee. But this route was blocked to water transportation by Muscle Shoals, effectively supplementing the barrier of encircling mountains. Most of Knoxville's traffic was by six-horse wagons, bringing goods from Richmond, Baltimore, and Philadelphia over the mountains and down the Virginia-Tennessee valleys. When these lumbering vehicles began the return trip, they were loaded with the farm produce which Knoxville merchants had accepted as payment for manufactured goods. After regular steamboat transportation was established on the Cumberland River in Middle Tennessee about 1820, some of these supply wagons traveled over the Cumberland Plateau between Nashville and Knoxville.[6]

---

[2] David Nelson's activities are indicated by many papers found in the Thomas A. R. Nelson Papers (McClung Collection, Lawson McGhee Library, Knoxville), hereinafter cited as Nelson Papers. See especially papers dated 1811 to 1839.

[3] Nelson Papers, May 20, 1817, contain a record of the purchase of a girl of about eighteen years for five hundred dollars.

[4] Nelson referred to this in an 1861 speech published in the Knoxville *Whig*, June 8, 1861. Benjamin White's war record was published in an article by Selden Nelson in the Knoxville *Sentinel*, July 19, 1925.

[5] Genealogical information on the Nelson family may be found in articles by Selden Nelson in the Knoxville *Sentinel*, July 5, 1923, and July 19, 1925. These articles and others are also to be found in a scrapbook entitled East Tennessee: History and Genealogy, located in the McClung Collection of the Lawson McGhee Library, Knoxville.

[6] Stanley J. Folmsbee, *Sectionalism and Internal Improvements in Tennessee, 1796-1845* (Knoxville, 1939), 10-14.

More than two dozen merchants were established in Knoxville when David Nelson decided to open a general store, and Tom became a part-time clerk in the heart of the town's economic life. Because of the heavy transportation expense, much of the corn growth in the area was fed to hogs and cattle, which were driven over the mountain to eastern markets. The merchants were in frequent conversation about Knoxville's need of improved transportation as the only bar to its becoming a great city, and an early essay of Tom's was concerned with the vital need for adequate transportation facilities.[7]

Knoxville of the 1820's was a stimulating community in ways other than the thriving commerce. Education was unusually popular for a frontier town, probably because of the presence of large numbers of Scotch-Irish Presbyterians, who furnished the presidents of the first three colleges in East Tennessee. Blount College of Knoxville was chartered in 1794 by the territorial assembly as a strictly non-sectarian institution of higher learning; and its trustees included William Blount (governor of the territory), James White (the founder of Knoxville), John Sevier (to become the first governor of Tennessee), and others prominent in the area. After a sporadic existence, Blount College gave way to East Tennessee College in 1807, which in turn closed in 1809. Reopened in 1820 with nineteen or twenty students, the college survived and slowly prospered.[8]

Tom was personally interested in this progress and entered the college as soon as he was prepared. He was also keenly interested in the' Knoxville girls, whose higher education was not neglected, for several were admitted to Blount College between 1804 and 1808. They probably received only preparatory training; nevertheless, coeducation was abandoned in favor of the prevailing idea that young ladies should be taught the finer arts and graces in separate institutions where the "ornamental branches" of knowledge and skill could be emphasized. An attempt in 1811 to establish the Knoxville Female Academy failed; but in 1827, while Tom was attending East Tennessee College, the academy was formally opened. The girls were taught piano, painting, drawing, lace making, and sewing in addition to the ordinary academy curriculum.[9]

East Tennessee College in these years provided the highest education available in the state although it bore not too much resemblance to later college programs. The new building for the college, situated on a hill outside the town, was not completed until Tom had graduated; but the interest in its construction added prestige to the college and stimulated

---

[7] *Ibid.*, 10. The essay may be found in the Nelson Papers under date of August 7, 1828.

[8] Stanley J. Folmsbee, "Blount College and East Tennessee College, 1794-1840," in East Tennessee Historical Society's *Publications*, No. 17 (1945), 22-50.

[9] Laura E. Luttrell, "One Hundred Years of a Female Academy: The Knoxville Female Academy, 1811-1846; The Tennessee Female Institute, 1846-1911," in East Tennessee Historical Society's *Publications*, No. 17 (1945), 71-83.

pride in its students. The faculty consisted of three professors including the president, the Rev. Charles Coffin, a graduate of Harvard. The student body totaled about thirty or thirty-five. The laws of the college provided for strict discipline, admission being based on examination, evidence of good moral character, and a pledge not to use profane language, gamble, behave indecently, or be disrespectful to the faculty. Careful rules of courtesy were required with regard to the professors, and studying was done in the hall except for superior students who might be excused to study in their rooms. Idleness or "bull sessions" in the evenings were prohibited. Bible reading was a daily exercise although the faculty was eventually required to refrain from comment on the scripture because of sectarian controversy outside the walls. Corporal punishment was allowable, and sources of information on student misbehavior were scrupulously protected by the regulation making it a punishable offense even to ask a student whether he gave information to the faculty. Attendance at dancing parties was forbidden until 1839 when the rule was repealed.[10]

The curriculum consisted of lectures and recitations in Greek and Latin classics, French, algebra and geometry, various branches of natural science, several aspects of political science, and in ethics and religion, including a study of the evidences of Christianity. In addition, great stress was placed on rhetoric and debate or declamation. Terms were held in the winter and summer, with vacations in fall and spring. Commencement was held at the end of the summer session, and commencement programs were designed to display the abilities of the students. The commencement program of 1827 lists fourteen items, beginning with the salutatory oration in Latin and concluding with the valedictory oration, presumably in English. Between these, the audience was treated to an oration in French, another oration in Greek, a panel discussion, and two debates. One of the debates, dealing with the question "Was it a more difficult work to establish our liberties than it is to maintain them?" was contested by George Lindsay and Tom Nelson.

While only fourteen, Tom had delivered the first speech of his own composition, at the First Presbyterian Church in Knoxville, defending the right of the Indians to the land of America. Twelve years later he would endorse it with the comment that he had stolen the greater part of it from Robertson's *History of America*, but that he had long since quit the habit of plagiarism.[11] He also saved his essay on "Enterprise," written at the age of sixteen, in which he placed emphasis on transportation. The

---

[10] Folmsbee, "Blount College and East Tennessee College, 1794-1840," *loc. cit.*; and *id.*, "The Laws of East Tennessee College, 1821," in East Tennessee Historical Society's *Publications*, No. 16 (1944), 97-108. These two articles provide very useful information on all phases of the early college life.

[11] The manuscript in Nelson's handwriting, with the endorsement on the back dated September 24, 1838, may be found in the Nelson Papers under date of October 5, 1826.

writing was in oratorical style induced by collegiate emphasis on debate and declamation and displayed a vocabulary that indicated wide reading.[12]

Tom had unusual opportunities to see books because his father handled book sales through his store at Knoxville and also later at Elizabethton. These books came from J. J. Woodward at Philadelphia and included a wider variety than might be expected to be available to even a college student of the town. Since he helped in the store, it is certain that he handled the books and probable that he read extensively in many. The books included many of the better known pieces of fiction such as *The Vicar of Wakefield*, *Don Quixote*, *Tom Jones*, *Robinson Crusoe*, and *Brambleton House;* works of Byron, Milton, Goldsmith, Johnson, Cowper, Scott, Pope, Burns, Addison, Moore, and Shakespeare; and historical works on Greece, Rome, England, India, and America. Biographical works were numerous, including Franklin's *Life*, Boswell's *Johnson*, Plutarch's *Lives*, Scott's *Life of Napoleon*, a life of Wallace, and a book on Scottish chieftains. In the shipments were various specialist volumes pertinent to law, medicine, religion, carpentering, and parenthood. One of the most expensive single volumes was the new edition of a carpenter's guide. Numerous collections of quotations, biographical sketches, songs, and *Gaities* and *Gravities* were included. *Songs for Ladies* and *Songs for Gentlemen* were properly offered in separate volumes, and even humor came collected in a *Galaxy*.[13] Since Tom's later speeches would reveal a familiarity with many historical and literary sources, it is probable that access to his father's book stocks considerably supplemented his college education.

In forwarding the books, the Philadelphia agent carefully directed the manner of sale. He priced each book at about twice what he hoped to get, and David Nelson was to announce an auction at a future date. Then every effort was to be made to sell privately at not less than half price before the auction. Those books not sold by auction time would go at the bidding price, which was sometimes well below half price.[14] Book sales in Knoxville were satisfactory, however, and additional shipments came from Philadelphia. Woodward was anxious to keep up the arrangement when David Nelson moved to Elizabethton.

When Tom graduated from college in October, 1828, his father transferred his business to Elizabethton in Carter County, far up the valley, almost to the North Carolina-Virginia borders of Tennessee, where there was to be little or no competition.[15] Tom's change of residence was a severe shock; for Elizabethton consisted of only a score of families and

[12] The manuscript in Nelson's handwriting may be found in the Nelson Papers under date of August 7, 1828.

[13] Invoices are in Nelson Papers under dates of October 6 and December 27, 1827, and March 19, 1828.

[14] J. J. Woodward to David Nelson, October 6, 1827, in Nelson Papers.

[15] A. M. Carter to Nathan Nelson, January 4, 1828, in Nelson Papers.

had no regular store, and Carter County was sparsely settled as compared with Knox County.[16] There was not even much actual money in circulation, bar iron serving as the principal medium of exchange.[17] For a sixteen-year-old, fascinated by town life, the adjustment was too difficult to be made quickly and the nostalgic memories too keen to be resisted. Back to Knoxville he intended to go, and at the first opportunity.

To a cousin he wrote that Carter County was as desolate as the mountains that surround it and was peopled by a half-civilized race. In detail he compared them to peoples of low civilization. Then revealing a great deal about himself and his early conditioning, he wrote:

. . . To a person who has been reared in a place where he has had the opportunity of associating with persons of his own age, possessing a temperament and disposition somewhat analagous to his own, and having inclinations and amusements which meet his approbation; and moreover having the privilege of occasionally enjoying the company of his superiors, who are persons of intelligence; where he could acquire wisdom from the experience of others and knowledge from observation; the removal to such a place as this, where there are none of his own age who deserve the appellation of civilized, and few whose superiority in years would crown them with a greater degree of knowledge, from whose conversation, and maxims he can derive no benefit but that of observing nature in its pristine deformity; is an event which a youthful mind would most heartily deprecate; and the only alleviation he can experience from the tedious monotony which daily is exhibited, is that pleasure which he derives from an agreeable epistolary correspondence with some of his relatives, his former friends or acquaintances, or his youthful companions and associates . . . . there is an extremely great destitution of young ladies; not that there are no females, but that that there are no girls here, whose intelligence and acquirements, or personal formation, would entitle them to the appellation of beautiful; but if an assortment of ugly, illiterate, simple, and foolish ladies was requisite I would point the inquirer to no other place than Carter County. The females here whose age would pardon jocularity or lightness are as solemn as matrons and ugly as Satan . . . . I would wager that the girls in Carter County never saw a corsette, a buckle, a girth or a circingle and other trappings of genteel females, during the whole course of their existence. I never wish to speak a word to the disparagement of the female sex, and therefore would not let the people here know my opinion of their ladies under any consideration, for I have seldom seen a woman who did not consider herself handsome, and never heard of one who was told she was the contrary, that did not become so egregiously incensed, that she never pardoned the crime. You may think strange, as I was not renowned in Knoxville for my devotion at the shrine of female excellence, that I should take much notice of the ladies here, but I do assure you, I experienced as much taciturn pleasure at beholding a Hebe or an Houri, or hearing the conversation of a girl of intelligence, as any other person could; and was as much disgusted at a fool of that sex, as I would be at an ignoramus of my own. Some how or other when I got in the company of females, my ideas all rushed in upon me in such a confused mass that I never could give them utterance

---

[16] Tennessee State Planning Commission, Preliminary Population Report (Nashville, 1935). See especially the population density maps.

[17] A. M. Carter to Nathan Nelson, January 4, 1828, in Nelson Papers.

and was utterly confounded, vox haesit faucibus as Virgil says, in plain English, my voice adhered to my jaws, and I was of course thought a simpleton, and correctly too.[18]

He also reported that his brother, Carrick W. Nelson, was considering marriage at the age of eighteen to a local girl whose family the Nelsons did not even know. "This mania of boys getting, or wishing to get married at 18, or before they are of age, at least, I am entirely opposed to, and then to cap the climax of foolishness by desiring to wed upon a three months courtship with a girl of whom you know nothing and have never taken the pains to inquire, and of whose relations you are alike destitute, is superlatively ridiculous. May the Lord never infuse into me such a preposterous inclination!!!"[19] Carrick was not impressed by Tom's fulminations, however, for on March 25, 1829, he did marry Eliza Drake of Carter County.[20]

Tom never for a moment abandoned the intention of returning to Knoxville and only a few months after reaching Elizabethton wrote a friend in Knoxville of his determination to return and study law.[21] His new home and position were not quite as desolate as he pictured it, however. An imposing academy building at Elizabethton served as school and church although no female academy was yet established. Common schools had been started in several neighborhoods of the county. More than a hundred families in the county were slaveowners, including Tom's father. Most of these families had only household servants, as forty-seven of them held only one slave each, thirteen more two each, and eight families three each. Another forty families probably held only one or two slave families, while but two slaveholders held as many as four or five families. David Nelson acquired seven slaves in a few years after moving to Elizabethton. He was immediately accepted as a leading citizen of the town, becoming chairman of the Carter County Court. Tom's brother, Carrick, quickly assumed an important position in the community, and was soon to become circuit court clerk.[22] Tom still had his father's book shipments to browse through, his employment as store clerk to occupy some of his energy, and his growing interest in politics to relieve his boredom until he could escape to his beloved Knoxville. While still in college, he had exchanged correspondence with a rising politician of Knoxville, Thomas D. Arnold.[23] At Elizabethton he sub-

---

[18] T. A. R. Nelson to "Cousin," November, 1828, in Nelson Papers.

[19] Idem.

[20] Genealogical article by Selden Nelson in Knoxville Sentinel, July 19, 1925.

[21] Andrew T. Jones to Nelson, December 28, 1828, in Nelson Papers, is a reply to Nelson's letter in which Jones refers to Nelson's letters and writes: ". . . it appears that you are determined to live in Knoxville."

[22] Frank Merritt, Early History of Carter County, 1760–1861 (Knoxville, 1950), passim. This is a very revealing collection of data which includes individual names in many valuable instances.

[23] Thomas D. Arnold to Nelson, July 27, 1827, in Nelson Papers.

scribed to a paper, to be paid for with iron received in his father's store, and indulged his fancy in the composition of a political satire in rhyme that was considered for publication in the newspaper.[24]

The big day was approaching in November, 1830, when David Nelson wrote his friend, Thomas L. Williams in Knoxville, that Tom would leave for Knoxville in January to study law under Williams if that were satisfactory.[25] A month of growing suspense passed before the answer arrived as a Christmas present. Williams, one of the best-known lawyers in East Tennessee, would with great pleasure receive Thomas. The delay had resulted from a month's trip to Nashville. However, an unexpected problem was posed. "My only requisition upon you or him, for what I may be able to put in his way, is a solemn promise that . . . he will not taste one drop of ardent spirits—nor any other liquid tending to produce intoxication. I believe he will be ready to come under such an engagement, and if entered into, that he has too much honor ever to violate it." [26] Tom was certainly not accustomed to drinking—had in fact used no alcoholic beverage since a Christmas drinking bout two years earlier.[27] But he was reluctant to enter into such a permanent commitment. Hoping that Williams would not insist, but undoubtedly with some pangs of misgiving, Tom objected. His father wrote back reporting Tom's reluctance and emphasizing his sobriety and good morals. This time without undue delay the answer ended the suspense. No pledge would be required. Williams had never doubted the boy's character and habits, so "signally manifested" as a college student.[28]

The preparations and finally the trip down the valley were made with excited anticipation. After he arrived and found Williams away, he made approving observation of events in Knoxville and especially of the impressive number of "handsome females" to be seen everywhere.[29] His *alma mater* now occupied its new building, described in the trustees' newspaper announcement as situated "upon a hill at once beautiful, elevated and picturesque, from which can be seen the Cumberland mountain, on the north, that of Clinch on the east, and the Alleghany ranges, on the south, and which is washed by a noble river, shortly to bear upon its bosom, by the agency of steam, the commerce of an extensive section of the country . . . ."[30] Landscaping and fencing the

---

[24] Thomas Stringfellow to Nelson, February 19, 1829; Joseph L. Williams to *id.*, April 21, 1829, in Nelson Papers.

[25] David Nelson to Thomas L. Williams, November 27, 1830, in Nelson Papers.

[26] Thomas L. Williams to David Nelson, December 17, 1830, in Nelson Papers.

[27] Andrew T. Jones to T. A. R. Nelson, December 28, 1828, in Nelson Papers, reveals that Nelson had written him of a drinking bout the previous Christmas and of his abstinence since.

[28] Thomas L. Williams to David Nelson, December 28, 1830, in Nelson Papers.

[29] Samuel H. Watson to T. A. R. Nelson, March 21, 1831, in Nelson Papers, is replying to a letter from Nelson in which Nelson described the events and people at Knoxville.

[30] Folmsbee, "Blount College and East Tennessee College, 1794-1840," *loc. cit.*, 42.

campus were just getting under way at the time of his return.[31]

Perhaps more intriguing was the newly completed building of the Knoxville Female Academy—"handsomely situated and . . . completely finished containing rooms to accommodate two hundred pupils in the various branches of education." A separate music building was also constructed, and another for science was proposed.[32] Thomas L. Williams's temporary absence from Knoxville was obviously no great disappointment to the returning exile, nor did he make too great an effort to discover just when his mentor would arrive. His exultation was interrupted, however, upon receipt of a note from Williams:

I have been at home since last Friday and have expected to meet you somewhere about town, but in this have been disappointed. If you will come to my house tomorrow at 9 o'clock I can furnish the books with which you may begin to study.[33]

---

[31] *Idem.*

[32] Luttrell, "One Hundred Years of a Female Academy: The Knoxville Female Academy, 1811-1846; The East Tennessee Female Institute, 1846-1911," *loc. cit.,* 74.

[33] Thomas L. Williams to Nelson, February 8, 1831, in Nelson Papers.

CHAPTER II

Rarely To Be Met With

NELSON APPLIED HIMSELF VIGOROUSLY to his readings in law under Williams's direction and made rapid progress. His planned period of study was interrupted, however, when financial reverses with the mercantile business in Elizabethton decided him to stop spending his father's money and seek admission to the bar.[1] This scheme he kept from Williams, whom he feared would never agree to the falsehood about his age that would be necessary to gain admission. Obtaining the necessary certificate of good behavior and of age from the county court through another lawyer, Nelson was granted a license to practice before his twenty-first birthday. Williams acquiesced gracefully and commended him as being among the best qualified of young applicants for bar examination.[2] Nelson returned to Elizabethton in the summer of 1832 with his teacher's familiar injunction of total abstinence from alcohol and his prediction that Nelson would rise to usefulness and eminence at the bar.[3] In addition to excellent direction in his study, he had gained acceptance and prestige among the best lawyers of East Tennessee during his year and a half in Knoxville.

Before the end of 1832 the death of the solicitor for upper East Tennessee provided an unexpected opportunity for the young lawyer. The former solicitor's brother recommended Nelson to the governor in his letter of notification of death,[4] and Nelson's family brought many influential friends into the effort to secure the place. Seventeen members of the Knoxville bar recommended him to the governor as having fine talents, industrious business habits, and considerable legal information.[5] Former United States Senator John Williams, brother of Thomas L. Williams, urged his appointment, advising that he had known him from infancy and considered him among "the most promising young men ever raised in the state." [6] Williams further informed the governor that the late solicitor expressed a deathbed wish that Nelson be appointed his successor. Thomas L. Williams, under whom Nelson studied, wrote

---

[1] David Nelson to T. A. R. Nelson, July 26, 1832, in Nelson Papers, reports that an inventory showed the poor condition of the business.

[2] Thomas L. Williams to David Nelson, June 21, 1832, in Nelson Papers.

[3] *Idem.*

[4] Alfred W. Taylor to Governor William Carroll, January 14, 1833, in Nelson Papers.

[5] Knoxville Bar to Governor William Carroll, January 18, 1833, in Nelson Papers.

[6] John Williams to William Carroll, January 18, 1833, in Nelson Papers.

the governor: "His education is equal to that of any person taught among us—and his activity in the business he has shown, is rarely to be met with amongst young members of the bar . . . . Few young men whom I have known, have attracted higher regard and esteem for talents and integrity." [7]

Nelson received the *interim* appointment from the governor and prosecuted the accused in his circuit so energetically as to become unpopular with the less law-abiding element of the various communities.[8] When the legislature met, his friends and relatives used their influence to win his election to a full term.[9] When he sought re-election in 1836, he was defeated by John M. Brabson, a former member of the legislature who had many personal friends in that body.[10] For Nelson, however, the position had served his purpose well in presenting him vividly to the various counties in the district; and he immediately began to achieve unusual success as a country lawyer, the career which was always to be his primary concern. Oliver P. Temple, one of East Tennessee's most prominent men, attributed his own choice of a legal career to the capture of his imagination by Nelson's phenomenal rise to eminence.[11]

A keen ambition to succeed characterized Nelson from boyhood.[12] Advocates of psychological compensation might make a case from the fact that Nelson was slight of stature and limped from infancy as the result of being dropped by a nurse.[13] Also he was unusually timid and reticent with girls as an adolescent.[14] Whatever the explanation, he was certainly fired with enthusiasm for law as a profession and a service to his fellow men, and his young associates remembered him as thirsting for knowledge.[15] His brief period of reading law was supplemented throughout his career by the most exhaustive examination of law and fact in every case. The law was neither trade nor business to him, but a

---

[7] Thomas L. Williams to William Carroll, January 18, 1833, published in the Jonesboro *Whig*, May 12, 1841. Nelson explained in a card he published in this issue of the *Whig* that Governor Carroll gave him the letters of recommendation that had been sent in Nelson's behalf.

[8] Nelson's obituary in Knoxville *Chronicle*, August 27, 1873, commented that he was long remembered as a "terror" to "evil doers." Brownlow, in editorials supporting Nelson, occasionally referred to the fact that Nelson had some enemies because of the vigorous manner in which he fulfilled his duties as prosecuting attorney.

[9] See petitions in Nelson's behalf during September and October, 1835, in Nelson Papers. Letters of recommendation were published in the Jonsboro *Whig*, May 12, 1841, in connction with a dispute between Nelson and Thomas D. Arnold.

[10] Nelson explained this in his card in the Jonesboro *Whig*, May 12, 1841.

[11] Oliver P. Temple, *Notable Men of Tennessee from 1833 to 1875* (New York, 1912), 12.

[12] Charles Scott to Nelson, April 16, 1833, in Nelson Papers, makes extended reference to this characteristic.

[13] Henry M. Ingersoll, "Biographical Sketch of Thomas A .R. Nelson," in Bar Association of Tennessee *Proceedings* (Nashville), Twelfth Annual Meeting (1893), 156.

[14] T. A. R. Nelson to "Cousin," November, 1828; Charles Scott to Nelson, April 16, 1833, in Nelson Papers.

[15] Charles Scott to Nelson, April 16, 1833, in Nelson Papers.

sacred trust, and he frequently voiced the opinion that the liberty of the American people was not that defined in the Constitution or enacted into statute but that which was enforced and secured in the courts.[16] His fervor imparted itself to younger men, influencing them to choose law.[17] He was a fighter in the courtroom and impressed his associates as glorying in the exhilaration that came from legal argument and debate. He vigorously contested ground in preliminary proceedings as well as in critical stages, and he was jealous of the rights of the bar—especially its right to be heard fully in behalf of a client. On one occasion, when a circuit judge instructed both sides to take thirty minutes for closing arguments, Nelson delayed the proceedings for an hour with an earnest argument against such limitation.[18]

However deeply immersed in his profession he became, politics was a vital interest. By the age of sixteen he was writing political rhymes, and immediately upon his return to Elizabethton as a lawyer he served as secretary of an anti-Nullification meeting approving Jackson's proclamation against Calhoun's doctrine.[19]

In 1836 David Nelson and his sons at Elizabethton made a basic political decision on a national topic, although their reasons were probably local and personal. They decided to join the revolt against Andrew Jackson's attempt to push Van Buren into the presidency, a revolt that was the first step toward eventual Whig party affiliation; and they were credited with important influence in making Carter County eighty per cent Whig by 1840.[20] While many interpretations of the rise of the Whig party have been offered, none furnishes an entirely satisfactory explanation without generous allowance for individual leadership and personal motives. Thomas Nelson was active in this 1836 movement to support East Tennessee's own Hugh Lawson White for the presidency, contributing as large a sum as anyone else in Elizabethton toward a public dinner for White and being among the signers of a letter to White praising him as true to Jackson's principles—from which Jackson had himself strayed.[21]

It is doubtful whether any profound thought or basic political or economic considerations entered into Nelson's decision to support White. He was merely concurring with a strong East Tennessee sentiment for

---

[16] The only extended account of Nelson as a lawyer is found in Ingersoll, "Biographical Sketch of Thomas A. R. Nelson," *loc. cit.*

[17] Matthew Nelson to T. A. R. Nelson, November, 1833, in Nelson Papers.

[18] Ingersoll, "Biographical Sketch of Thomas A. R. Nelson," *loc. cit.*

[19] Nelson to Jacob Harding, December 20, 1832, in Nelson Papers.

[20] Merritt, *Early History of Carter County, passim.*

[21] A list of contributions and a copy of the public letter may be found in the Nelson Papers under dates of July 18 and September 20 and 21, 1836. A biographical sketch of White is L. Paul Gresham, "The Public Career of Hugh Lawson White," in *Tennessee Historical Quarterly*, III (1944), 291-318. This article is a brief abstract of the author's Ph.D. dissertation at Vanderbilt University, 1943.

its favorite-son candidate and also honoring the son of the founder of his beloved Knoxville. Other personal contacts, such as the one with Thomas D. Arnold, who was an anti-Jackson leader of East Tennessee, sustained his position. Also the implacable anti-Jackson stand of former Senator John Williams, who had so highly recommended Nelson to the governor, must have been influential. Senator Williams's dislike of Jackson stemmed from his Senatorial contest defeat by the general in 1823. Furthermore, Thomas L. Williams, Nelson's law teacher and life-long friend, was Senator Williams's brother and a brother-in-law of Hugh Lawson White.

Local politics also commanded Nelson's attention, for in 1838 he apparently served as secretary for a citizens' protest meeting in Elizabethton asking the legislature to repeal the town charter of incorporation on the grounds that they were not receiving corresponding benefits. The petition cited that taxes were employed to pay a recorder and a constable, two useless officials in a town the size of Elizabethton. The village was hardly capable of polling fifty votes, and only nine and fourteen had voted respectively in the last two town elections for seven aldermen. The petitioners also objected to some of the laws passd by the aldermen as being "conceived in the spirit of the Blue Laws of Connecticut." Particularly objectionable was a law imposing a fine on any man "who might happen to kiss his wife on Sunday." This petition was favorably received by the legislature, which did repeal the charter.[22]

County school matters interested Nelson during his years at Elizabethton. In 1836 he accepted appointment as county agent to collect the state tax for common schools at a commission of half the allowable amount, and later he became clerk of common school commissioners.[23] At this time the county was divided into ten school districts with the number of pupils ranging from 88 to 213 per district and totaling 1,357. Only men were acceptable as teachers, and one-teacher schools were the rule.[24] Nelson devoted much time and correspondence to this work.

In 1838 Nelson bought a town lot for $100;[25] and the following year his father named him executor in his will. Phoebe was to receive the house and lot in Elizabethton, where the family was living, including the household and kitchen furniture. Thomas was to have exclusive management of the store for five years after his father's death and was to support the family from the profits. At the end of the five years the value of the store was to be divided among the three sons and their mother. The married daughter, Mary, was to gain title to a slave girl she

---

[22] Merritt, *Early History of Carter County*, 51-52.

[23] Robert H. McEwen to Nelson, March 26 and May 9, 1836, in Nelson Papers. The Nelson Papers contain many items relevant to schools under dates from 1833 to 1839.

[24] Merritt, *Early History of Carter County*, 140-42.

[25] Record in Nelson Papers, April 26, 1838.

already was using; and the two minor girls, Lydia and Martha, were each to have a slave girl at their maturity or marriage date. Thomas was to have a slave family of three, and was also bequeathed lands on Indian Creek and charged to support his mother and the young girls if the store would not do so.[26] This suggests that Nelson considered at that time making Elizabethton his permanent home.

The topography of his adopted area predisposed Nelson to favor the rapid development of railroads. Upper East Tennessee consists of a series of rolling-floored valleys lying in a northeast-southwest pattern between the principal Appalachian Mountain watershed on the southeast and the Cumberland Plateau on the northwest. Within the valley system lower ranges running parallel to the Appalachians and the plateau escarpment subdivide the area. These are locally called Iron, Holston, Bays, Clinch, and Powell mountains. The principal streams flow between the ridges or from the Appalachian Mountains and Cumberland Plateau, generally southwestward, forming or joining the Tennessee River near the site of Knoxville. Water transportation on these streams above Knoxville was not suited to steamboats, and by the late 1830's the railroad fever was rising in the region. As early as 1835 Nelson was corresponding with politicians and editors on the feasibility of state financing of railroads and roads since it appeared by that date that Jackson's administration would not sponsor federal aid.[27] The Cincinnati to Charleston railroad project interested Nelson considerably as a way to open the transportation pocket in which the eastern part of the state was situated. He collected and published evidence of its value to East Tennessee and engaged in an acrimonious press debate with a Greeneville, Tennessee, citizen over the relative merits of Greeneville and Elizabethton as points through which the railroad should pass.[28] Acting for a committee of correspondence, Nelson sent a detailed letter to Robert Y. Hayne expounding the advantages of routing the railroad through Elizabethton.[29] Although this visionary project was buried in an uncompleted tunnel into the first major ridge attacked, Nelson did not abandon his interest in rail outlets for his region. Later, the more feasible project of the Virginia and Tennessee railroad, running parallel with the main mountain masses rather than directly across them, received his support.

In 1839 Nelson accepted as a law student in his office a prominent young man of Elizabethton, four years his junior, who had recently graduated from Washington College near Jonesboro. Landon Carter Haynes would be Nelson's most persistent political opponent in their

---

[26] The will of David Nelson may be found in the Nelson Papers under date of July 4, 1839. It is endorsed with a revocation, dated May 16, 1843.

[27] Hiram Daily to Nelson, December 17, 1835, in Nelson Papers.

[28] Green Moore to Nelson, December 20, 1835; Nelson to editor of the *Washington* [County] *Republican* [Jonesboro, Tennessee], February 22, 1836, in Nelson Papers.

[29] Nelson to Robert Y. Hayne, April 18, 1836, Nelson Papers.

congressional district, and in the years to come these two men would represent their parties from every platform in upper East Tennessee in hundreds of joint debates. Haynes was the son of David Haynes, a successful businessman and land speculator in Carter and Washington counties. He was named for General Landon Carter, for whom Carter County was named. The family was recognized as aristocracy in Elizabethton, and Landon was provided with the best environment and education available in the vicinity. Landon had distinguished himself at Washington College as a debater and orator. He was six feet tall, slender, and broad shouldered and was to become recognized as the most polished orator in his legal and political circuit although he could never match Nelson in logical analysis and marshaling of arguments.[30]

It was at Elizabethton that Nelson formed a life-long friendship with William G. Brownlow that was not destined to be untroubled. Brownlow, born in Virginia on August 29, 1805, was brought into East Tennessee and left an orphan at eleven. After distasteful years as farm helper and carpenter's assistant, he was converted amid the emotional scenes of a frontier camp meeting and chose preaching as a career. With only one year of formal study, Brownlow, at the age of twenty-one, was admitted to the Holston Conference of the Methodist Episcopal Church and sent on circuit. For the next ten years he rode circuit in the highland conference which embraced parts of East Tennessee and adjoining sections of four other states. In this rough-and-tumble life Brownlow distinguished himself for durability and ferocity. The Devil, Presbyterians, and Baptists felt his heavy hand as the Methodists engaged in a four-way struggle for the souls of the mountaineers. Meanwhile, he considered himself to be of sufficient importance to have a biography; therefore he wrote and published one. He listed the charges which could be made against him, such as inconsistency of character, quarrelsome nature, violent style of writing, poor talents as a preacher, unmannerliness, and unpopularity. Having catalogued, he vigorously defended himself against all of these charges. Other writings of Brownlow castigated Baptist and Presbyterian doctrine and practice.[31]

After a decade of circuit riding, Brownlow met Eliza O'Brien, hurried her into marriage, gave up his riding, and settled in Elizabethton. His large, lank appearance contrasted as much with Nelson's as did the radical nature of his thinking and the paucity of his formal education. But his earnestness and passionate devotion to the emerging Whig principles were compatible traits; and Brownlow's warm, sprightly, and selfless private personality attracted Nelson. As the political pot began to boil for

---

[30] James W. Bellamy, "The Political Career of Landon Carter Haynes (M.A. thesis, University of Tennessee, 1952), 1-12.

[31] E. Merton Coulter, *William G. Brownlow, Fighting Parson of the Southern Highlands* (Chapel Hill, 1937), 1-32.

the exciting presidential election of 1840, Nelson encouraged Brownlow to establish a newspaper in their small village for the election campaign.[32] Thus was born the *Whig*, which immediately plunged into the vitriolic personal controversies that were to characterize the paper and its editor to the end. After a few months of publication, the *Whig* had the town torn with strife, and its editor had opened a feud with Nelson's law student, Landon C. Haynes. At this time Brownlow was even fired at by an unknown assailant, whom many suspected to have been Haynes.

The young Nelson had become an uncle by the time he returned to Elizabethton, as Carrick and Eliza had a girl by the end of 1831. Another girl was born to them three years later, and in May of 1838 their first son was born. Perhaps despairing that his twenty-six-year-old brother would ever have a namesake of his own, Carrick named this son Thomas A. R. Nelson, II.

Soon, however, Nelson was courting twenty-two-year-old Anne Elizabeth Stuart, daughter of Montgomery Stuart of Nolichucky. On July 30, 1839, they were married. This connection resulted in a change in Nelson's plans; for he moved with his bride to Jonesboro, one county seat nearer Knoxville and the second largest town in East Tennessee. Here Nelson settled permanently until he was driven out by war. Haynes followed to Jonesboro to continue reading law under Nelson; and here also came Brownlow with his *Whig* a few months later, heralding his arrival with a street brawl with Haynes in which Brownlow was shot through the leg.[33] Marriage at the age of twenty-seven was a great delight to Nelson, who wrote so frankly to a friend of his happiness as to evoke a concurring answer in which extensive praise of married life culminated in the exclamation: "I would rather have a wife & *twenty children Squalling* on every side, & my wife occasionally, to scold me for not helping to nurse them, than be single!"[34] The first child, Alice, was born a year later, and five other children were born eighteen months to two and a half years apart.[35]

Nelson's new home town, Jonesboro, was situated in Washington County in rolling hills between the principal Appalachian watershed and Bays mountain range. It boasted a male and a female academy with a total of about two hundred students. Presbyterians, Methodists, and Baptists had church structures, and the former two operated Sunday Schools of about one hundred each. A Masonic Lodge was located at Jonesboro, and several merchants and professional men made the town their residence. Seven mercantile stores were in operation. There were some Democratic lawyers and another Whig lawyer besides Nelson. Six

---

[32] Temple, *Notable Men of Tennessee*, 179.
[33] Bellamy, "The Political Career of Landon Carter Haynes," 15-17.
[34] Robert H. McEwen to Nelson, November 4, 1839, in Nelson Papers.
[35] Selden Nelson, East Tennessee: History and Genealogy (scrapbook in the McClung Collection of the Lawson McGhee Library, Knoxville).

doctors practiced there, five of whom were Whigs. Two taverns competed along political party lines, one being operated by a Whig and the other by a Democrat. Many old log or frame buildings, including churches, were being torn down and replaced by brick ones. The former habits of wintering cows under porches and emptying refuse in the front streets had not been corrected by the time the Nelsons established residence in Jonesboro, but some progress was soon made. In mid-winter the morass that was main street sometimes could be forded at only selected places.[36] The county had one concern of considerable proportions, John Blair & Company, which was engaged in iron manufacturing —from blast furnace to nailery. More than a score each of blacksmiths, millers, and saw mill operators and a dozen tanners supplemented the basic agricultural economy of the county. A very few workers skilled in making wagons, furniture, leather goods, or guns also were located in the county, but most of these workmen probably farmed also.[37]

Before Nelson had resided in Jonesboro long, he ordered a carriage for his family from the Blairs. It was an elaborate one to be used with either one or two horses, and although open it was fitted with curtains to close it entirely when desired. The carriage required six months in building and was paid for with bar iron, doubtlessly received by David Nelson at his store in Elizabethton. Half the iron, in fact, was to be paid at the Elizabethton warehouse.[38]

For a home the Nelsons acquired "Buckhorn," an excellent place situated on a rise about a mile east of Jonesboro.[39] It had formerly been used as an inn. The gates to the semicircular drive had a frame superstructure holding a buck's horn. The house was strongly built with a brick bond foundation of seven or eight feet providing a full basement under the entire house. The sills were whole tree trunks simply laid across the foundation and hewed flat on top to receive the flooring. The exterior of the house was sheathed in yellow poplar with wide, vertical boards, stripped with narrow ones. Only small stoops sheltered front and side entrances; there were no wide verandas so characteristic of houses of similar size in lower parts of the South. The house was two-story with the familiar "L" floor plan. On the main floor there was an

---

[36] For a descriptive article on Jonesboro in 1844 see Jonesboro *Whig*, February 7, 1844.

[37] Unpublished schedules for Washington County for the *Seventh Census of the United States*, deposited in the Duke University Library, Durham, North Carolina.

[38] Carriage Agreement, June 10, 1843, in Nelson Papers.

[39] Nelson's Jonesboro home and barn, still in excellent condition, have been inspected by the writer through the kindness of the present owner, Mr. Joe McCoy. Mr. McCoy and Mr. Paul Fink of Jonesboro provided useful information about the appearance of the house before it was remodeled. The office has now been replaced by a double carport, and a wide veranda has been added across the front and down the side opposite the carport. The stripping of the vertical sheathing boards has been removed, and horizontal sheathing boards have been placed directly on the vertical poplar boards.

entrance hall containing the stairs to the second floor with a door opening on the back porch. On either side of the hall were two rooms, one
large and the other small. The "L" extension contained two more rooms,
and beyond them, without inside connection, was a brick storehouse
and kitchen opening on the extended back porch. Upstairs were two very
large bedrooms in the main part of the house, with windows in the gable
ends but without front dormer windows. These rooms were situated
over the center of the downstairs floor plan and stopped several feet
short of roof eave at front and back. The remaining generous space was
utilized for fifteen-foot-long, walk-in closets from each room and from
the hall. Small windows in the gable ends of the house gave light and
air in these closets. The upstairs of the "L" extension contained one finished bedroom and an unfinished attic room. Every room had a fireplace. Attached at the right front of the house was Nelson's office, a
large room with its own fireplace and with no entry except from outside.

A well and three cisterns served the place excellently in this respect.
The barn was as sturdily built as the house, being framed with whole
tree trunks as uprights from ground to roof peak and hewed tree trunks
as crossbeams and braces, all joints being mortise and pin. The driveway
was lined with cedar trees, evenly spaced, and the lawn was shaded by
sugar maples. A visiting Methodist minister who sayed with Nelson at
"Buckhorn" wrote: "We were in clover. The entertainment, materially
and intellectually, was up to the high-water mark. He put his carriage
and driver at our service all the time, and anticipated every want. Before
we left he had all our horses shod afresh . . . ." [40]

The circuit that Nelson regularly rode in his legal practice (and also
in political campaigns) was a rough one that sometimes exhausted horses
and exasperated riders. Nelson was recognized as one of the best horsemen in the area, and his skill was not allowed to grow rusty. Part of his
territory was itself mountain country, and the Holston, Bays, and Clinch
mountains had to be crossed and recrossed in regular circuit. On some
occasions business required crossing the Great Smokies to North Carolina or winding up the valley into Virginia. A favorite location for political gatherings was Cumberland Gap at the juncture of Tennessee,
Virginia, and Kentucky, where tri-state conventions provided opportunities for mutual encouragement and attraction of nationally known
speakers. Bays Mountains and Clinch Mountains lay between this point
and Jonesboro. But difficult to traverse though his circuit might be,
Nelson never again longed for Knoxville. His growing business took
him there frequently; but the valleys and mountains of his home area
grew to be familiar and beloved landmarks, his "secluded land of gentle
hills and mountains grand." [41]

[40] Paul M. Fink, "Methodism in Jonesboro, Tennessee," in East Tennessee Historical Society's *Publications*, No. 22 (1950), 56.
[41] These are the opening lines of Nelson's poem, "East Tennessee," published
anonymously in 1864 under the title, *Secession; or, Prose in Rhyme, and East Tennessee, a Poem* (Philadelphia, 1864).

Portraits of Anne Elizabeth Stuart, the first Mrs. Nelson, and of her children, Alice (b. 1840), Alexander Williams (b. 1841), Stuart (b. 1843), David Montgomery (b. 1845), Thomas A. R., Jr. (b. 1847), and Anne Helen Cunningham (b. 1849). The portraits are by Samuel Shaver and are owned by Mrs. J. H. Stewart of Knoxville, Judge Nelson's granddaughter.

A photograph of "Buckhorn," Nelson's home at Jonesboro, Tennessee. Extensive remodeling of the exterior has changed the appearance.

CHAPTER III

For the Good of Rome

NELSON'S FIRST SERIOUS plunge into political activity was in behalf of the presidential candidacy of William Henry Harrison. Between 1836 and 1840 the opposition to Andrew Jackson in Tennessee had crystalized as a strong Whig party. Nelson's adherence to the Whigs rather than the Democrats was ultimately to prove of considerable importance to that party, and there is evidence to indicate that the political bisection of the state was partly a matter of just such individual leadership. In an understandable desire to reduce this problem of party division to simple and meaningful terms, some interpreters have sought one or two bases of opposition to be applied to the whole state. But a detailed comparison of the twenty-seven consistently Whig counties with the sixteen consistently Democratic counties, together with a comparison of generally Whig with generally Democratic counties, fails to sustain any simple formula.[1] Rich and poor counties were found in both camps, and the effects of slaveholding seem to have been negligible in East Tennessee, only modest in Middle Tennessee, and not even uniformly significant in West Tennessee. Counties with the heavier concentrations of business and professional men did show Whig preferences, but there were notable exceptions. Manufacturing and trade people were not numerous enough in the overwhelmingly agricultural population to make a decisive impression upon political geography, even assuming that they had a definite political bent. Those counties with the heaviest in-

---

[1] Data for these comparisons are found in *The Tribune Almanac for the Years 1838 to 1868, Inclusive* (New York, 1868); Austin P. Foster, *Counties of Tennessee* (n.p., 1923), and *Sixth Census of the United States* (Washington, 1841). The literature concerned with the origins of the Whig party in general, the Southern Whigs as a special group, and the Tennessee Whigs in particular is extensive. Some of the more scholarly investigations or analyses include: E. Malcolm Carroll, *Origins of the Whig Party* (Durham, 1925); Arthur C. Cole, *The Whig Party in the South* (Washington, 1913); Ulrich B. Phillips, "The Southern Whigs, 1834-1854," in *Turner Essays in American History* (New York, 1910); Charles Grier Sellers, Jr., "Who Were the Southern Whigs?" in *American Historical Review*, Volume 59 (1953-54), 335-46; Thomas P. Abernethy, *From Frontier to Plantation in Tennessee* (Chapel Hill, 1932); *id.*, "The Origin of the Whig Party in Tennessee," in *Mississippi Valley Historical Review*, XII (1925-26), 504-22; Stanley J. Folmsbee, *Sectionalism and Internal Improvements in Tennessee, 1796-1845* (Knoxville, 1939); Albert V. Goodpasture, "John Bell's Political Revolt and His Vauxhall Garden Speech," in *Tennessee Historical Magazine*, II (1916), 254-63; Powell Moore, "The Political Background of the Revolt Against Jackson in Tennessee," in East Tennessee Historical Society's *Publication*, No. 4 (1932), 45-66; *id.*, "The Revolt Against Jackson in Tennessee, 1835-1836," in *Journal of Southern History*, II (1936), 335-59; Joseph Howard Parks, *John Bell of Tennessee* (Baton Rouge, 1950).

vestment in commerce, manufacturing, or mining were most often Whig in their alignment, but moderate or light investments in such business seemed to exercise no decisive influence. Economic considerations suggest tendencies but fail to furnish a satisfactory explanation of the origin of the Whig party in Tennessee.

Issues in the state elections from 1835 to 1840 provide only a partial explanation of the party pattern. The gubernatorial election of 1835 was largely a preliminary contest in behalf of the presidential candidacy of Hugh Lawson White, for the gubernatorial candidates divided on that subject and merged their own contests inextricably with the national one. Numerous personal reasons for enmity toward Jackson and a general desire not to be dictated to with regard to the next President, combined with some concern over Federal aid to transportation, aided the anti-Jackson faction to elect its candidate.[2] In the presidential contest of 1836 the Hugh Lawson White faction denied being Whigs and claimed to represent the principles on which Jackson had been elected and from which he had strayed. The national questions of banking and internal improvements at Federal expense were not vocal issues in the Tennessee contest although men who opposed Jackson on those subjects probably voted against Jackson's hand-picked successor.[3] Personalities dominated issues in the gubernatorial election of 1837, a generally spiritless affair in which anti-Jackson Governor Newton Cannon's re-election was assured by the depression for which Jackson's party was blamed. Cannon took a far weaker position on Federal aid to transportation than he had in 1835 and was unpopular in both East and West Tennessee. But his opponent was no more satisfactory on that subject.[4] The determination of the Democrats to recapture the governorship in 1839 led to a vigorous campaign in which a great many issues were raised; however, the notion that the contest was essentially agrarianism versus commercial interests is clearly an oversimplification. The Democratic candidate, James K. Polk, had been induced to leave the speakership of the national House of Representatives to do battle against Governor Cannon. Cannon was already widely disliked by transportation advocates because of his coolness toward state assistance, so Polk was able to neutralize that issue, if not to gain support on it, by proposing a system of aid in which the state would subscribe to a part of the stock of private turnpike and rail-

---

[2] Abernethy, *From Frontier to Plantation in Tennessee*, 299; Philip M. Hamer, ed., *Tennessee, A History, 1673-1932* (New York, 1933), I, 290-91; Folmsbee, *Sectionalism and Internal Improvements in Tennessee*, 130; Robert Cassell, "Public Career of Newton Cannon" (Unpublished M.A. thesis, Vanderbilt University, 1938), 52-55.

[3] See the Nashville *Banner* and the Nashville *Union*, February to November, 1836, for the progress of the campaign. Abernethy, *From Frontier to Plantation in Tennessee*, presents an economic interpretation of the contest.

[4] Nashville *Union*, July to August, 1837; Abernethy, *From Frontier to Plantation in Tennessee*, 301; Cassell, "Newton Cannon," 65-68; Folmsbee, *Sectionalism and Internal Improvements in Tennessee*, 151-53.

road companies. Neither candidate became specific and no real issue on this subject developed.[5]

During these campaigns the Tennessee opponents of Jackson did not sponsor protective tariffs, bringing themselves to do so only in 1840 after decisions as to party alignment had already been made by most of the Tennessee electorate. It is difficult to see that real issues were the dominant factors in that alignment. Both parties claimed direct descent from the party of Jefferson, and the voters were generally presented with a question of faith in a set of leaders rather than clearly defined alternative policies. Since economic considerations fall far short of explaining the political geography of Tennessee between 1835 and 1840, and since the issues advanced throw inadequate light on the basis of party division, there remains ample room for the effect of personal leadership on the county level in determining the political complexion of the state. It is significant that the most prominent political figures in the Tennessee scene from the origin of the Whig party to the outbreak of the Civil War were generally able to keep their home counties firmly aligned in their respective party columns.[6] Of course, there was an obvious advantage to a man seeking political preferment to be gained from living in a county where a majority of the voters supported his party, or even choosing his party according to the prevailing majority sentiment. Yet the high correlation between the party affiliations of Tennessee's United States Senators and Representatives and the party majorities of their home counties suggests the considerable effect of prestigious leadership in establishing traditional party alignments. Nelson's decision to support the Whigs probably had much to do with the strength of that party in Carter and Washington counties.

Why Nelson chose as he did cannot be discerned with certainty. His earliest step toward Whiggery was the support of Hugh Lawson White on personal and regional grounds, and the influence of other men he admired was probably a factor. The national position of the Whigs on Federal aid to transportation was certainly attractive to one as conscious as Nelson of the transportation problems of East Tennessee. And conservatism of attitude may have affected him as much as anything else. The Whigs nationally were evidently attracting the bulk of the profes-

[5] E. I. McCormac, *James K. Polk, A Political Biography* (Berkeley, 1922), 139-54; Powell Moore, "James K. Polk and Tennessee Politics, 1839-1841," in East Tennessee Historical Society's *Publications*, No. 9 (1937), 33-39; Abernethy, "The Origin of the Whig Party in Tennessee," *loc. cit.*, 504-22; J. L. Williams to William B. Campbell, June 30, 1839, David Campbell Collection (Duke University Library, Durham, North Carolina). This collection is hereinafter cited as the Campbell Collection.

[6] Tennessee members of Congress in these years with their counties of residence may be found in the *Biographical Directory of the American Congress* (Washington, 1928). An extremely interesting account of a Jackson favorite who became an opponent of Jackson is Arda S. Walker, "John Henry Eaton, Apostate," in East Tennessee Historical Society's *Publications*, No. 24 (1952), 26-43.

sional and business men; and the tenor of their newspaper support suggested the conservative nature of the party interests, however radical
the vote-garnering campaign techniques might become.[7] Nelson's environment at Knoxville, in college, and in his father's store contributed
to his conservatism of outlook, a conservatism well illustrated in his
agitation over his brother's hasty marriage and in his almost anguished
longing to return to Knoxville and to people who had a "temperament
and disposition somewhat analagous to his own" and whose "inclinations
and amusements" met his "approbation." Maturity eliminated the crav-
ing to return to Knoxville but only deepened the underlying consciousness of intellectual aristocracy which may have contributed to his
sympathy with a conservative party spirit. In the last analysis the
causes of such attitudes may be beyond recapture, but conservative his
temperament was, and the Whig party found in him an ardent champion.

The presidential election contest between William Henry Harrison
and Martin Van Buren produced a new high in fanfare and emotional
appeal and aroused the Whigs to a fever pitch. With Jackson in retirement and his hand-picked successor, Van Buren, discredited by the panic
of 1837, the Whigs were inspired by sanguine hope. Defeat in the state
elections of 1839 only redoubled the Whig determination to carry Tennessee for their party in 1840. Harrison was nominated in the Whig
National Convention at Harrisburg, Pennsylvania, in December, 1839,
leaving ten months for the campaign. State party organization was completed in February when both parties held conventions in Nashville and
the Whigs a second one in Knoxville. Principal speakers in each campaign were to be the presidential electoral candidates. The electors-at-
large were expected to speak in every county while the district electors
would repeatedly canvass each county in their districts and interchange
with each other. The chief hope of the state Democrats was to tie the
popular name of James K. Polk to the campaign as vice-presidential
candidate. When this failed, Polk entered the canvass as a candidate for
re-election to the governorship thirteen months before the gubernatorial
election. Newspapers, from the major dailies to the temporary county
weeklies, were all party organs; and most counties had a journalistic
advocate for each party. Brownlow's Jonesboro *Whig* was one which
survived and became permanent. The Whigs employed local, district,
and even regional camp meetings very much resembling contemporary
religious camp meetings, supplementing this colorful activity with mon-
ster parades of uniformed "Harrison Guards" and floats of all kinds
including the ubiquitous log cabin with the latch string out. Scores of

---

[7] The conservative spirit of the Whig party in its early stages is well documented in
Carroll, *Origins of the Whig Party*, 171-227.

campaign songs were written and set to popular tunes for lusty singing, and ladies were encouraged to turn out for rallies as never before.[8]

By the end of 1839 Nelson's name was being mentioned as a possible district presidential electoral candidate. His teacher and friend, Thomas L. Williams, counselled caution, however. In a meeting with Nelson, Williams (now chancellor of equity court) expressed his pride in his student's most commendable progress in law and predicted a success that would gratify all his well-wishers if he would avoid political candidature. Chancellor Williams warned Nelson not to follow his example because his own single excursion into politics, election to the legislature in 1819, had checked his legal career so badly that it had never fully recovered. Although gratified at having Nelson's name offered for posts of honor and distinction, Williams urged declination and suggested that Nelson's father advise the local delegates to the Knoxville Whig Convention of February, 1840, not to make Nelson's decision more difficult by tendering him the nomination.[9] But political ambition was already touching Nelson, and he found it difficult to resist the temptation involved in a canvass as presidential elector—for a good showing in such a contest would establish a fair prospect of going to Congress in the next election. And Nelson was already convinced that he would very much like to have a seat in Congress, although he acknowledged that he was "poor and in debt" and that other duties compelled him to bridle his inclinations and attend closely to his professional business for some years to come. His compromise was to assure his friends that if they could prevail upon no one else to run, he would engage "personally as a drafted soldier" or assume responsibility for securing a substitute.[10]

The substitute Nelson sought was Thomas D. Arnold of Greene County, who had failed to sustain some of the Whig party platform planks in a previous congressional election and had been accused by some Whigs of courting Democratic votes. Nelson wrote asking Arnold if he would accept nomination as Whig elector in the first district and offering to nominate him at the district convention, adding with typical candor:

---

[8] The nature of the campaign is revealed in the files of the Nashville *Whig*, Nashville *Republican Banner*, and Nashville *Union*. Many letters addressed to William B. Campbell during 1840, found in the Campbell Collection, as well as the published correspondence of James K. Polk and Andrew Jackson, throw much light on the behind-the-scenes operations. See letters to Polk in *Tennessee Historical Magazine*, Series II, Volume II (1931-32), and John Spencer Bassett, ed., *Correspondence of Andrew Jackson* (Washington, 1926-35), Volume VI. This campaign is treated in Thomas B. Alexander, "The Presidential Campaign of 1840 in Tennessee," in *Tennessee Historical Quarterly*, I (1942), 21-43.

[9] Thomas L. Williams to David Nelson, January 20, 1840, in Nelson Papers.

[10] Nelson's attitudes are revealed in letters and comments published by Nelson in the Jonesboro *Whig*, April 28, 1841.

While, at the risk of offending you, I must be permitted to say, as I have heretofore told you, that I do not now, and never have approved of your course in your last canvass for Congress; yet I have every reason to believe, that under existing circumstances, the Whig cause would probably gain more by your nomination than that of any other man in the District—provided you should bring into the contest your usual energy and determination. . . . By doing so—if you will permit one who has always voted against you to express an opinion on the subject—you will, in my judgment regain the confidence of the Whig party in this District, which—your own opinion to the contrary notwithstanding—was impaired by your course in the last canvass. . . .

I have addressed you thus frankly, not because I have a *mental reservation*, that I hope you will in reply *insist on my running* but in sincerity and good faith, because I wish to see the Whig cause prosper, and am willing to do any honorable act that will promote its success. . . .[11]

A week later Nelson, having received a protesting letter from Arnold, wrote: "I have for sometime past been *scheming* in your favor, 'not for the weal of *Caesar*, but for the good of *Rome*.'"[12] Arnold accepted the nomination.

Although Nelson did not actually become presidential elector for Harrison, he perhaps devoted more energy to the campaign than did Arnold. Nelson drafted a long preamble and set of resolutions for the Jonesboro Whig convention, which he described as "somewhat *peppery* in their character, but embodying our whole political creed, which I design as a set off against the Nashville doings of the 8th of January, and which I have the vanity to believe will be of great service when circulated. . . ."[13] By invitation Nelson spoke at various places in the district during the contest; and before the campaign was a month old, his speeches had brought a personal attack in the columns of the local Democratic paper. Revealing a sensitiveness about personal honor that would not mellow with age, he penned a protest to the editor warning that he would hold the editor responsible for another personal attack "if my life pays the forfeit." He continued:

In the course of my address . . . I did not allude personally to any Democrat in this County, nor did I mention the newspaper under your control. As my personal relations with yourself and a great many gentlemen of your party in this County have been of the most amicable nature, I was studious to avoid doing or saying anything that ought to disturb these relations. I attacked the public men and measures of your party with the boldness and independence that should ever characterize an American citizen in the investigation of political subjects. I have never questioned the right of any gentleman Democrat to pursue the same course in regard to the public men and measures of the party to which I belong, but I deny the right of the Sentinel, when it was not assailed, to wage a personal warfare against me, and if it does, *its Editor* shall abide by the consequences, as I will not deal with every

---

[11] Nelson to Arnold, January 20, 1840, published in the Jonesboro *Whig*, April 28, 1841.

[12] *Id.* to *id.*, January 29, 1840, published in Jonesboro *Whig*, April 28, 1941.

[13] *Idem.*

contemptible puppy who may choose to scribble against me in its columns.

I intend freely and fearlessly to continue the discussion of Whig principles before the people but I do not wish to court a personal quarrel. I will endeavor, however, not to flinch, if one is forced upon me and you can pursue whatever course your inclinations may prompt.[14]

The above letter illustrates one of the interesting anomalies in Nelson's nature—an essentially careful, conservative mentality clothed in an always vivid and sometimes pugnacious manner of speaking and writing.

By June, Nelson and Brownlow had about taken control of Whig activities in Washington County, and both were involved in arranging for a great camp meeting at Nelson's Camp Ground seven miles east of Jonesboro. Nelson was chairman of the local arrangements committee and spent much time on the elaborate facilities for the three-day meeting early in October.[15] Meanwhile, he spoke by invitation in five of the six easternmost counties of the state; and he was asked to speak also in Greene County but was prevented by urgent business with an out-of-state client. He attended the tri-state convention at Cumberland Gap in September and was invited to address the crowd there.[16]

It was easy to conduct a campaign of popular appeals to the voters on the grounds of Harrison's sympathy for the common man as contrasted with Van Buren's alleged aristocratic tendencies and of references to the extravagances of Van Buren's administration in such matters as the size of the standing army.[17] But when it came to issues of a more substantial sort, the Tennessee Whigs were far from united; and Whigs of neighboring states were even less willing to accept the Henry Clay philosophy of national bank, protective tariffs, and Federal aid to the states for the construction of transportation facilities. Before Nelson went to the tri-state convention at Cumberland Gap, he was advised that the resolutions being drawn up for that convention had to be stripped of references to the national bank and to the superiority of the convention to the caucus as a nominating agency. It appeared that the Virginians attending the convention were against a national bank, preferring a state chartered bank for the same purposes, and were also partial to the caucus system on the grounds that it was Jeffersonian doctrine.[18]

The elderly Governor David Campbell of Virginia was prevailed upon by the Whig Vigilance Committee of Washington County to attend the Nelson Camp Ground convention, and upon his return to Virginia he wrote:

---

[14] Nelson to Daniel Kenney, February 9, 1840, in Nelson Papers.

[15] Jonesboro *Whig*, July 22, August 12, and October 7, 1840.

[16] A public letter signed by Nelson and published in the Jonesboro *Whig*, May 12, 1841, gives information on his activities during the 1840 canvass.

[17] A report in the Jonesboro *Whig*, November 4, 1840, indicated that Nelson stressed currency and standing army issues in a debate with Andrew Johnson.

[18] William R. Caswell to Nelson, September 14, 1840, in Nelson Papers.

I was invited to a great Convention at Nelson's Camp Ground . . . to commence on the 5th last Monday, in honor of the battle of the Thames and to continue 'till the 7th the 60th anniversary of the battle of Kings Mountain.
. . . The first day we had a speech from Preston and then one from Genl. Leslie Combs of Kentucky. [Preston was William C. Preston of South Carolina.] This brought evening—We adjourned for dinner and after dinner I went a mile into the country to lodge for the night—A large number of persons remained in the camp all night and had speaking until 12 Oc at night—Tuesday we had one of the finest bursts of eloquence from Genl. Combs that I ever listened to and several other very capital speeches. One from Mr. Senter [William T. Senter, Second District electoral candidate]—a speech of the first order. Combs left us in the evening for another gathering some twenty miles off—It was exciting in the highest degree to hear the cannon roaring from a hill near us and see the preparations to bear Combs off as soon as he was ready to go—He left the speaker's stand and ran off to get a mouthful of dinner—Near the camp stood ten or twelve young gentlemen waiting for him holding their horses by the bridle. As soon as he was ready they mounted him on a fine charger and all jumped into their saddles and were off at a gallop. This was Tuesday evening. Speaking was kept up till late at night.
Wednesday morning as I awoke the cannon began to roar—We took breakfast & repaired to the camp. There at 10 Oc we found the people in waiting to hear Preston make one of his best efforts . . . as soon as he ended I closed the Convention & we took dinner and started for home—
Some five hundred or a thousand ladies attended each day and I suppose three or four hundred encamped on the ground during the whole time.[19]

The ladies were provided with seats, but men stood for hours at a stretch listening to speeches by the dozen orators, interspersed with band music, choir singing, marching, and mass singing. One popular song at this gathering was sung to the tune of "Yankee Doodle" and ran as follows:

> Come here's a health to Harrison
>   The old log cabin farmer
> When he commands the ship of State
>   The Tories cannot harm her.
>
> Chorus: Yankee Doodle, fill a mug
>   A pewter mug of cider
> When he commands our gallant ship
>   No evil can betide her.[20]

Before the canvass ended, Nelson met in full debate the rising Democratic leader of East Tennessee, Andrew Johnson, of Greeneville. Johnson was a Democratic elector-at-large and spoke over the entire state. He met Nelson on October 29, and the friends of each were satisfied that their spokesman had triumphed.[21]
Election returns brought rejoicing to the Whigs, for General Harrison had won a sweeping victory in the electoral count, carrying nine-

[19] David Campbell to Virginia Campbell, October 9, 1840, in Campbell Collection.
[20] Jonesboro *Whig*, October 7, 1840.
[21] *Ibid.*, November 4, 1840.

teen of the twenty-six states, including Tennessee. Nelson's home county of Washington went Democratic by a narrow margin, but East Tennessee showed great Whig strength and the state was won by a popular margin of more than ten per cent. Nelson was made Washington County manager for the Harrison victory ball,[22] and his services to the party were known outside East Tennessee. John Bell, stalwart Whig of Middle Tennessee, wrote Nelson rejoicing in victory.[23] Nelson tried to persuade Bell to run against Polk for the Tennessee governorship, but Bell could not agree that he should do this and thought that there were many Whigs who could defeat Polk, suggesting that Nelson himself could do so. Bell asked Nelson for his candid opinion as to whether he should accept a cabinet post or stay in the House of Representatives and become speaker.[24] A few weeks later Bell expressed to Brownlow a wish that Nelson would get himself elected to Congress so that he could help the Whigs on the national stage.[25] Nelson, at twenty-eight, was thus firmly established as a party leader.

Even before the dust of the presidential melee had settled, Nelson was corresponding with Chancellor Williams about a suitable Whig gubernatorial candidate and about the possibility that Williams should seek election to the United States Senate when the next legislature met.[26] The Chancellor was pressed by many friends and even by his daughters to enter the political lists, but his essentially ascetic nature recoiled from the temptations involved. "The solidarity of a man's virtues may, and no doubt often is tried by exposure to seductive influences," he wrote Nelson, "still it is the dictate of infinite wisdom to ask that we may not be led into temptation." He continued:

It is true as you state that a man may escape the contagion of evil examples —yet how many are overcome and fall away forever . . . . The question therefore is—ought a man to encounter these perils for the sake of a little, a fleeting distinction—a morsel of that honor that cometh from men . . . . Now if there were great national calamities impending [over] our Country, a time when every man should step forward in its defense, the crisis would create obligations essentially different from such as now exist.[27]

After further importunities from friends, the Chancellor put his final refusal on essentially the same basis: the temptations a politician must endure, the difficulty a politician must suffer in his growth as a Christian, and the absence of any impelling peril to the nation. "He therefore who looks beyond the present sphere of existence expecting a day of retribution sooner or later . . . ought to abstain from the strife of

---

[22] Indicated by a paper in the Nelson Papers under date of November 27, 1840.

[23] John Bell to Nelson, November 9, 1840, in Nelson Papers.

[24] Id. to id., December 21, 1840, in Nelson Papers.

[25] William G. Brownlow to Nelson, February 12, 1841, in Nelson Papers.

[26] Thomas L. Williams to Nelson, February 12, 1841, in Nelson Papers.

[27] Id. to id., February 19, 1841, in Nelson Papers.

politics. . . . 'What will it profit a man to gain the whole world and lose his own soul, or what will he give in exchange for his soul.' " [28] The correspondence between Nelson and Chancellor Williams continued over many years and was supplemented by occasional visits. It is likely that the Chancellor's views of politics tempered Nelson's own fascination with it and kept his activities on a national plane of interest, generally above seeking local preferment in offices. His ultimate achievements as a lawyer may have been saved from engulfment in politics by Williams's counsel and example.

A local newspaper altercation ensued in the spring of 1841 between Nelson and Thomas D. Arnold, stemming from the fact that Arnold would not submit his claim to the Whig nomination for Congress to a district Whig party convention. Nelson tried to argue him into accepting the authority of the convention; but when Arnold defied it and denounced it as a rump convention, Nelson strongly urged that opposition be offered to Arnold and tried to persuade Robert J. McKinney to seek the nomination. The district convention did nominate McKinney, who had not sought the nomination and would not canvass. There was no Democratic nomination, so Arnold won the election without organized opposition. On April 17, 1841, Arnold published a long denunciation of Nelson, Brownlow, and McKinney, charging Nelson with desiring to split the Whig party and improperly conniving to defeat him. In the Jonesboro *Whig* of April 28, Nelson replied at great length and published the correspondence between himself and Arnold in justification of his course toward Arnold. Arnold replied at length in the Democratic paper; and Nelson again answered in the Jonesboro *Whig* in what he called a defense of his character before the Whigs of Middle and West Tennessee, who did not know him personally.[29] After publishing various letters from prominent East Tennesseans attesting to his character and ability, he further refuted Arnold's charges and concluded:

I now dismiss this controversy, unless Gen. Arnold will take issue upon the charges I have made against him. In view of his repeated falsehoods and perversions, I feel constrained to publish him as *a liar a scoundrel and a Coward.* I hope he will not bind me to the peace, as he did one or more citizens of Knox County; for I shall make no threats against him. And while I do not claim to be Gen. Arnold's equal in point of *station,* I claim to be his superior as to *character* and every thing else, except bodily size and physical strength. The future shape of this controversy will, therefore, depend on Gen. Arnold himself.[30]

Arnold chose not to avail himself of the thinly veiled invitation to a duel but busied himself with a massive pamphlet of forty-eight pages

---

[28] *Id.* to *id.,* June 14, 1841, in Nelson Papers.
[29] Jonesboro *Whig,* May 12, 1841.
[30] *Idem.*

denouncing Brownlow and Nelson, which he circulated through the congressional district.[31] In this pamphlet he had the bad taste to refer to Nelson as a cripple and as too small for him to cane or cowhide, to which Brownlow replied editorially: "Mr. Nelson claims no favors on the score of his being a cripple—he never did, as the whole country can testify. He puts himself in line with able-bodied men, and he expects to take what follows." [32] While it is easy to understand the frustration of a politician who had alienated the support of the most influential paper of his party's persuasion in his congressional district, the evidence still convicts Arnold of serious half-truths and of deliberately fostering false impressions at Nelson's expense. That Nelson's sensitive honor was directly attacked accounts for his rather explosive second reply.

While still involved in the unpleasantness with Arnold, Nelson must have been in a singularly receptive mood for another of Thomas L. Williams's strictures against political ambition. Williams, noting that reports had reached him that his own name would be presented as a candidate for governor to the Murfreesboro Whig convention of March, 1841, and that he had unequivocally refused, commented:

. . . Offers of such promotion [from chancellor of court of equity to governor] (if promotion it can be called) are destitute of all attraction, in them there is everything to forbid and nothing to invite acceptance. . . .

The other station to which you allude [probably a United States Senatorship] is less repulsive to my sense of duty—still it is without charms. Several years ago when hurried along the stream of life, by the winds of ambition, I might have been tempted to desire such a station. For some years past it has been my desire to be freed from the dominance of that maddening, that tyrannical passion. A man much subject to its sway stands (as we lawyers say) in vinculis; he is led about and over ruled by a most domineering and capricious despot. Hence he cannot be a free man, cannot be a happy man.

Besides this consideration, the votary of politics is in the way of temptation —he will be assailed by thousands of extraneous and corrupting influences, not one of which would be felt in the private walks of life. . . .[33]

Then, referring to his one entry into elective politics, a single term in the Tennessee legislature, he added: "I thought our Nation was in jeopardy and that every one loving his country ought to bear some part in its reformation. This work is accomplished and I am satisfied."

Displaying his customary lack of enthusiasm for state politics, Nelson played no prominent part in the gubernatorial election of 1843. He had suffered a prolonged illness during the preceding winter from which his recovery was agonizingly slow for a person accustomed to ride circuit so vigorously.[34] His third child was born in June, 1843, and three days later he celebrated by signing the agreement for his elaborate carriage

---

[31] *Ibid.*, September 14, 1842.
[32] *Ibid.*, September 21, 1842.
[33] Williams to Nelson, June 14, 1841, in Nelson Papers.
[34] Thomas A. R. Nelson to David Nelson, April 7, 1843, in Nelson Papers.

to be built—"similar to John F. Deaderick's to differ in the following particulars: body 4″ wider, 6″ longer, 2″ higher; hull of body 4″ deeper. . . ."[35] He was not, however, uninterested in the Senatorial contest in the legislature in the fall of 1843 and still hoped Thomas L. Williams would seek the seat. Williams, although still resolutely refusing to consider politics, was interested in the possibility that a state supreme court seat might be vacated by the election of a judge to the Senatorship. He wrote Nelson that he planned to accept the supreme court position if elected to it by the legislature.[36]

Before 1843 was ended, Nelson had occasion to show that his quick temper where personal honor was involved was not entirely reserved for the political arena. He was attempting a collection for a Baltimore firm and received an insulting letter from them insinuating an absence of professional integrity. His long reply was couched in blistering language, which probably evoked smiling approval from his friend Brownlow. After inferring that the members of the firm were not gentlemen, Nelson concluded:

I do not imagine that I should miss the mark were I to guess that I am now addressing a set of Shylocks of the first water. Be that as it may, I will receive no further letters from you. It gives me no pleasure to be engaged in an angry correspondence, especially with strangers who live at such a distance that it must all end in words.[37]

Whig bad luck in Harrison's death and bad judgment in the selection of Tyler kept politics stewing during Tyler's term. Brownlow applied the heat in East Tennessee; and the political lull for Nelson ended abruptly with the beginning of the presidential election year, 1844. On New Year's day the Whigs of Washington County met in the Methodist Church at Jonesboro to form a Clay Club and to select delegates to a young Whig's national convention at Baltimore and to the Knoxville convention to be held on Washington's birthday. According to Brownlow's report, Nelson was called on by the club for a speech and "addressed it in a thrilling and off hand speech, of more than one hour, in which he glanced at the political topics of the day—spoke of the campaign of 1840—and of the cheering prospects now before the Whigs." "Mr. Nelson's speech was full of genuine Whig enthusiasm," continued Brownlow, "and the manner in which his fine anecdotes were applauded, and his eloquent eulogy upon Clay received, attested that the Whig spirit of 1840 still breathes and burns in the hearts of those who contributed to the election of Harrison, and have been betrayed by Tyler."[38]

The day after the meeting, Nelson began receiving letters urging him to be electoral candidate for the first district, an honor and an oppor-

[35] Carriage Agreement, June 10, 1843, in Nelson Papers.
[36] Williams to Nelson, August 26, 1843, in Nelson Papers.
[37] Nelson to R. R. Griffith and Co., December 12, 1843, in Nelson Papers.
[38] Jonesboro *Whig*, January 3, 1844.

tunity he had evidently decided to accept.[39] In February Nelson was one of a committee appointed to draft a constitution for the Washington County Clay Club, and he received in invitation from the Knoxville Bell Club to speak at the Knoxville Whig convention of February 22.[40] He spent his spare time polishing this major effort and set out with Brownlow and others in high spirits for Knoxville. The weather was soft and balmy, adding to the cheerfulness of the party. Their entry into Knoxville was exhilarating, for they were met by a delegation and fell in with the procession behind a band. The town was alive with more than a thousand delegates from almost all of East Tennessee's counties, and much marching and band playing added to the rising party spirit. Nelson had the satisfaction of doing justice to a thoroughly prepared speech— thus launching himself on a broader theatre than one congressional district. As was customary for a political *piece de resistance* of the period, he spoke for two hours; and his voice and memory both served him well. He made his arguments firmly and rose to eloquence at will—winning accolade as the equal of the best stump speakers of the day. The convention elected Nelson as Whig electoral candidate for his district, and even the weather continued to smile as he returned to Jonesboro in triumph.[41]

A schedule of speeches throughout the district was immediately arranged, and Nelson began canvassing in a matter of days. Enthusiastic audiences repeatedly interrupted him with applause and laughter. He did not use one prepared speech but rather developed new speeches constantly. In three weeks he delivered three major addresses entirely different. He invaded rock-ribbed Democratic Sullivan County and managed to hold a large crowd at the courthouse for hours.[42] His health suffered from the exertions, however, and the latter part of April and early May were spent fighting a chest cold that was epidemic in East Tennessee.[43] In early May the expected nomination by the Whig National Convention of Henry Clay as the party's standard bearer was eminently acceptable in Tennessee and added fervor to the Whig campaign. But as circuit court started the first Monday in May and continued until the end of July, Nelson announced that he would make no more speeches except at the court meeting places until August and September. Six court meeting speeches were scheduled for the months of May, June, and July; and thirty-one engagements were announced for the period from July 29 until October 28, with almost every day in August scheduled. The Democratic candidate for elector was Landon

[39] See E. Alexander to Nelson, January 2, 1844, in Nelson Papers.
[40] Jonesboro *Whig*, February 7 and 28, 1844.
[41] *Ibid.*, February 28, 1844.
[42] *Ibid.*, March 13 and 27, 1844.
[43] *Ibid.*, April 17, 1844. References to the epidemic of sickness appear in the Jonesboro *Whig* throughout May and June of 1844.

C. Haynes, Nelson's former law student, who now edited the Democratic paper at Jonesboro, the *Tennessee Sentinel*. He met Nelson at most of these engagements in joint debate.[44]

Turning his hand to a diversion that always interested him, Nelson composed some doggerel poetry to be sung in the typical campaign rally fashion. Noting that Democrats were taunting the Whigs for having only a now-useless batch of anti-Van Buren songs (since James K. Polk's unexpected upset of Van Buren at the Democratic Convention), he published in the Jonesboro *Whig* a thirteen-stanza piece on Polk "in the hope that some of your numerous readers will take the hint and furnish something better." Two of the stanzas read:

> They met and they chattered, like so many birds,
> And, quarrelling, fixed on the rule of two-thirds,
> While,—awful to tell—Matty vanished in smoke
> And the sins of the party were packed upon Polk.

> The cause of their party is *poking* along
> And the Whigs will still *Polk* them with laughter and song;
> Their doom by the people was long ago spoke,
> And now they're self murdered by taking to Polk.

> Chorus: Oh! dear, what a fine joke
>   To have such a leader as little Jim Polk.[45]

In June Nelson accepted an invitation to speak at Abingdon, Virginia, not far from the Tennessee line, concerning which the opposition paper in Abingdon commented that the audience would be condemned to boredom for three hours.[46] Long speeches were undoubtedly in the normal order; at the Jonesboro Methodist Church on June 24, Nelson and Haynes spoke from 1:00 P.M. until near sunset—one of the longest days of the year. The lead-off speeches were of two hours each, followed by rebuttals and cross questions.[47] A month later, in Jonesboro again, Nelson opened with an hour-and-twenty-minute speech as a prelude to the major address by the Whig candidate for elector-at-large, Spencer Jarnigan, before a crowd of more than five hundred.[48] In October he was host to a tri-state convention at Elizabethton to which several thousand Whigs came. As local district electoral candidate he was made president of the three-day convention and delivered as his presidential address the usual two-hour effort.[49]

In this contest the Whigs were more united on issues than in 1840 and

---

[44] Bellamy, "The Political Career of Landon Carter Haynes," 30-33; Jonesboro *Whig*, April 17, June 12, 1844.

[45] Jonesboro *Whig*, June 12, 1844. Polk was pronounced "poke" in Tennessee.

[46] *Idem.*

[47] *Ibid.*, June 26, 1844.

[48] *Ibid.*, July 24, 1844.

[49] *Ibid.*, October 9, 1844.

resorted less to ballyhoo. Henry Clay's whole American System was sustained by John Bell and the other Whig electoral candidates—protective tariffs, Federal aid to internal improvements, and a national bank. In response to the surging Democratic appeals to expansionist sentiment, the Whigs sought to puncture the eagle flights of oratory with sharp, common-sense references to the questionable ethical position of the United States in regard to the Texas question and to the eminent danger of a costly war with Mexico. While Haynes argued for the immediate annexation of Texas, Nelson insisted that the only honorable way the United States could annex would be with the consent of Mexico.[50]

Both Democrats and Whigs were driven to unusual lengths in Tennessee by the nomination of the Tennessean, Polk. The Whigs had long found him a thorn in their political hides and were hysterically anxious to defeat him in his home state, but it was an unavoidable fact that Polk was a drawing card greatly enhanced by the prospect of another Tennessee President. His victory in the nation by the narrowest of margins sent a pall of gloom over the Tennessee Whigs as dark as anywhere in the nation, relieved only by the pale gleam of pleasure that Polk had not quite carried his own state. Nelson had done effective work in his district and had held the Whig vote high although he could not keep Polk from polling more votes than did Van Buren in 1840. His trip to Nashville to cast the electoral vote of Tennessee for Clay he made one leg of a vacation. In Nashville the Whigs celebrated their state victory with dinners for Whig leaders and by a flamboyant display in casting their electoral vote for Henry Clay. The presidential electors assembled at the home of John Bell; and riding in four open carriages accompanied by fifty other carriages, a band, uniformed companies of Whigs, and other pedestrians, they rode through town and around the city square before going to the state capitol building to cast their votes.[51] After two more evenings of celebration, Nelson boarded the steamboat *Talleyrand* for a trip to Memphis via the Cumberland, Ohio, and Mississippi rivers.[52]

National politics were not taking all of Nelson's political interest, for he was at this time an alderman of Jonesboro and soon became one of seven commissioners appointed by the county court to arrange for the construction of a county courthouse at Jonesboro. The commissioners named Nelson to act for them in letting contracts, thus placing on him the burden of detail for the undertaking.[53] His interest in the economic progress of East Tennessee was attested by his attempts to get a pottery industry into the section to make use of local clay and by his assistance

[50] *Ibid.*, June 26, 1844.

[51] Parks, *John Bell*, 206-07.

[52] W. G. Brownlow to Nelson, November 29, 1844, in Nelson Papers; Nelson to Brownlow, December 5, 1844, published in the Jonesboro *Whig*, December 18, 1844.

[53] Information on Nelson's local activities is found in the Nelson Papers under dates in April, 1845, and April 9, 1846. See also the Jonesboro *Whig*, January 17, 1844.

to the East Tennessee Bank in handling subscription stock sales.[54] Transportation continued to be one of his principal interests, and he was named as a delegate to Lynchburg, Virginia, in September, 1847, to consider river and railroad facilities for the valleys.[55]

On September 8, 1847, Brownlow's Jonesboro *Whig* fired the first gun in what Nelson considered at the time to be his major political battle by suggesting his name for the United States Senate. His talents, staunch Whig principles, and long unrewarded service to the party were mentioned. But before a month had passed, Nelson's relations with Brownlow were clouded by a religious controversy. Brownlow had been an active Methodist preacher before he turned editor, and Nelson was a Presbyterian elder. The Methodists were engaged in a clash of some bitterness with a Presbyterian minister, Frederick A. Ross, whose book attacking Methodists in reply to an attack on Presbyterianism had caused some sensation. In September of 1847 the Jonesboro meeting of the Methodist Circuit denounced the Presbyterian laymen who had financed Ross's book and called upon all Methodists to refrain from supporting these men for any public office. The donors were also called upon to admit their "guilt" in contributing to "a secret fund to destroy Methodism." Nelson published in the Jonesboro *Whig* of October 6, 1847, a statement that he had contributed twenty-five dollars and solicited fifty more dollars in order that Ross should have as wide a hearing as the Methodists, whose book was circulated by itinerant preachers. He denounced political proscription for supporting a religious publication as unheard of and subversive of the American system. In the same issue of the paper, editor Brownlow answered the Nelson position by reference to many instances in which Presbyterians tried to mix church and political affairs. The tone of both letters was sharp, but comity was maintained in a manner not customary to Brownlow in his press altercations. Brownlow's son, John Bell Brownlow, wrote later that this was the only thing in a warm friendship of over forty years that ever seriously threatened their personal relations. "After a few months the parties were as cordial as ever," he concluded, "and Nelson was the first choice of the editor for Congress, Gov. & Senator." [56]

---

[54] Ezekiel Birdseye to Nelson, August 17, 1846, in Nelson Papers; Jonesboro *Whig*, January 17, 1844.

[55] Jonesboro *Whig*, September 1, 1847.

[56] This is an undated note in the handwriting of John Bell Brownlow, son of William G. Brownlow, found unbound in the 1847-48 volume of the Jonesboro *Whig* in the Library of Congress. This was the editor's own file and contains many marginal notations by John Bell Brownlow as well as some inserted notes such as this one.

CHAPTER IV

Not Killed But Only Banished

A S EARLY AS THE FALL OF 1847, a *Whig* editorial by Brownlow had suggested Nelson's name for a United States Senatorship.[1] The presidential contest of 1848 won Nelson serious consideration for that office. He did not wish to sacrifice time and legal business as a presidential elector and early announced that he did not want to be placed on the Whig ticket for 1848. He pointed out that he had served in 1840 and 1844 at considerable cost in time, labor, and money; that he had not asked for the nomination in 1844 as elector; and that since he was asking no office from the party, it should not expect him to again make such sacrifices.[2] He was interested in the contest, of course, and at a Jonesboro gathering successfully opposed a motion by Brownlow to commit the Whigs against General Zachary Taylor prior to the meeting of the Whig National Convention.[3] The *Whig* kept hinting that Nelson might run as electoral candidate even if it was asking too much of him, but Nelson announced to a local Whig meeting he was addressing in support of General Zachary Taylor that he would not accept if nominated by the district convention.[4] Since he had to be out of town when that convention met at Jonesboro on July 8, he left a letter explaining in detail how his court commitments in the circuit and at Knoxville made it impossible for him to canvass.[5] The convention elected Thomas D. Arnold and adjourned before Arnold's refusal was received.[6] Election time was approaching, and the Democrats began to taunt the Whigs about having no candidate for elector. Therefore, when the Whig district convention hastily reconvened on July 26 and asked Nelson to accept, he cast aside his reasons and consented.[7] He did insist that he would meet every court and would speak generally on court days. Landon C. Haynes, who was serving his second term in the state legislature, was again the Democratic electoral candidate in the district.

During the following month Nelson made sixteen major addresses be-

---

[1] Jonesboro *Whig*, September 8, 1847.

[2] Nelson's card in the Jonesboro *Whig*, February 23, 1848.

[3] Jonesboro *Whig*, February 23, 1848.

[4] *Ibid.*, June 28, 1848.

[5] *Ibid.*, July 12, 1848.

[6] Arnold's letter declining the nomination for much the same reasons as Nelson had given was published in the Jonesboro *Whig*, July 26, 1848.

[7] Jonesboro *Whig*, August 2, 1848.

fore going to Knoxville for a month-long session of the state supreme court.[8] Before he left, he had a six-hour debate with Congressman Andrew Johnson at Washington College, between Jonesboro and Greeneville (Johnson's home). Nelson opened with a two-and-one-half hour discussion of the Mexican War and the whole expansion problem and other Whig differences with the Democrats, including the perennial Whig denunciation of the presidential veto power. Johnson replied for more than two hours, devoting an hour to defending the veto power. Nelson's rebuttal lasted more than a half hour, and Johnson's almost that long. The discussion was reported to be courteous and free from everything light and trifling.[9] Nelson spoke the next day in a strongly Whig community, and Johnson declined to appear to debate—probably recognizing that, since Nelson would have the privilege of speaking last, no advantage for the Democrats could be gained in that neighborhood. After Nelson returned from Knoxville and resumed the canvass, he again met Andrew Johnson, this time in Johnson's home town. All comments indicated that the discussion was creditable to both men. The Knoxville *Tribune* reported that there had not been a more fair and candid discussion since the canvass began—both men arguing their subjects and avoiding tricks and anecdotes.[10]

On the eve of the election Brownlow felt it necessary to urge every Whig to vote for Nelson. Some few, he said, were prejudiced against Nelson because he had been a severe prosecuting attorney and others because of the religious controversy. There was no occasion for this, argued Brownlow, as "he has acted more nobly and openly than any Presbyterian in all this county—and we know."[11] Evidently Brownlow's pique over the religious controversy with Nelson had been entirely mollified.

Election results gave Tennessee and the nation to General Taylor over the Democratic candidate, Lewis Cass; and Nelson's district was lost to Cass by less than fifty votes—a much smaller margin than customary in the district. John Bell acknowledged Nelson's service by asking him to suggest someone for the office of First Assistant Postmaster General of the United States,[12] and there was a flurry of suggestions that he be rewarded with political office. The governorship was repeatedly mentioned in the following months, and Brownlow editorially advocated supporting him for any office he wanted—citing his long and

---

[8] *Ibid.*, September 6, 1848.

[9] See *idem* for a detailed report of the speeches in this debate with editorial comment.

[10] Cited in *ibid.*, October 25, 1848. See also Oliver P. Temple to Nelson, October 20, 1848, in Nelson Papers.

[11] Jonesboro *Whig*, November 1, 1848.

[12] Bell to Nelson, January 28, 1850, in Nelson Papers.

expensive services to the Whig cause without reward.[13] Nelson indicated that he would not seek election to Congress from the district and declined to consider the governorship because the salary was inadequate to the needs of his large family, which was soon to include six children.[14] It was the United States Senatorship that Nelson desired.

Meanwhile, he was active in the chartering of a railroad to open up the East Tennessee Valley. In the spring of 1849 he had tentatively agreed to seek election to the state senate in behalf of the railroad project, but he changed his mind when conditions upon which he had counted failed to materialize.[15] A railroad convention met the following September at Greeneville and accepted a charter offered by the state. Nelson was appointed on a three-man committee of publicity.[16] When the stock did not sell adequately and the charter was about to expire, Nelson joined thirty other men in subscribing the balance of $450,000 in stock to save the charter.[17] More than ten years later, the railroad was finally completed.[18]

Nelson's political ambitions faded into insignificance before the events of 1850. The application of California for admission had precipitated the whole gamut of sectional issues into Congress, where the fateful controversy raged. A Southern convention was to assemble at Nashville in June, perhaps to consider secession; and John C. Calhoun's dying words urged Southern opposition to Henry Clay's plan of compromise. And then Nelson's concern was suddenly drawn home. Mrs. Nelson's winter illness failed to improve with the coming of spring, and she died on May 23, 1850. At the age of thirty-eight, he was a widower with six children between the ages of nine and one. At the end of the summer his father died at Elizabethton.[19] By fall the nation's travail was postponed as President Taylor's death on July 9 made possible the victory of compromise, but Nelson was hardly even reading the newspaper accounts. The following summer he would write that, owing to the great family affliction with which he had been visited, he had read the newspapers less in the fifteen months since his wife's death than ever in any equal period of the preceding fifteen or twenty years.[20]

[13] Jonesboro *Whig*, January 10 and 17, 1849; W. H. Sneed to Nelson, January 22, 1849; Ebenezer Alexander to *id.*, February 1, 1849; W. H. Sneed to *id.*, February 9, 1849, in Nelson Papers.

[14] Nathaniel G. Taylor to Nelson, June 7, 1849, in Nelson Papers, reveals that Nelson had indicated that he would not run for Congress. For Nelson's public letter expressing appreciation to those who had urged him to seek the governorship and giving his reasons for declining see Jonesboro *Whig*, February 12, 1849.

[15] Revealed in a letter from Nathaniel G. Taylor to Nelson, June 7, 1849, in Nelson Papers.

[16] James W. Holland, "The Building of the East Tennessee and Virginia Railroad," in East Tennessee Historical Society's *Publications*, No. 4 (1934), 87.

[17] Knoxville *Whig*, December 22, 1849.

[18] Holland, "The Building of the East Tennessee and Virginia Railroad," *loc. cit.*

[19] See genealogical article by Selden Nelson in the Knoxville *Sentinel*, July 5, 1923

[20] Nelson to William B. Campbell, July 9, 1851, in Campbell Collection.

The governorship was to be contested in the 1851 election; and by the fall of 1850, Brownlow's *Whig*, now operating on a wider scale from Knoxville, was urging Nelson for the governorship and quoting other papers in the state to the same effect.[21] The Franklin (Tennessee) *Review* was quoted as saying that Nelson ought to be the Whig candidate for the governorship because he was a fluent and eloquent speaker, a sound logician, and an able advocate of the Whig cause. He was further commended for his ready and easy manner of address, high moral character, unbending integrity, and undeviating support of sound morals, public education, and internal improvements.[22] Nelson firmly declined to be considered, nonetheless, on the grounds of pressing professional and family problems.[23] His chief interest in politics at the moment was to urge the passage of a bill through Congress creating a new Federal district judgeship for East Tennessee and to obtain the appointment of his mentor, Thomas L. Williams, to the post.

In a letter to John Bell on the subject of the judgeship in January, 1851, Nelson commented upon Bell's reference to forming a Union party:

I have no objections to the Whigs becoming the chosen champions of the Union. I would make that a question in the next elections. But I am opposed to the idea of changing our name or abandoning our old standards. There is not a doctrine of our party that cannot be vindicated and successfully vindicated on the stump—whether we believe they can be accomplished now or not—U. S. Bank—"*judicious* tariff"—Distribution—internal improvements by the General Government—and the sturdiest hostility to the annexation of Texas and the Mexican War and the train of evils which has followed.[24]

The Whig governorship nomination went to William B. Campbell despite his protestations, and he accepted. Before this had happened, however, Nelson's imagination had been challenged by hearing that he had been appointed by President Fillmore as Commissioner to China.[25] While the problem of his children's care troubled him, it did seem an opportunity to change setting and escape from the restlessness of his still new bereavement. John Bell sent word that Secretary of State Daniel Webster was anxious for him to accept;[26] and he began to clear his professional business in preparation, under a misunderstanding as to salary and allowances. By late April he had reluctantly concluded it was financially and domestically impractical and declined the nomination.

No sooner was one challenge removed than another arose. The Whig gubernatorial candidate, William B. Campbell of Middle Tennessee, be-

[21] Knoxville *Whig*, November 9 and 16, 1850.
[22] *Ibid.*, November 16, 1850.
[23] *Ibid.*, January 4, 1851.
[24] Nelson to John Bell, January 10, 1851, in John Bell Papers (Division of Manuscripts, Library of Congress).
[25] Knoxville *Whig*, March 15, 1851.
[26] S. D. Mitchell to Nelson, April 5, 1851, in Nelson Papers.

came ill and was forced to abandon his joint speaking engagements with William Trousdale, the Democratic nominee. When Trousdale reached Jonesboro on his speaking tour, eighty Washington County Whigs petitioned Nelson to replace Campbell in the canvass. As some Knoxville and some Middle Tennessee Whig leaders had written to the same effect, and as he had been so prominently considered for the nomination before his refusal, Nelson concluded that he would attempt the awkward task.[27] After ascertaining that Trousdale had no objections, Nelson joined him on July 4, 1851. Although he had heard none of the previous speeches and was not even well informed on the newspaper accounts, Nelson was required to speak before Trousdale at Jonesboro. This caused some difficulty, but after the first encounter Nelson swiftly gained the advantage. At the cost of abandoning his legal cases Nelson thereafter accompanied Trousdale throughout East Tennessee and across the Cumberland Plateau into Middle Tennessee, speaking almost daily.

Nelson feared that he had "no reputation to make and probably some little to lose by engaging in the canvass with such a total want of preparation," and he earnestly hoped that Campbell could resume the contest at Sparta as he disliked "to cross the mountains and speak among strangers when so unprepared with facts & that thorough knowledge of the topics, which is desirable." [28] Nevertheless, reports from various points were highly favorable to him. William B. Campbell learned from his uncle that at Jonesboro Nelson answered Trousdale "most effectually." [29] The Nashville *Republican Banner*, a Whig paper, reported repeatedly that Nelson was doing extremely well.[30] Felix K. Zollicoffer reported to Campbell that, although his judgment had been against Nelson's taking the stump, he was "not sure now but that it will do you a good deal of good." He had a letter from Elizabethton giving a "very satisfactory account of the results of the speaking" there, and his news from East Tennessee was "all cheering." [31] Another account of the Elizabethton debate recorded that Trousdale tried to show that the 1850 compromise measures were all for the North and against the South and that President Fillmore and Daniel Webster were agitators and abolitionists, insisting that Webster favored repeal or essential modification of the one measure the South most favored—the strong fugitive slave law. Of Nelson's reply, it was reported to Campbell:

Nelson had profited by the discussion at Jonesboro; had got his documents arranged and was completely *himself*. He made one of the most forcible and

---

[27] The details of Nelson's decision to enter the canvass were explained in the Knoxville *Whig*, July 12, 1851.

[28] Nelson to William B. Campbell, July 9, 1851, in Campbell Collection.

[29] David Campbell to William B. Campbell, July 7, 1851, in Campbell Collection.

[30] Nashville *Republican Banner*, July 11, 1851, and subsequent issues throughout July and early August, 1851.

[31] Zollicoffer to Campbell, July 14, 1851, in Campbell Collection.

happy efforts I have ever heard him make. Nobly and most effectually did
he sustain and defend the Compromise. He scattered to the winds the Governors [sic] assertions that the President and Mr. Webster were abolitionists.
He passed a handsome . . . eulogy upon you; explained your absence &
exorted [sic] the Whigs & all the friends of the *Union* to activity and effort
on your behalf. His speech, taken all together, was an able and effective effort . . . .[32]

Brownlow wrote Campbell that Nelson was a prudent, sensible man,
discussing only the issues already raised in the contest and having a good
effect in East Tennessee. "Nelson's turning out, as well as his speeches,
pleases the whole Whig party in this end of the State, except *a few leading men*, who don't care to see Nelson do anything that will *tend to increase his already strong claim upon his party.*"[33] The Knoxville Whig
group was grooming one of its members, John Netherland, for the next
United States Senate seat that East Tennessee could claim from the
Whigs of the state and were naturally nervous about Nelson's speaking
throughout East Tennessee and perhaps even into Middle Tennessee.

The Democratic papers made much of Nelson's initial difficulties in
speaking without having heard Trousdale's previous speeches, and accused him of conceit in entering the race. They commented upon Nelson's explanation of his willingness to represent Campbell (because he
had been considered for the nomination himself) by saying that "it is
very evident that Mr. Nelson has an exalted opinion of himself . . . ."[34]
Nevertheless, accounts of the canvass continued to grow warmer in
Nelson's behalf; and his courteous and gentlemanly treatment of Trousdale so impressed the governor that at Clinton, when he had concluded,
he requested the Democrats in the audience to remain and hear Nelson
as he had "found him to be a man of honor, a gentleman in every sense
of the word, and a gentleman of whose talents his party had a right to
be proud."[35]

By late July Campbell was hearing that his friends were of the opinion
that Nelson was demolishing Trousdale and making "a most glorious
impression"—managing the discussion with great prudence by com-
plimenting Trousdale's military character and stating that he did not
accuse Trousdale of being a disunionist—but most effectually proving
it nonetheless. When Nelson said he stood ready to abandon the canvass
whenever Campbell's friends thought best, they urged him to continue.[36] Zollicoffer had so completely revised his original doubting position that he wrote Campbell a suggestion emanating from some of the

---

[32] E. Alexander to Campbell, July 15, 1851, in Campbell Collection.
[33] Brownlow to Campbell, July 16, 1851, in Campbell Collection. For further comments by Brownlow about the group of Whigs in Knoxville who were jealous of
Nelson's success see Knoxville *Whig*, July 26, 1851, and W. G. Brownlow to Nelson,
August 28, 1851, in Nelson Papers.
[34] Nashville *American*, July 15 and 22, 1851.
[35] Quoted in the Knoxville *Whig*, July 19, 1851.
[36] H. S. Carrick to W. B. Campbell, July 24, 1851, in Campbell Collection.

Nashville Whigs that Nelson might well be called upon to conclude the campaign there with "an eloquent defense of the Whig cause" if Campbell himself were still unable to speak.[37]

Nelson did continue over the Cumberland Plateau and concluded at Gallatin, in Middle Tennessee, on August 7. Campbell spoke at Nashville on August 8, and Nelson refused an invitation to speak there until a considerable group of Whigs insisted on hearing him. He began in the hall of the house of representatives, expecting no large crowd; but within fifteen minutes a crowd had gathered outside and sent word asking him to come out. He then spoke for two hours to a very receptive audience and made a strong impression.[38] When this news reached Knoxville, Brownlow led off the campaign to reward Nelson with a Senate seat.[39] The Nashville Democratic paper had already had its word on that subject. Commenting derisively upon a twenty-five dollar, gold-headed cane presented Nelson by the Nashville Whigs as a token of appreciation, the Nashville *American* described this as a cheaper way of paying Nelson than by election to the Senate—concluding with: "we greatly fear this is the only present the Whigs of Middle Tennessee will ever be willing to make Mr. Nelson." [40]

As the fall session of the legislature in which a Senator would be elected was only two months away, the Knoxville *Whig* intensified its campaign for Nelson until its editor, Brownlow, left for Nashville to work for Nelson on the scene.[41] Meredith P. Gentry, one of the most prominent Whigs of the state, wrote Nelson that he was for Nelson from East Tennessee and John Bell from Middle Tennessee for the Senate seats. He said that he considered Nelson "a man of noble principles, engaged in a protracted struggle, against adverse circumstances, & fighting the battle of life heroically—scorning the while to make the smallest sacrifice of honour or independence, to shield himself from the kicks and cuffs of unkind Fortune." [42] Senator John Bell took no open stand for any candidate but appears to have favored Nelson.[43] The Nashville *Republican Banner*, generally thought to reflect the views of Governor-elect William B. Campbell, announced that it would not weaken its general influence in the Whig ranks by supporting any one candidate for the Senate.[44]

When the October session of the legislature opened, the Whigs held a narrow margin in the joint convention of the two houses—fifty-five

[37] Zollicoffer to Campbell, July 26, 1851, in Campbell Collection.
[38] Knoxville *Whig*, August 16, 1851.
[39] *Idem.*
[40] Nashville *American*, August 13, 1851.
[41] Knoxville *Whig*, August 23, September 6 and 13, 1851.
[42] Gentry to Nelson, September, 1851, in Nelson Papers.
[43] Parks, *John Bell*, 267.
[44] Issue of September 11, 1851.

seats with fifty-one votes needed to elect a Senator. Twenty Whigs were from East Tennessee, of which sixteen were pledged to Nelson, and two more were considered probable supporters if John Netherland could not win. Netherland, outvoted sixteen to four in the East Tennessee Whig caucus, would not withdraw or release his support to Nelson; and Brownlow's rival newspaper in Knoxville, the *Register*, was proclaiming that East Tennessee was for Netherland. Nelson's strongest opponent proved to be James C. Jones from West Tennessee, who had beaten the leading Democratic campaigner, James K. Polk, for the governorship, in 1841 and 1843. Another West Tennessean, Milton Brown, had the support of the West Tennessee delegation at the outset; but when his election became evidently hopeless, his support switched to Jones as another West Tennessean. Two Middle Tennesseans were also seeking election—but without much hope because Middle Tennessee held one of the existing Senatorships, that occupied by John Bell.

At the first meeting of the Whig caucus trouble developed as to whether to elect two Senators or one. John Bell's term was to expire before another session of the legislature, and his seat would be vacant in the event of a special session of the Senate in the spring or summer of 1853. Furthermore, both parties had previously elected Senators two years before the expiration of the incumbent's term. East Tennesseeans felt certain that Nelson and Bell would be elected if two seats were filled simultaneously, but they were less certain of Nelson's election if only one seat were filled. Hence, they resolved not to go into caucus unless it was agreed that two Senators were to be elected. Particularly were they determined to have an East Tennessean elected because the narrow margin by which the Whigs controlled the legislature was due to the zeal of the East Tennessee Whigs in increasing their vote totals and electing five new Whig members from customarily Democratic districts. At the first meeting of the Whigs a few Middle Tennesseans announced unilaterally that they were pledged to their constituents not to elect more than one Senator and, in conjunction with the Democrats, would prevent election of a second Senator regardless of what the Whig caucus decided. The East Tennessee delegation then walked out—claiming that party apostasy on the part of the Middle Tennesseans had released them from any obligation to the caucus.[45]

The Nashville Whig papers immediately set up a clamor for Whig

---

[45] A running account of the entire Senatorial contest was carried in the Knoxville *Whig*, October 18 through November 22, 1851. Extended explanations of the actions of the East Tennessee delegation were published by Nelson in the Knoxville *Whig*, November 29 and December 20, 1851, and by twelve members of the East Tennessee Whig caucus in the Knoxville *Whig*, March 6, 1852. This latter explanation and statement concludes with the comment that the other members from East Tennessee would have signed the statement except for its prediction that East Tennessee could not hope again to have a Senatorship, and that they agreed with all the rest.

unity and condemned the East Tennesseeans for not rejoining the caucus.[46] As October wore on and the discord continued, Nelson announced his position, pursuant to the will of the majority of the East Tennessee delegation: if fifteen of the twenty Whigs from East Tennessee voted for him, and if sufficient Democrats voted with them without any bargain, he would consider that he could accept election without violation of his political integrity. At the end of October, all efforts at compromise having failed, the Whig caucus invited all candidates to appear and address them. The East Tennesseans met and disagreed vigorously as to whether Nelson should attend—a majority opposing. Nelson stated that if uninstructed by the delegation he would attend; and a majority then instructed him to attend, but without authority to pledge the delegation to any particular course of action. At this meeting Nelson and three other candidates agreed to submit their claims to caucus if fifty-one Whigs (the number necessary to elect in the legislature) would pledge themselves to abide by the majority action of the caucus. Jones and Netherland wanted a majority of all the Whigs (fifty-five), or twenty-eight votes, to be required for nomination. The caucus finally voted to adopt the scheme Nelson had agreed to, and thereafter he considered himself bound to abide by the caucus action. When a dozen of the East Tennesseans decided just before balloting to absent themselves, thus preventing any nomination, Nelson used his influence to get them to attend although he was at the time resigned to defeat.

As eight ballots were taken, Nelson was consistently in the lead with about twenty votes and began to feel that he would win. On the sixteenth ballot, taken on the night of November 10, Nelson reached twenty-one, with Jones sixteen. On November 13 the Whigs found their hand forced by a resolution passing both houses of the legislature to hold the Senatorial election the following day—some Whig members joining the Democrats in so voting in the belief that it would aid the chances of their choices for the Senatorship. Therefore, on the night of November 14, the Whig caucus made a final effort; but only forty-eight members could be convened—less than the fifty-one agreed upon as a minimum action number. When the caucus was on the point of dissolving without a nomination, threats of saddling party dissensions and failure on the absentee members finally brought in a total of fifty-four. As the ballots proceeded, Nelson's vote climbed steadily until it reached twenty-three (five from victory) on the ninth ballot—Jones receiving only fifteen. On the tenth ballot, however, a Jones surge brought him up to twenty-one and Nelson down to twenty.

Sharp recovery on the eleventh ballot pushed Nelson to twenty-five, with Jones receiving twenty. At this point one Middle Tennessean with-

[46] Nashville *Republican Banner*, October 14 and 30, 1851; Nashville *True Whig*, November 5, 1851.

drew as did the East Tennessean, Netherland, whose votes were not swung to Nelson, however. On the twelfth, thirteenth, and fourteenth ballots Nelson pushed up to within one vote of victory and three votes ahead of Jones. With victory for an East Tennessean near, the remaining three votes being cast for the West Tennessean, Brown, were hastily swung to Jones, as was the single vote remaining for a Middle Tennessean. The West Tennesseans had never had a Senator from their division of the state and were determined to break the East-Middle Tennessee arrangement. The fifteenth ballot nominated Jones with a margin of twenty-eight to twenty-five over Nelson.[47] Which two deserted Nelson at that juncture is not known, but his supporters in East Tennessee blamed members of the East Tennessee delegation who had not supported Nelson in the beginning and who had received certain letters of questionable authenticity from home concerning their political future. Middle and West Tennessee had united in opposition to East Tennessee's claim and, with the aid of four anti-Nelson East Tennesseans, had elected Jones. Nelson had to work hard to keep some of his friends from opposing Jones in the legislative election the following day, but in the end the Whigs voted unanimously for Jones.

During the last meetings of the caucus, Nelson passed the time at one of his favorite hobbies—composing political doggerel. He described the proceedings in 166 lines of rhyming couplets, replete with twenty-three explanatory notes. Of the final night he wrote:

> The victory Nelson seems to clasp,
> But quickly it eludes his grasp;
> The strife is o'er, Jones wins the day,
> No man can stand where friends betray.
>
> Ah! Nelson, thou most luckless bard!
> Thy doom is fixed—thy fortune's hard!
> Oft did'st thou mingle in the fray,
> And raise the flag for MONTEREY,
> But now his weight you're doomed to bear,
> Who honors with you will not share!
> Yet ever cherish love of duty,
> Nor say despairing, "*et tu brute:*" [48]

This latter reference was, of course, to Campbell, whose gratitude to Nelson did not extend to refraining from indirectly opposing him in the Senate race. Nelson read the poem to Jones the day of his victory and showed it to most of the Whigs in the legislature. So many asked for a copy that he arranged a private printing with precautions that it should not be published, but some how the Democratic papers in Nashville got it in print. Friends of Governor Campbell were incensed. Nelson later

---

[47] The tabulations on the last ten ballots were printed in the Knoxville *Whig*, March 6, 1852.

[48] Knoxville *Whig*, November 29, 1851.

felt called upon to explain that he never intended publication but that his charges against Campbell, from whose county the three legislators voted for Jones, were justified.[49] Campbell privately wrote that the reason for Nelson's defeat was the bad behavior of East Tennessee Whigs in helping Democrats to elect a Democrat over a Whig for comptroller of treasury, thus causing much feeling among other Whigs against East Tennessee.[50]

Nelson commented in his poem, "And tho' thy hopes have strangely vanished, Thou are not killed but only banished!" When the election year for President approached, the Whigs were anxious to heal rifts and close ranks for the contest, so Nelson was nominated as elector-at-large by the Whig state convention meeting in February in Nashville. Nelson was from many quarters urged to accept, and Jones indicated his desire that Nelson accept as a peace step.[51] Recognizing that a state-wide canvass would put him in a position where a Senatorship could hardly be denied him the next time, Nelson struggled for weeks to arrange his family and professional affairs to free himself for such a canvass. But he reluctantly concluded that he must decline in justice to his family.[52] This decision greatly weakened, although it did not eliminate, his chances for a Senatorship in 1853.

Meanwhile, Nelson's interests were again centered at home. By the summer of 1852 he had been a widower for more than two years. Personal inclinations, custom, and the need of his six children for a mother encouraged remarriage. On August 7, 1852, he married Mary Jones, the daughter of George Jones of Greeneville. The wedding was an occasion of much satisfaction to Nelson's friends and of evident joy to him.[53]

One more effort from Washington to appease Nelson was an offer of the position of Land Commissioner of California, which he declined as unappealing.[54] It is quite possible that Senator John Bell procured the appointment for Nelson to remove a probable opponent from the next Senatorial election.

Although the Democratic leader of East Tennessee, Andrew Johnson, won the governorship in the 1853 elections, the Whigs retained

---

[49] *Ibid.*, December 20, 1851. Unfortunately, no discussion of the details of this election is found in Ray Gregg Osborn, "Political Career of James Chamberlain Jones, 1840-1857," in *Tennessee Historical Quarterly*, VII (1948), 195-228, 322-34.

[50] Letter to "My Dear Uncle," presumably from William B. Campbell to David Campbell, November 20, 1851, in Campbell Collection.

[51] James W. Gillespie to Nelson, February 10, 1852; G. A. Henry to *id.*, February 10, 1852; James W. Deaderick to *id.*, February 10, 1852, in Nelson Papers; Knoxville *Whig*, March 6, 1852.

[52] Public letter by Nelson, dated May 1, 1852, published in Knoxville *Whig*, May 15, 1852.

[53] Nelson's high spirits were commented upon in Caroline J. Aiken to Nelson, August 13, 1852, in Nelson Papers.

[54] Nelson's declination of the position is revealed in Allen A. Hall to Nelson, November 16, 1852, in Nelson Papers.

control of the joint convention of the two houses of the legislature, which was to elect a new Senator. Nelson received much correspondence concerning the seat; and Brownlow continued to advocate his election, even when it meant opposing his political idol in Tennessee, John Bell.[55] For Bell finally decided to seek re-election; and, having decided, hastened from his mountain vacation to Memphis, where he might use the platform at the Southern and Western Commercial Convention to garner West Tennessee support by urging a transcontinental railroad with Memphis as its eastern terminus.[56] When the legislature convened, the Whigs were unable to agree on a candidate from among Nelson, Bell, and Gustavus A. Henry.

The East Tennesseans, standing on their section's historic claim to one of the seats, flatly refused to go into caucus unless guaranteed the seat for East Tennessee. Some hints from Democrats to East Tennesseans that they would support Nelson in the open election stiffened their resistance.[57] Nelson categorically refused to submit his claim to a Whig caucus again on the grounds that to do so would be surrendering East Tennessee's claim to a seat based on fifty years usage by both parties, that he believed the caucus principle wrong and to have been rejected by the Whigs of Tennessee in 1836, that he had information leading him to believe that he was cheated of the nomination by the midnight caucus two years before, and that he was obeying the instructions of a majority of the East Tennessee Whig delegation.[58] The Democrats held the balance and prevented an election until Governor Johnson's state bank directors had been approved, and then they threw support to John Bell and elected him.[59] This ended Nelson's ambitions for office holding— or so he thought, at the time. As Brownlow had said after Nelson's first defeat for the Senate, he was an able, popular lawyer with a good practice and would probably attend to business and let politics alone.[60] Nelson's comment on the same occasion had been: "It is an incident to every election that some of the opposing candidates must be defeated, and, as I never was a candidate or applicant for any office but one previous to the late election, (aside from my position on the whig Electoral Ticket in 1844 and 1848.) I trust that my conduct through life, as well as when the result of the late election was ascertained, affords a sufficient guaranty of my ability to live without the honors of office as well as to submit to disappointment without indulging in useless and unavailing regrets." [61]

---

[55] See Nelson Papers, August to November, 1853; Knoxville *Whig*, September 17, 1853; R. L. Caruthers to W. B. Campbell, September 30, 1853, in Campbell Collection.

[56] Parks, *John Bell*, 278-79.

[57] William G. Brownlow to Oliver P. Temple, October 26, 1853, in Oliver P. Temple Papers (University of Tennessee Library, Knoxville).

[58] Knoxville *Whig*, November 5, 1853.

[59] William G. Brownlow to Oliver P. Temple, October 26, 1853, in Oliver P. Temple Papers; Parks, *John Bell*, 279-81.

[60] Knoxville *Whig*, November 22, 1851.

[61] *Ibid.*, December 20, 1851.

A portrait of Mary Jones, the second Mrs. Nelson, owned by
Mrs. W. W. Carson of Knoxville, Judge Nelson's granddaughter.

CHAPTER V

Without the Honors of Office

NELSON HAD EVERY REASON to be satisfied with his position and achievements as he looked forward from his forty-second birthday to the flowering of a precociously developed career in law. While he did not expect to again seek political office, he fully anticipated a congenial and gratifying influence in future Whig party affairs in East Tennessee.

His fine home, "Buckhorn," provided quiet, beautiful surroundings for living and working, and it enabled him to dispense hospitality of a generous caliber.[1] He owned enough slaves to provide household servants, a carriage driver, and field hands to tend his two hundred acres of grain and hay and his cattle and hogs.[2] He acquired lands for speculation or later development to the extent of more than ten thousand acres in Washington County by 1860, and valued his holdings in that year at more than twenty-six thousand dollars. In a county of general agricultural prosperity, only nine agricultural holdings were valued at more than Nelson's. Jonesboro, on whose eastern outskirts he lived, reached a population total of 1,300 by 1860 and was the largest town in upper East Tennessee, being third only to Knoxville and Chattanooga in the eastern part of the state.[3] Educational opportunities were unusually good in Jonesboro for Nelson's family, which was to include six boys and five girls, as there were academies for both boys and girls with enrollments of more than one hundred each.[4] His eldest child, Alice, was now old enough to be pleasant company at home and to send him amusing letters when he was away. It was nice to receive a long letter about rain, fires, marriages, and the girl Alice didn't like—"but as she has the big head we can account for her meanness very well." A wish that he could come home and write her a composition was followed by the playful signature, "Ecila Noslen."[5]

Washington County provided Nelson with a prosperous population

---

[1] For an example of enthusiastic appreciation from a guest see Fink, "Methodism in Jonesboro, Tennessee," *loc. cit.*, 56.

[2] Detailed information on Nelson's holdings and production for 1860 may be found in the unpublished census schedules for Washington County, Tennessee, for the *Eighth Census of the United States*, located in the Duke University Library, Durham, North Carolina.

[3] Tennessee State Planning Commission, Preliminary Population Report (Nashville, 1935). This is a mimeographed, bound volume.

[4] Unpublished census schedules for 1860 for Washington County (Duke University Library).

[5] Undated letter to Nelson, signed Ecila Noslen, in Nelson Papers, undated group.

from which to draw legal business. Of the nearly thirteen hundred farms in this fertile, limestone-soil county, only a tenth were valued at less than $500. Many of these small farms probably belonged to the numerous part-time artisans. Almost half of the farms were valued from $500 to $2,500, and a fourth were in the $2,500 to $5,000 range. Fifteen per cent of these farms were worth from $5,000 to $10,000, and almost one hundred farmers (more than seven per cent) valued their holdings at above $10,000. While there were few who might be called wealthy, one valuing his holdings at $86,400, and only a dozen at above $25,000, the agricultural base of the county provided a sound income for almost everybody. More than one hundred full-time or part-time blacksmiths, tanners, millers, carpenters, wagonmakers, and other artisans reported good incomes. Half of these valued their annual output at between $1,000 and $2,500, and a few reported from $3,000 to $8,500, principally in flour milling. Washington County had one important manufacturing firm, John Blair and Company, with a $65,000 production value of iron products in 1850.[6] Elizabethton to the east and Greeneville to the west, in neighboring counties, were almost as large as Jonesboro.[7]

Legal circuit-riding as well as political campaigning required Nelson to make frequent trips through the counties of upper East Tennessee and sometimes beyond. This was rough country for riding, interlaced with small ridges and sharply segmented by several major mountain chains. Fords were numerous, and floods made travel all but impossible. The best of riding conditions seldom permitted more than five miles in an hour, and in much of Nelson's territory an hour was required to cover one or two miles. He was an outstanding horseman, but his impatience in times of stress occasionally caused him to wear out his horses.

As he rode circuit in the first district, year after year, the varied landscapes were etched upon his mind. There was the cascading creek, as he wound steadily upward toward Taylorsville and the easternmost corner of the state, with the contrasting repose of the valley nestled high in timbered mountains—a true frontier, hardly touched by the ax. The loftiness of Iron Mountain, blocking the passage westward, was each time surprising anew; beyond its crest lay the cove of treetops in Shady Valley, stretching out only briefly to the rampart of razor-backed Holston Mountains. And from that range the sunset view across the depths of Holston Valley, with its rolling hills rising to the unbroken escarpment of the Clinch Mountains—a day's ride westward—was inspiring in its grandeur. The sharp downward winding of the road to Bristol brought the relief of valley riding to Blountville, broken only by the mild barrier of Chestnut Ridge. The pleasant ride around the north end of Bays Mountains to Kingsport revealed the sparkling waters of Holston River. And, as the road followed the stream southwestward, the sharp

[6] Unpublished census schedules for Washington County, Tennessee, for the *Seventh Census of the United States* (Duke University Library).
[7] Tennessee State Planning Commission, Preliminary Population Report.

rise of Bays Mountains furnished a stage-set backdrop less than five miles to the south across the rolling valley floor. When the road approached Rogersville, the looming mass of Clinch Mountains rose on the right. From Rogersville to Morristown and on to Knoxville was easy riding along Holston Valley to its juncture with the principal East Tennessee Valley, where thoughts of "Buckhorn" were encouraged by turning eastward through Greeneville to complete the circle.

On other occasions, there was the ride to Knoxville through relatively flat country for supreme court meetings or political conventions, followed by the trip through ever rougher country toward Cumberland Gap, while the rugged rampart of Cumberland Mountain dominated the northwestern horizon and lifted the eyes to the azure clouds of a mountain dusk. Or Knoxville might be a point of departure for the southern sweep of upper East Tennessee—eastward to Sevierville, directly into the smoky gray mass of the Great Smoky Mountains, then northeastward under the morning shadow of this massive highland to Parrotsville. Near Greeneville the country became more open, and the homeward ride was through fields of yellow wheat and waving corn, banked by evergreen forests.

In welcoming Swiss immigrants to East Tennessee, Nelson concluded that the Switzer could find much to remind him of home:

> He who first meets the highland's swelling blue
> Will love each peak that shows a kindred hue
> Hail, in each craig, a friend's familiar face,
> And clasp the mountain in his mind's embrace.[8]

After thirty years of riding his circuits, he revealed his own "mind's embrace" in his lines:

> East Tennessee! secluded land,
> Of gentle hills and mountains grand,
> Where healthful breezes ever blow,
> And coolest springs and rivers flow;
> Where yellow wheat and waving corn
> Are liberal poured from plenty's horn,—
> Land of the valley and the glen,
> Of lovely maids and stalwart men;
> Thy gorgeous sunsets well may vie,
> In splendor, with Italian sky;
> For, gayest colors deck the clouds,
> As night the dying sun enshrouds,
> And heaven itself doth wild enfold
> Its drapery of blue and gold,
> And, pillowed in the rosy air,
> The seraps well might gather there,
> And, in the rainbow tinted West,
> Be lulled by their own songs to rest!

[8] He employed these lines from Byron to conclude a short address at a Swiss celebration. The manuscript is in the Nelson Papers, undated. Evidently he was very fond of the lines since he used them on the title page of his published poems.

Thy bracing Winter, genial Spring,
The ruddy glow of rapture bring;
Thy Summer's mild and grateful heat,
From sweltering suns gives cool retreat;
White frosty Autumn, full of health,
Fills crib and barn with grainy wealth,
And challenges the earth to dress
Its leaves in richer loveliness!

Enchanting land, where nature showers
Her fairest fruits and gaudiest flowers;
Where stately forests wide expand,
Inviting the industrious hand,
And all the searching eye can view
Is beautiful and useful, too;—
Who knows thee well, is sure to love,
Where'er his wandering footsteps rove,
And backward ever turns to thee,
With fond, regretful memory,
Feeling his heart impatient burn
Among thy mountains to return! [9]

Nelson's prestige as a lawyer, his primary concern throughout life, was gratifyingly high. By the time he was forty, he was acknowledged leader of the bar of his judicial circuit, and by 1860 was recognized as one of the best trial lawyers in East Tennessee.[10] Oliver P. Temple, a contemporary East Tennessee leader, said of him that "he underwent no long probation at the bar, as most young men had to do in that circuit, but leaped at once into a full practice. . . ." He added that in nearly fifty years of observation he had seen no parallel to Nelson's early success. Temple considered what he called Nelson's "phenomenal rise at the bar" to be the result of a combination of natural ability, unusual educational opportunities and a habit of thorough study, the physical stamina to bear long-continued and intense effort, a voice that held attention with its strength and deep pitch, moral and physical courage, candidness and directness tempered by generosity and sympathy, rigid personal integrity, and a compelling ambition. Of Nelson's ambition, Temple observed: "To excel, to deserve success, rather than to gain a mere empty triumph, spurred him to almost superhuman efforts. But all this toil, all this boundless ambition was regulated and controlled by the keenest and the highest sense of honor and right and the most sacred regard for truth." [11]

---

[9] These are the opening stanzas of a long poem entitled "East Tennessee," written by Nelson during 1863-64 and published anonymously in *Secession; or, Prose in Rhyme, and East Tennessee, A Poem* (Philadelphia, 1864).

[10] The most fruitful source of information on Nelson as a lawyer is an account by a younger colleague, Henry H. Ingersoll, "Biographical Sketch of Thomas A. R. Nelson," *loc. cit.* Additional intimate information is available in a sketch by a contemporary East Tennesseean, "Thomas A. R. Nelson," in Oliver P. Temple, *Notable Men of Tennessee,* 166-81.

[11] Temple, *Notable Men of Tennessee,* 166-67.

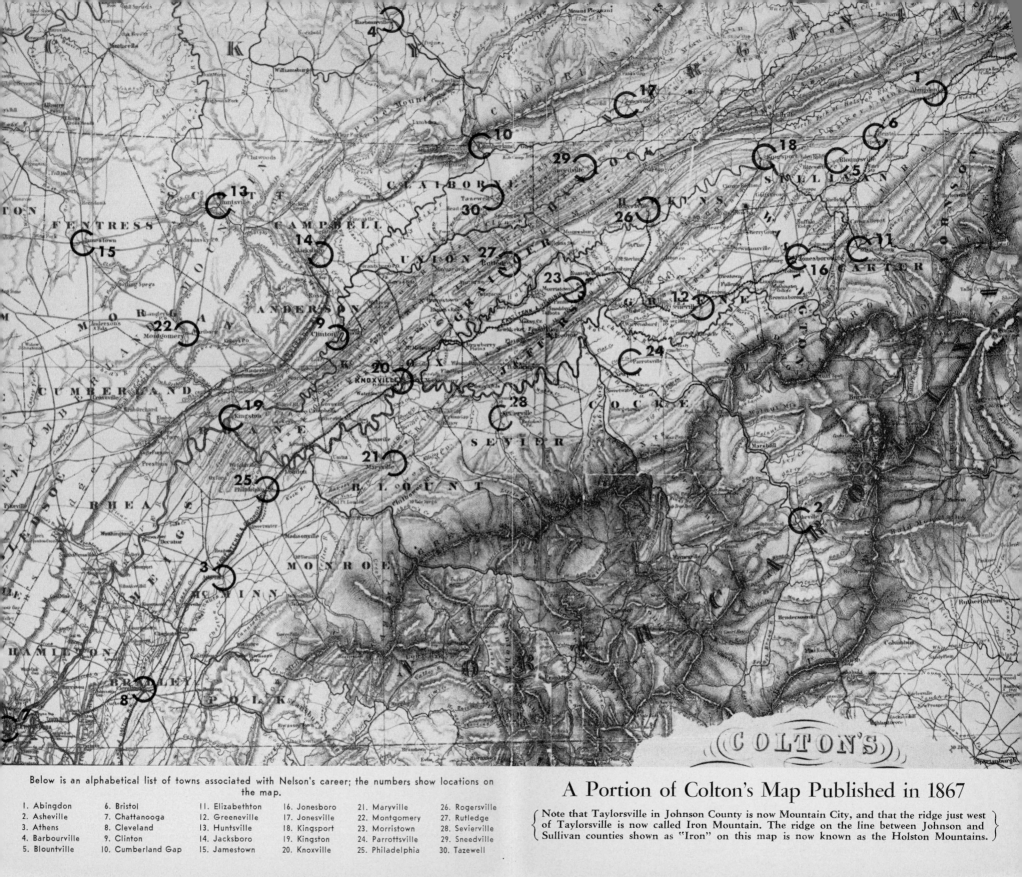

1. Abingdon	6. Bristol	11. Elizabethton	16. Jonesboro	21. Maryville	26. Rogersville
2. Asheville	7. Chattanooga	12. Greeneville	17. Jonesville	22. Montgomery	27. Rutledge
3. Athens	8. Cleveland	13. Huntsville	18. Kingsport	23. Morristown	28. Sevierville
4. Barbourville	9. Clinton	14. Jacksboro	19. Kingston	24. Parrottsville	29. Sneedville
5. Blountville	10. Cumberland Gap	15. Jamestown	20. Knoxville	25. Philadelphia	30. Tazewell

A Portion of Colton's Map Published in 1867

Note that Taylorsville in Johnson County is now Mountain City, and that the ridge just west of Taylorsville is now called Iron Mountain. The ridge on the line between Johnson and Sullivan counties shown as "Iron" on this map is now known as the Holston Mountains.

Since specialization in law was impossible for a rural, circuit-riding lawyer of the day, Nelson never considered the idea of such limitation of practice. He was generally considered equally at home in any type of case before any court. According to a younger associate at the bar, passing judgment twenty years after Nelson's death, he lacked the outstanding tact in cross-examination possessed by some of his fellow counselors although he was always careful and precise in following the rules of practice. He was also exceeded by one or another of his colleagues at the bar in such matters as mathematical accuracy, analytical power, eloquence, brilliance of wit, or power of arousing emotion. But, concluded this associate, "in the average possession of all those faculties which go to make a great lawyer, he seemed to me the best balanced and strongest all-around lawyer I ever knew." [12]

In his manner at the bar he was unaffected and candid, avoiding histrionics always. Some considered this an explanation of his influence over judges and juries. Without entertaining the court with sparkling sallies of humor, and without concise statement or pointed epigram, he nonetheless made an effective impression. This was generally due to the earnestness and transparent sincerity of his often copious presentation. He was nearly always successful in avoiding the impression that he was sly or clever in twisting the facts of the case to suit his client, and he won an unusually high reputation for being perfectly frank with the court. In personal appearance he was of medium height and rather robust figure. His limp was always noticeable, but his face commanded attention. The features were strong, with broad, full brow, massive jaw, prominent Grecian nose, and steel gray eyes that "beamed with joy and merriment and flashed with anger and disdain." In legal or political speeches his delivery, though earnest and serious, was vigorous and involved continuous bodily action.

He was considered an example of high professional ethics and correct deportment. He almost always maintained an attitude of dignified respect toward the bench, regardless of how great his contempt for its occupant might be; and he deplored the advent of judicial elections as undermining the dignity of the bench. He was zealous in his defense of the rights and privileges of the bar but resentful of any suggestion of unethical behavior on the part of an attorney. On one occasion, inadvertently overhearing the opposing counsel, in a night visit to the judge's chamber, submitting a decision as an authority for his case and commenting on it, Nelson entered the judge's chamber as soon as his opponent was gone and announced: "I have heard, sir, because I could not help hearing, the supplemental argument and authority of Mr. ——— in the ——— case; and I only wish to say now that tomorrow morn-

---

[12] Ingersoll, "Biographical Sketch of Thomas A. R. Nelson," *loc. cit.* The following description of Nelson's courtroom personality is based on Ingersoll's account.

ing, after your honor shall have opened court, in the courthouse, and in the presence of opposing counsel, and by daylight, I will reply to his argument, and comment upon his authority. Good night." [13] He stated his own position on this subject late in his career when he said:

In the whole course of my professional career . . . I have never had the impudence or presumption to talk to a judge out of court about any case in which I was concerned. . . . I have had sufficient respect for the independence of the judges before whom I have had the honor to practice my profession to take it for granted that they were men of honor, men of intelligence, and that they would not hear any remarks that I would attempt to infuse into their understandings out of doors, and not in the presence of my adversary." [14]

Duties as well as rights of the bar were rarely forgotten in the excitement and exhilaration Nelson experienced in the heat of legal dispute. When a junior member of the bar declined the court's appointment as counsel for a Negro accused of larceny, Nelson looked up from his writing in the courtroom and rose to deliver an earnest lecture to the effect that a lawyer owed it to himself, to the profession, and to the state to defend the lives and liberties of those who could not pay, in preference even to paying clients. He volunteered his services and won acquittal in a difficult case.

In his preparation he was always thorough in searching out precedent or fact and in preparing every avenue of attack or defense he could think of that might aid his client. During the trial he contested points in preliminary skirmish and in decisive combat with equal tenacity. Some considered it a failing that he employed as much vigor, learning, and labor on small points as in maintaining the essential points of his case. But "abundant caution" was his self-imposed rule of practice, for he maintained that no one could tell what might happen to strike the mind of a juror or on what point in the case the judge might accidentally hinge his decision.

To Nelson the law was not a business, and he resented efforts to bring business methods into the profession. Soliciting cases or advertising were considered disgraceful. He often expressed his high estimate of the role of the law in the thought that the liberties of the American people are not those in constitution or statue but those which are enforced and secured in the courts.

To his eminence at the bar and in local and state political matters, Nelson early added local church leadership. He joined the Presbyterian Church after moving to Jonesboro and soon became an elder, bearing a disproportionate share of church expenses over many years. [15] He took

---

[13] *Idem.*

[14] From Nelson's address in the impeachment trial of Andrew Johnson. Quoted in *idem.*

[15] R. P. Wells to Nelson, July 14, 1858, in Nelson Papers.

his church duties seriously enough to devote many hours of his brief visit home in the midst of a vigorous political campaign to reconciling a controversy among five members of his church and thereby avoiding a church investigation—"believing it to be my duty as an Elder of the Church to endeavor to reconcile the parties without the ill feeling which I feared would be the consequence of the investigation." [16]

In religious matters he seems to have conformed to the general tendency away from Eighteenth Century rationalism that characterized the mid-Nineteenth Century South. If he held any beliefs that were not orthodox Protestant, he saw to it that none became public. To a friend, who drew him into a doctrinal discussion, he curtly excused himself with the statement: "I am not in the habit of parading my opinions on such topics." [17] He read widely on religious topics in orthodox books and magazines, and in one speech expounded a literalistic interpretation of the Bible. "Who that believes in the truth of revelation," he asked, "can for a moment doubt that there are national sins, and that war, pestilence, and famine, are scourges which an Almighy Power brings into requisition in order to rebuke those sins, and show his abhorrence of them?" [18]

Newspaper and pamphlet material on political, religious, or other topics that he wished to have in handy form were clipped and mounted in scrapbooks. He amassed nineteen volumes in the years between the age of twenty-seven and his death. For each volume he prepared an index and copied it into the book. A speech outline might consist of little more than topic headings with volume and page references to his scrapbooks for items which he might want to read or on which he might be challenged. [19]

Although disappointed in his Senate ambitions, Nelson had every reason to look forward from his forty-second year to many years of peaceful and rewarding leadership. His home, profession, and avocation were well ordered; his economic status was sound and improving; and his labors in every field were meeting with satisfying success and appreciation. It was true that Democrats occupied the governor's mansion at Nashville and the White House, but that could be corrected in the next election. The Compromise of 1850, so staunchly defended by Nelson in his last two political efforts, seemed to have calmed a nation already sobered by realization of how near the brink of disaster the controversy had swept them. The deep-seated forces propelling the nation toward schism were for the moment obscured, but Stephen A. Douglas's Kansas-Nebraska Bill was only weeks away as Nelson settled down at "Buckhorn" to "live without the honors of office, attend to business, and let politics alone."

---

[16] Jonesboro *Whig*, September 27, 1848.
[17] The direct quotation is employed in a letter from R. J. Meigs to Nelson, September 6, 1857, in Nelson Papers.
[18] *Congressional Globe*, 36 Cong., 1 Sess., Appendix, 190-95.
[19] For an example of such an outline see Nelson Papers under date of April 26, 1861.

CHAPTER VI

The American Order in Tennessee

THE OPEN COLLAPSE of the superficial sectional amity under the impact of the Kansas-Nebraska Bill, and the subsequent series of events plainly threatening the Union, shattered Nelson's plans for a quiet life far from the acrimony of politics. He must have thought of his friend and teacher's justification of entering the political lists despite an overpowering fear of political ambition: "I thought our Nation was in jeopary and that every one loving his country ought to bear some part in its reformation." [1]

The American party, popularly known as the Know-Nothing party, emerged from a welter of sporadic nativistic movements. After some local successes in political action, it adopted a platform at Philadelphia in June, 1855, and thereafter the element of secrecy was rapidly dropped. Its chief platform planks centered around keeping native-born citizens in complete control of local, state, and Federal governments, excluding Catholics from political power on the assumption that they owed a loyalty to the Pope higher than their loyalty to the United States and hence were subversive, and restricting immigration and naturalization in the interests of weakening the political influence of non-native stock. Another point included in the platform was antagonism to all political office seekers who were in favor of dissolving the Union. The rise of Know-Nothingism in the South probably was due less to any great antipathy either to foreigners or Catholics than to the reluctance of Whigs to join their historic opponents, the Democrats, and to the assumption that naturalized citizens generally voted the Democratic ticket. The Whigs had no particular objection to the idea that America should be ruled by Americans and surely approved the Unionist platform. Above all, the American party was a place to go when their own national party organization crumpled under the pressure of sectional animosity.[2] Hence,

---

[1] Thomas L. Williams to Nelson, June 14, 1841, in Nelson Papers. For study of the impact of the Kansas-Nebraska Bill on Tennessee Whigs see Joseph H. Parks, "The Tennessee Whigs and the Kansas-Nebraska Bill," *Journal of Southern History*, X (1944), 308-30.

[2] For treatments of the Know-Nothing party in Tennessee see Murry Bryant Measamer, "A History of the Know-Nothing Party in Tennessee" (M.A. thesis, University of Tennessee, 1931); W. Darrell Overdike, *The Know-Nothing Party in the South* (Baton Rouge, Louisiana, 1950), 40-43; Ray Allen Billington, *The Protestant Crusade, 1800-1860* (New York, 1938), 380-97; Sister Mary de Lourdes Gohmann, *Political Nativism in Tennessee to 1860* (Washington, D. C., 1938), 65-177. This latter reference contains the texts of the Tennessee American party platforms for 1855, 1856, and 1857. The first reference contains the Tennessee American party platforms and the national American party platforms for 1855 and 1856.

although every effort was made to present the new party as a fusion of conservative men from all parties, Tennessee Americans were nearly all Whigs.

Nelson joined the ranks of the American party in the summer of 1855, presumably soon after he read the platform adopted at Philadelphia. A call to duty immediately came from the new organization, because the American party candidate for the governorship against Andrew Johnson, Meredith P. Gentry, a Whig of long-standing leadership, became ill during the canvass. Nelson was asked to repeat his performance of 1851 and substitute for Gentry.[3] He rode the one hundred miles to Knoxville in two days to answer this call, but when he arrived on July 23 Johnson and Gentry had agreed to close the canvass. Former Governor William B. Campbell, with animosity from the Senatorial contest of 1851 buried under the weight of threatening national disaster, persuaded Nelson to accompany him back to Middle Tennessee to speak for the American party cause.[4] For more than a week he addressed large audiences in Middle Tennessee towns before returning to Jonesboro in early August. Gentry lost to Johnson by about two per cent of the total popular vote, but the American party won half the congressional elections and more than half the seats in the state legislature, controlling the state senate.

Encouraged by the good showing in several states in 1855, American party leaders launched ambitious plans for a national presidential campaign in 1856. Nelson, unexpectedly, was named as a delegate to the National Council of the party, which was to meet in Philadelphia in February, 1856. Attendance required him to leave some of his cases, but he thought that this service would exempt him from any demand that he be a presidential elector candidate in the state, for which he explicitly declined to be considered by the state convention.[5] Also, his friend and loyal advocate throught the columns of the *Whig*, Brownlow, was to be a delegate. Since Brownlow had moved his paper to Knoxville, their close association had been changed to infrequent contacts, and the trip together would provide an opportunity to discuss the problems facing the country. Arriving in Philadelphia in the midst of a cold and snowy season, Nelson and Brownlow encountered sharp controversies within the council over both slavery and Catholicism.

On the day the council organized, an effort was made to repeal the twelfth section of the June, 1855, platform guaranteeing protection to slavery. Fearing that enough votes might be mustered to achieve this purpose, the Southern members caucused to discuss what action they might take. Motions were introduced that the Southern delegates should

---

[3] Alex E. Smith to Nelson, July 20, 1855, in Nelson Papers.

[4] Knoxville *Whig*, August 11, 1855.

[5] A public letter from Nelson, published in the Knoxville *Whig*, June 7, 1856, explains fully his role during the entire 1856 campaign.

withdraw if the slavery guarantee were repealed and that the anti-Catholic clause ought to be repealed in behalf of the Louisiana Catholic members of the party, who denied the claim of the Pope to political allegiance. After some favorable discussion of a general nature, it appeared that these resolutions might be adopted by the caucus—an action Nelson considered undesirable. He therefore undertook to prevent a favorable vote by objecting on the grounds that the Southerners should not begin agitation and threatening on the assumption that the Northerns would do something, in advance of any definite action on their part, and that the Catholics of Louisiana who were American-born and did not acknowledge the temporal supremacy of the Pope should find nothing objectionable in the existing clause on that subject. After some further discussion the resolutions were withdrawn at the request of Brownlow, and no action was taken.

The following day the council conducted angry discussions about slavery throughout the day, and in the evening session comity had been so completely broken that the following exchange took place: Governor Call of Florida turned to the Massachusetts and Ohio delegations and requested them to visit his slaves and see how they were clothed, fed, and housed. Brownlow jumped up in the middle of the hall and requested the governor to withdraw that invitation as he would be sorry to see the breed of that delegation introduced among the Negro women of Florida. The governor responded that there need be no fears on that score because (turning to the Ohio delegation) the Negro women would scorn to associate with them. The session broke up with loud and long applause from the floor.[6] Again the Southern delegates held a caucus and wrangled until after midnight. Nelson grew weary and doubtful of any advantage to be gained and went to bed before any votes were taken on resolutions, comforting himself with the thought that his duty was clear—"to maintain the position which Tennessee has always occupied between the secessionists on both sides of Mason and Dixon's line: to do nothing which would be calculated to increase the excitement on either side, but to act with the South and to retire from the Convention whenever its final action was calculated, in my judgment, to peril Southern interests."[7]

As the snow and ice had delayed many delegates, the council increased in attendance each day until it was evident that the anti-slavery group could not win. A vote on repeal of the slavery clause in the platform sustained the South. Then, in a hasty effort at compromise, the entire existing platform was annulled and replaced by one the delegates were given no opportunity to debate or amend. Moved with the previous question, and with only three minutes for a delegate to explain his vote

---

[6] Knoxville *Whig*, March 1, 1856.

[7] Nelson's explanation was published in the Knoxville *Whig*, June 7, 1856.

if he wished, the new platform was adopted. The anti-slavery extremists walked out as they could not accept even the reworded platform. Nelson refused to vote for it on the grounds that prevention of debate was detestable and that he had not had time to read the new platform carefully enough to know whether he approved its contents. He did announce that, if upon careful reading he could accept it, or if the convention nominated the right kind of man, he would give his support.[8] This cautiousness is illustrative of one of Nelson's traits of mind, described by an associate in the following manner: "He unquestionably had a strong mind, but he was so honest that it made him slow and cautious in his mental operations. He arrived at conclusions on important questions only after the most careful reflection. On new questions he would express no opinion until he had looked into them most carefully and thoroughly."[9] When the convention nominated former Whig President Millard Fillmore and Andrew Jackson Donelson, a former Democrat, Nelson was satisfied.

The question of admitting the Louisiana delegation, who represented groups containing Catholics, was settled after a floor fight in which the Louisiana delegates insisted that none of their members maintained the temporal supremacy of the Pope. Nelson and Brownlow spoke and voted with the majority in seating this delegation.[10]

Upon returning to Tennessee, Nelson was faced with the fact that the state convention of the American party had nominated him as candidate for elector-at-large, entailing a state-wide canvass, in the face of his flat refusal to be considered. Again accepting what he considered a draft call, he struggled for weeks to arrange for substitute counsel for all of the cases he would have to abandon. Finding this impossible on such short notice, he resigned the nomination with a letter, dated May 30, 1856, in which he delivered a full length "campaign speech," expounding and defending the essential points in the national platform of the American party. Brownlow thought enough of the speech to print five thousand copies in booklet form for distribution and to comment that, could the booklet be placed in the hands of every voter, he would be willing to excuse Nelson and all other speakers on his side.[11]

The first part of Nelson's 1856 campaign address dealt with the Democratic party and all the things its leadership had done that allegedly brought on the sectional controversy, even accusing them of favoring Northern abolitionists and Southern secessionists in the search for votes, for "when did modern Democracy ever display the moral courage to denounce the aberrations of its followers if there was the slightest danger

[8] *Idem.*

[9] Temple, *Notable Men of Tennessee*, 180.

[10] Overdyke, *The Know-Nothing Party in the South*, 134.

[11] Nelson's speech is printed in full in the Knoxville *Whig*, June 7, 1856.

of losing a single vote." He then tried to show that the American party had been necessary because even in the Whig party some prominent leaders had been abolitionists or secessionists. "Under these circumstances, that portion of both the old parties, North and South, who regard the Union as in danger and believe that this danger has been fearfully augmented by the appalling increase of foreign immigration, sundered the ties that bound them to their former associations and attached themselves to the American Order." After recounting the presumed offenses of immigrants which caused the formation of the order, he continued:

. . . Although, there are other organizations which claim to be American, the American Party of Tennessee has no alliance, or sympathy, with any organization which does not regard the Union as the "palladium of our safety"—the jewel above all price . . . . the American party claims to contain sound Northern men and Southern men, who consider the Union of paramount importance; and . . . although, it does not claim, in Congress, the strength which belongs either to the Democrats or Black Republicans, yet it does claim to be the nucleus around which true hearted men everywhere, North and South, can rally, and fearlessly proclaim to the people that its only object is our country's good—its only aim that the Union shall be preserved "one and indissoluble now and forever."

After further exhorting all "patriotic and Union-loving men" to rally to the American party, he urged the change of naturalization laws so that immigrants unfamiliar with American laws and political systems should not be able to vote after only five years residence—the national party platform calling for twenty-one years residence. He blamed the Democrats for catering to immigrants, conniving in fraudulent naturalizations, and encouraging the flood of immigrants which reached half a million in 1854.

In dealing with Catholics, Nelson accepted uncritically the whole gamut of conspiracy literature launched in 1834 by Samuel F. B. Morse in his attack upon the Austrian Catholic missionary organization, the Leopold Association. The general theme was that the reactionary monarchical leaders of Europe feared the democracy of the United States as a source of all their troubles and intended to stem its flow at the source by overthrowing the government of the United States. Unable to do this by direct war, according to the conspiracy theory, they had enlisted the aid of the Catholic Church and were encouraging millions of Europe's Catholic masses to migrate to the United States, ultimately to gain political control, and then to establish the Catholic Church and monarchy upon the ruins of democracy. Toward this presumed menace Nelson stated that the American party policy was not disfranchisement of Catholics, nor disqualification for office holding, nor interference with their private religious practice—but was to organize public sentiment against electing Catholics to public office and against too quick and easy naturalization and enfranchisement of aliens. After portraying in unflattering terms the Catholic religious practices which he did not propose to interfere with, he concluded with another long attack on twenty years of treason by the Democratic party in the interest of victory at the polls, pleading with his Whig associates not to be misled into that party.

Nelson delivered the essence of this speech at Asheville, North Carolina, at the request of Zebulon B. Vance,[12] and in Knoxville, where the Fillmore Club insisted upon a second speech from him before he left for home.[13] Numerous other invitations to speak were received in October and November.[14] When the returns were in, Fillmore ranked below James Buchanan and John C. Frémont, the Republican nominee. Fillmore had received only about twenty per cent of the popular vote, carried only Maryland, and lost Tennessee by a margin of the popular vote wider than that between Gentry and Johnson in the gubernatorial contest of the preceding year.[15] This defeat in Tennessee and even greater defeat in the gubernatorial and legislative elections of 1857 ended the organization of the American party in Tennessee. By 1858 Neill S. Brown wrote to John Bell: "And now Whigs and Americans have become synonymous, & of the tenets which marked the origin of the American party, none remain, save the exclusion of foreign paupers & criminals and the extension of the time necessary to naturalization. The opposition party [to the Democrats] is made up almost entirely of Whigs —the Democrats who formerly acted with us having gone off." [16]

As Kansas and Sumner continued to "bleed" in the anti-slavery press, Chief Justice Taney inadvertently added lightwood to the sectional fires while Lincoln startled and chilled the South with his "House Divided" speech. And as the panic of 1857 added economic distress to moral indignation in parts of the North, and talk of "higher law" than the Constitution became more general among the abolitionists, and *Uncle Tom's Cabin* became the first American best-seller, Nelson was steadily driven to reconsider a decision of long-standing—not to seek election to Congress as a representative from the first district. He went as a delegate to the Whig district convention to work for the nomination of Nathaniel G. Taylor on February 15, 1859; but, when the convention unanimously adopted a nominating committee recommendation for Nelson, he accepted in an unaccustomed manner—with a *brief* speech, promising to battle for party, Union, and the whole country.[17] The Democrats nomi-

---

[12] Vance to Nelson, September 10, 1856; E. J. Austin to *id.*, October 14, 1856, in Nelson Papers; Knoxville *Whig*, November 14, 1856.

[13] Knoxville *Whig*, October 18, 1856.

[14] These may be found in the Nelson Papers under dates in October and November, 1856.

[15] Overdyke, *The Know-Nothing Party in the South*, 154.

[16] *Ibid.*, 268.

[17] Knoxville *Whig*, February 12, 19, and 26, March 3, 1859.

nated Landon C. Haynes, against whom Nelson had so often debated; and almost fifty joint debates were scheduled.

Politeness and courtesy characterized this otherwise strenuous struggle. Not only were the usual Democratic alignment of the district and the obviously disorganized condition of the Opposition party handicaps to Nelson, but also four of the five papers in the district and one of the major Knoxville papers opposed him—only the Jonesboro *Vindicator* and Brownlow's Knoxville *Whig* favoring his election. The Democrats tried to discredit him by associating his name with the Republicans, a Greeneville paper carrying an untruthful story that he had said he would vote for a Republican before a Democrat—a trick Haynes was fair enough to repudiate from the platform. Another line of attack was the proposition that the Southern Opposition party to the Democrats (erstwhile Whigs) planned a fusion nationally with the Republicans for the 1860 presidential election. To take full advantage of this thrust, Haynes asked Nelson on the platform whether he would support John Bell in 1860 if he should be nominated by the Black Republicans of the North and the Opposition party of the South. Nelson's reply created a sensation, for he replied in the affirmative—injecting the very important proviso, if "the Black Republicans will drop their abolition tendencies." [18]

This contest brought a revival of the Methodist-Presbyterian controversy of the 1840's during which Nelson and Brownlow had briefly disagreed. Democrats in the district conducted a systematic campaign among Methodists, urging them not to vote for Nelson. Brownlow, the principal protagonist of the Methodists in the earlier controversy, hastened to Nelson's defense and insisted that he had acted honorably in publishing his views and privately writing to the Presbyterian author of the attacks on the Methodists, asking him to disavow some of the charges made against Methodist women or, if misinterpreted, to announce that he had not intended to imply what was charged against him.[19]

A final, largely irrelevant, attempt to discredit Nelson came in connection with the Bank of East Tennessee, which had been chartered by the State of Tennessee in 1843,[20] and had failed after the panic of 1857 with great loss to its depositors. Nelson had condemned its officers repeatedly for illegal practices which resulted in the failure and had claimed to be able to send the bank's former president to prison if he could be indicted and tried before an impartial jury. The Knoxville *Register* was financially controlled by officers of the bank, and its columns were used during the 1859 campaign to publish private dealings Nelson had had with the bank in such a way as to imply that his attacks had been nothing

[18] Philip M. Hamer, ed., *Tennessee, A History, 1673-1932*, 4 vols. (New York, 1933), I, 515.

[19] Knoxville *Whig*, July 5, 1859.

[20] *Acts of Tennessee*, 1843-44.

A Brady photograph of Landon Carter Haynes, Nelson's political opponent in hundreds of campaign debates. The negative is in the National Archives.

more than private resentment of the bank's placing an overdue note out for collection. Nelson made one reply to these charges, explaining that he had borrowed about two thousand dollars in 1855 and had been unable to meet the note on the date it came due. The bank had placed it in the hands of an attorney within ten days although it was endorsed by men of unquestionable financial status. Nelson paid the note and charges within four months.[21] He repeated his reasons for considering the bank president guilty of a felony—generally circumstantial evidence —and concluded by saying that he could spare no more time from the canvass to debate the matter.[22]

In the discussion of issues in the election, Haynes emphasized the danger of Negro insurrection under the stimulation of Republican propaganda, the prospect of Republican fusion with the Southern Opposition (Whigs) in 1860, and the national nature of the Democratic party as the only guarantee of the Union and the South's rights within the Union. Nelson denied repeatedly the charge often published in Democratic papers that he favored a Republican over a Democrat for the presidency. His chief dependence, however, was upon a catalogue of Democratic corruption, extravagance, and subversion of American institutions, and the charge that the existing danger from the Republican party was due to the fact that the Democrats invited the Old World's "paupers and criminals," who first became Democrats and then abolitionists and Republicans.[23] President Buchanan, he charged, was the first President to be guilty of personal corruption.[24] As a positive policy Nelson stated that he had always supported and still did support the American System of Henry Clay, "comprising Bank, Tariff, Internal Improvements of a National Character, Distribution, economy in the public expenditures and devotion to the American Union. . . ." [25] Some other issues were injected, of course, such as the soldiers' pension bill recently defeated in a Democratic-controlled Senate and Haynes's attempt to gain votes by implying that the Democrats would obtain Cuba. Nelson deplored the danger of plunging the United States into war with Spain.[26]

The results of the election were elating to Nelson and the Opposition party throughout Tennessee. Nelson won by a margin of less than one hundred, but in a district that had been in the Democratic column in the preceding presidential and gubernatorial elections. After the dissolution

---

[21] A statement by Nelson, found in his Scrap Book Number 7 (1859), page 20, in Nelson Papers.

[22] Nelson's card in Knoxville *Whig*, May 31, 1859.

[23] The notion that immigrants became abolitionists and then Republicans has been challenged by recent scholarship but was widely held in the Nineteenth Century.

[24] Knoxville *Whig*, May 10, 1859, reports this charge in an account of the Nelson-Hayne debate at New Market, Tennessee. For another account of the canvass see Bellamy, "The Political Career of Landon Carter Haynes," 51-57.

[25] Quoted in the Knoxville *Whig*, June 5, 1859.

[26] *Ibid.*, May 10, 1859.

of the national organization of the Whig party, Nelson's district had drifted toward the Democrats, and in the 1857 gubernatorial election had given a majority of 651 for the Democratic candidate.[27] It was this trend that the Tennessee Whigs were struggling to counteract without the prestige of a national party organization, and they were encouraged by having won six of the ten congressional seats in Tennessee although they lost the governorship.[28] John Bell's name had been intimately associated with the whole contest as a prospective national leader in some capacity in 1860, and much effort had been expended by the Democrats to discredit him. Bell, therefore, although having sought election to no office, considered the results as something of a vindication and participated in a torchlight celebration at Knoxville on August 19, where Nelson introduced him as the "Nestor of the Whig party." [29]

In his congressional district Nelson won by a few votes less than the gubernatorial candidate of the Whigs, perhaps because of the personal popularity of his opponent, Landon C. Haynes, who was, two years later, to be selected as Senator from Tennessee to the Confederate Congress. Most of the counties in the first district yielded about the same party division as in the presidential election of 1856 and the gubernatorial contest of 1857. In Nelson's home county of Washington, normally Democratic, which had given the Democrats a majority of 406 in 1857, Nelson lost by only 339, running several votes ahead of his party's gubernatorial candidate. Although Nelson's victory could hardly be described, as in Brownlow's words, the "greatest victory of modern times," it did reverse a recent trend in the district.

As the nation staggered under the repercussions of Harper's Ferry, where "an old man, half mad, who knew naught of peace or calm save in strife, accepted the responsibility for a nation's failure to get on with its problems," [30] Nelson took his seat in a House of Representatives that was so torn with strife it could not even elect a speaker.

---

[27] Election returns are taken from *The Tribune Almanac . . . 1838 to 1868* (New York, 1868).

[28] Parks, *John Bell*, 342.

[29] *Ibid.*, 343.

[30] Avery O. Craven, *The Growth of Southern Nationalism, 1848-1861* (Baton Rouge, 1953), 305.

CHAPTER VII

Under Malign Influence

THE PANDEMONIUM IN THE HOUSE of Representatives when it convened in December, 1859, centered around a determination on the part of many Southern representatives and Northern Democrats to deny the speakership to any member who had endorsed Hinton R. Helper's *The Impending Crisis*. Since the Republicans had a plurality they would normally have expected to choose the speaker; but with the Democrats and Southern Opposition (ex-Whig) members and other non-Republicans holding a majority of seats, this could not be achieved without co-operation. Therefore, as the candidates proposed by the Republicans had endorsed the book, a deadlock ensued. A resolution was on the floor specifically excluding from the speakership any endorser of *The Impending Crisis;* and another was introduced more broadly resolving that no member should be elected speaker whose political opinions were not known to be opposed to renewing the slavery controversy, in Congress or out, under any guise. To this latter resolution Nelson spoke on December 7, explaining that no member had discussed the resolution which he thought should be adopted and that he felt he should comment upon it—although he "had hoped that it would have fallen into abler hands to do so." [1]

His beginning was repetitive and ill-organized; evidently he was feeling the pressure of speaking in the halls of Congress so soon after his arrival. His major points were that great danger threatened the country from extremists in both sections—to buttress which he cited or quoted several sentiments from North and South—and that he was opposed to the feeling of disunion, "no matter whence it comes." Having built up to that avowal by a rather oratorical reference to the Hartford Convention and to treason, he received prolonged applause from the floor and gallery. Warming to his task under these assurances of approval, he nonetheless was sufficiently out of his familiar setting to require some moments to order his thinking—to gain which moments he simply repeated the same avowal to further applause. He then gained aplomb and improved his organization—going on to stress the absence of any concrete issue of slavery that required settlement or that would require settlement for years.

After the usual attacks on the Democratic party for nurturing abolitionism as a vote-getting deal until the Republican party had suddenly become dangerously large, he expressed "one or two old-fashioned sen-

[1] *Congressional Globe*, 36 Cong., 1 Sess., 46.

timents which, in days past and gone, were common to the whole American people":

It may excite the derision of a portion of the disunionists of the North, and it may provoke the contempt of the fire-eaters of the South; but I say there is one class of sentiments which, although the leaders in the excitement may strive to create a feeling of discord in the minds of our citizens, I trust all will hold in common. What are they? We love our country; we love its mountains, its hills, its valleys, and its streams; we love its peaceful Sabbaths, its church-going bells, its English Bible, and its glorious liberty of conscience. [Applause] We love that feature in every American constitution which abolishes all hereditary honors and distinctions, and enables the poor man's child if he have talent and genius, to climb "The steep where fame's proud temple shines afar." [Applause in the galleries] We love the star-spangled banner which has waved in triumph over many a field of battle, and protects our commerce upon every sea. We love the memory of the world's only Washington. [Applause on the floor and in the galleries.] We love the name and the fame of every hero who has fought or bled or died upon the battle-fields of the country. [Renewed applause.] [2]

He then quoted ten lines of poetry on the fame of the country's heroes; and the galleries, not knowing that he was just warming up, gave him a thundering and presumably final applause. He continued with a long peroration to the Union, evoking further loud applause in the galleries, and concluded with renewed pleas to Northerners and Southerners to abandon theoretical claims and meet on practical ground. The audience undoubtedly liked his militant Unionism and gave him a final tribute.

The afternoon session heard a speech from Roger A. Pryor of Virginia, considered by Nelson a Southern extremist. Pryor made the mistake of including personal references to Nelson, implying that he was collaborating with the Republicans and referring to his having been a member of the American party as a disgraceful thing. Nelson gained the floor on a point of personal privilege, and the remainder of the afternoon was taken up in an exchange among Nelson, Pryor, and other Representatives. Sharp words were passed, including thinly-veiled references to physical assault or a duel. Under badgering from the floor, Nelson asserted that if a Republican were elected President he would not favor resistance or secession unless and until he "committed some overt act leading to the peril of the South." The moment that act should take place, he stated prophetically, "I would be willing, humble as I am, to link my shield to the shield even of these secessionists, to repel the wrong, just as soon as I would repel wrong from any quarter."

In this congressional counterpart of the stump speech debates so familiar to him, Nelson was thoroughly at home. He made pointed rebuttal to a thrust when possible and evaded the point adroitly when necessary, but above all had the courage to state his position squarely regardless of the opportunity it afforded his opponents to aim more

---

[2] The address and subsequent exchange of comments is in *ibid.*, 46-48 and 50-52.

effectively. These qualities endeared him to the visitors in the galleries and even to many of the Representatives just as they had to countless East Tennessee crowds. He drew repeated outbursts of laughter or applause, concluding with the mirth-provoking observation: "I wish merely to say, in courtesy to the gentleman from Virginia, that I intended no disrespect to him in the observation I made that I saw no logical sequence in his remarks. The gentleman has won a reputation as one of the ablest editors in the South, of his party, and I do not, by any means, wish to discredit his intelligence, though owing to the unfortunate sentiments he has advocated, I do not wonder that he did not come up to the reputation I have heard of him."

Nelson's first appearance on the floor of Congress stimulated considerable interest in the editorial columns of papers in many parts of the country, and glowing reports appeared in the friendly papers of Tennessee.[3] The Nashville *Republican Banner* reprinted the entire speech and exchange of remarks with the editorial comment that the "speech of Col. Nelson comes like a bright gleam of sunshine from a clouded sky." It was described as masterly and impressive—with the prediction that it would be more widely read than any similar document the paper had published for years. On December 9 the Baltimore *Patriot* stated that the speech had had a happy effect and that "men who had begun to quail under the insolence of the disunionists, wore radiant faces yesterday." Brownlow, of course, outdid himself in praise in his Knoxville *Whig*. Numerous letters reached Nelson from North and South praising his speech and his handling of Pryor.[4] One of his Asheville, North Carolina, friends wrote a warning, however, that his hatred of the Democratic party should not prevent a solid Southern stand against the Republicans.[5]

Patriotic fervor from Nelson or others seemed powerless to stem the strife; and members carried daggers and guns, which they considered necessary for personal protection. Many physical clashes between members occurred, and parliamentary decorum was rare. Nelson had to sit with growing forebodings as the deadlock over the speakership dragged through December and January and threats of open break were heard from all sides—supplemented by such ominous steps as assurance from the governor of South Carolina that he could have a regiment in or near Washington on short notice.[6] When the wrangle was compromised by electing a New Jersey Whig as speaker, conditions did not improve

[3] Knoxville *Whig*, December 22, 1859, refers to sixteen favorable comments the editor had seen in papers from various sections of the country. See also Washington *Star*, December 8, 1859; Louisville *Courier*, December 12, 1859; Nashville *Republican Banner*, December 13, 1859; Knoxville *Whig*, December 17, 1859, and January 7, 1860.

[4] These letters are in the Nelson Papers under dates in December, 1859, and January and February, 1860.

[5] E. J. Acton to Nelson, December 28, 1859, in Nelson Papers.

[6] Craven, *The Growth of Southern Nationalism*, 317-18.

much; for "men were in no mood for looking after the business of the nation. Instead they threatened and talked of things sectional." [7]

Meanwhile, Nelson's reputation as a Unionist brought him an invitation to speak in Baltimore at a benefit gathering on January 16, 1860. The audience was extremely large, and Nelson was escorted to the hall by a committee of city dignitaries. As the party entered, a band struck up a lively national tune which was quickly drowned in the thunderous cheering and applause of the festive-minded audience. Nelson spoke extemporaneously with ease and was frequently interrupted by applause. At the conclusion of the address, he was presented with a flower basket by the woman's group sponsoring the benefit lecture and was made a life member of their society. Many of the men accompanied Nelson to his hotel, taking the band along to serenade him. After making another appearance to compliment the band and thank the crowd for the kindness of his reception, he retired to his room to the sounds of three cheers and Yankee Doodle. [8]

While Nelson was still in Washington and unable to volunteer his aid, Brownlow suffered a severe shock. Brownlow's young son, John Bell Brownlow, a student at Emory and Henry College, killed a fellow student, James W. Reese. Young Brownlow, who weighed only a little more than a hundred pounds, was being mercilessly beaten on the ground by Reese, who was much heavier. He grabbed a stick and struck Reese over the head with it, accidentally killing him. When the news reached Brownlow, he knew instantly that his own pugnacious and even ferocious public personality would be attributed to his son and perhaps prejudice his case. In probably the only instance in which Brownlow ever begged, he published a plaintive description of his son as not at all like himself and concluded: "I respectfully suggest to newspaper editors and their correspondents, the great injustice of visiting upon him, the political or personal sins of his Father, over whom he has never exercised any control!" [9] Although the evidence seemed fully to exonerate young Brownlow, there was naturally a restless and suspenseful six weeks before a jury acquitted him on three minutes deliberation—after which Brownlow regained his almost swaggering style in reporting the trial. [10] Nelson must have regretted the fact that his first extended absence from home should have made it impossible to aid the Brownlows as legal counsel. Sooner than he could have imagined, this harrowing experience was to be his—when Brownlow would be in Congress.

Nelson's only other major effort in this first session of Congress was an address on polygamy in Utah, delivered on April 4 and 5, 1860. [11] In a

---

[7] *Ibid.*, 318.

[8] Baltimore *Patriot*, quoted in Knoxville *Whig*, February 4, 1860.

[9] Knoxville *Whig*, March 3, 1860.

[10] *Ibid.*, April 21, 1860.

[11] *Congressional Globe*, 36 Cong., 1 Sess., Appendix, 190-95.

long and ornate speech, he asked the repeal of the Utah territorial act because it granted the Mormon Church unconstitutional powers. He leveled a blistering attack on the Mormon Church itself, accusing its official leaders of planning and executing robbery and murder and ridiculing Joseph Smith as a "man more ready to live by his wits than by the labor of his hands" who manifested a turn for pious frauds early in life.

The most scathing part of the speech called for the passage of a bill outlawing polygamy and its enforcement, if necessary, by the dispatch of army and *navy* [?]. His argument against polygamy was based on a literal interpretation of the *Bible*, dismissing the polygamy of the *Old Testament* as a dispensation superseded by Jesus' injunction. He warned that God would punish the nation if the sin of polygamy were not eradicated, and cited instances at length in which he discerned the hand of God punishing nations. He also dwelt on the debasement of woman involved in polygamy; in fact his address could have been changed into a philippic against slavery by substituting the word "slave" for the word "woman." But, under questioning, he affirmed that polygamy was a sin while slavery was not. If he felt any incongruity in this juxtaposition, he revealed none. His deadly earnestness in the matter was revealed when he sternly rebuked his fellow Tennessean and Whig colleague, Emerson Etheridge, who agreed with him on polygamy but had referred to the matter in a light and humorous vein.

When the old-line Whigs of the border states brought together delegates to a Constitutional Union party national convention at Baltimore, Nelson attended. The convention assembled on May 9, 1860, with more than forty Tennesseans present, pledged to work for their favorite son, John Bell. Although no Tennessean spoke a word on the convention floor until Bell's nomination, they were not so silent in the all-night work in the hotel rooms; and Bell ultimately won. A Central National Executive Committee was set up to run the presidential campaign, composed of seven free-state members and seven slave-state members, including Nelson.

The Democrats were already split at Charleston and would soon have a Southerner and a Northerner in the race against each other. When the Republicans met at Chicago on May 16 and nominated "house divided" Lincoln, it seemed to Nelson that the issue was finally free from every cloud of ambiguity. Lincoln could get only Northern votes; Stephen A. Douglas could hope for few votes outside the North; John C. Breckinridge could expect only Southern votes; but John Bell and his running mate, Edward Everett of Massachusetts, could hope for national support. Three sectional candidates against a "national man" was the clearest call to duty Nelson had heard in a quarter century of political interest.

No sooner was he back in Tennessee than Nelson started his speaking campaign at every circuit court opening day. He invited opposing party speakers to divide time with him, but when none appeared he would speak for three hours.[12] He did not confine his efforts to the first district but invaded the Knoxville area and went on into southern East Tennessee.[13] On October 24, during the Knoxville fair, Nelson spoke at the invitation of the Knoxville Bell-Everett Club to a crowd representing nearly every county in East Tennessee. When William L. Yancey spoke in Knoxville on behalf of Breckinridge, Bell supporters petitioned Nelson to be present and answer him; but Yancey did not share time on the platform except to let Brownlow, who could hardly talk because of a sore throat, make a few remarks.[14] While few, if any, of Bell's supporters considered a clear victory at the polls as possible, they did hope to see the election deadlocked and thrown into the House of Representatives where either Democrats or Republicans might ultimately support Bell to prevent the other party from winning.

The results, giving Lincoln a majority of electoral votes with only about two-fifths of the popular vote, shattered the hopes of the Bell followers; and Nelson could take small comfort in the fact that Tennessee was one of the three states to cast their electoral votes for Bell. As alarming preparations for secession conventions took place in the lower South, Nelson journeyed to Washington anticipating a momentous short session of Congress—his mind excited to a vigorous canvassing of all compromise possibilities. The House immediately appointed a committee of thirty-three to recommend measures of reconciliation, and Nelson was placed on this committee. He was ready with a set of resolutions which he submitted to the committee, proposing a satisfactory settlement in the form of three constitutional amendments, which were surely not original proposals. The first would restore the Missouri Compromise line and guarantee slavery in any territory south of that line until statehood had been granted, deny Congress power to interfere with slave trade in the South or abolish slavery in the District of Columbia, and forever prohibit foreign slave trade. The second was a fugitive slave amendment compelling Congress to provide a fugitive slave law and permitting Congress to collect indemnities from persons, counties, or towns by whom or in which a fugitive slave was aided in escaping. The final proposal called for the President and Vice-President always to be from opposite sides of the Missouri Compromise line. Nelson explained that these did not represent his own political sentiments but only such middle ground as he thought had a chance for acceptance.[15]

---

[12] Knoxville *Whig*, August 18, 1860.

[13] *Ibid.*, September 22 and 29, 1860.

[14] *Ibid.*, August 10, 1861, makes reference to this affair of September, 1860. For the general picture of this campaign see Margaret B. Hamer, "The Presidential Campaign of 1860 in Tennessee," in East Tennessee Historical Society's *Publications*, No. 3 (1931), 3-22.

[15] *Congressional Globe*, 36 Cong., 2 Sess., Appendix, 106.

Shortly thereafter, Senator Crittenden introduced his compromise resolutions in the Senate. Nelson, wishing to concentrate effort on one possibility, withdrew his resolutions from the committee of thirty-three and submitted for consideration instead the Crittenden proposals, which essentially called for the same points as Nelson's first two proposals.[16] Then, as the haggling in the House committee of thirty-three and the Senate committee of thirteen seemed to indicate the futility of compromise proposals and as South Carolina's secession on December 18 was followed within six weeks by the remaining states of the lower South, Nelson worked on a major plea to the House and the country to save the Union. He was encouraged by the Tennessee vote on February 9 which rejected the proposition to call a state convention to consider secession; but as he struggled in committee and with the preparation of his address, disheartening news kept coming from home.[17]

One close observer of East Tennessee politics, Andrew Jackson Fletcher, after completing his legal circuit and talking with people at each county seat, wrote Nelson an extended commentary on December 18, 1860. Having heard that Nelson was solicitous to hear from his constituents, Fletcher opened with a warning of his dread responsibility:

. . . I feel that it will be unsafe for you to look to your constituents in this crisis to govern your course in the momentous matter upon which you have to act. . . . It is well enough in minor concerns or mere party matters for a valuable statesman to make such a record as he can stand by when he is again to pass through the hands of his people. But, I need not say to you, my dear sir, that you are now acting upon questions which are vitally to affect unborn millions of posterity. And knowing you, as I do, I know that you will rise infinitely above every thing but your Country's good. I mean *your whole Country*. The eyes of a mighty but tottering nation as well as your constituents are upon you. . . . I have met with no man of any party but who has the utmost confidence that you will do your whole duty.[18]

Nelson could not have been unaware that this last sentiment was substantially true. A contemporary colleague in the struggle for the Union, who later differed strenuously with Nelson, wrote after Nelson's death that: "No man has lived in East Tennessee, except possibly [Meredith P.] Gentry and W. B. Campbell, in whose honesty there was more universal confidence. His influence was therefore marked. All parties, even in times of highest excitement, admired him." [19]

[16] *Idem.*

[17] For a study of the February 9 election see Mary R. Campbell, "The Significance of the Unionist Victory in the Election of February 9, 1861, in Tennessee," in East Tennessee Historical Society's *Publications*, No. 14 (1942), 11-30. Letters from Tennessee to Nelson containing disheartening news include: Dr. W. R. Sevier to Nelson, December 11, 1860; Andrew Jackson Fletcher to *id.*, December 18, 1860; E. G. Sevier to *id.*, December 25, 1860; N. G. Taylor to *id.*, January 3, 1861; O. P. Temple and W. G. Brownlow to *id.*, January 12, 1861; A. A. Kyle to *id.*, January 14, 1861; W. P. Hunt to *id.*, February 2, 1861, in Nelson Papers.

[18] Fletcher to Nelson, December 18, 1860, in Nelson Papers.

[19] Temple, *Notable Men of Tennessee*, 42.

Fletcher's letter further reported that a change in popular opinion had occurred since Nelson left for Washington—a growing fatalistic acceptance of secession as a foregone conclusion and a tendency to overlook the question as to whether Southern secessionists were wrong in their action. Attention was centered on the "first sin," which was found at the "door of the North." Either the Republican party, right or wrong, must surrender "*the* principal [*sic*] upon which it stands" or the Union would be dissolved. The people generally considered the time for theorizing past and the time to face facts arrived. Fletcher, himself, feared that there was no hope of saving the Union but only a hope that it could be reconstructed if economic distress in the North should persuade the abolitionists to abandon their fanaticism. It might work out its own cure, he suggested, "not it is to be hoped, like the Crusades of old, or the fanaticism of Cromwell and Mohammed, through seas of blood. . . ."

Looking gloomily forward to the prospects of a Southern confederacy with its broadside exposed to a hostile nation, Fletcher predicted, more than a year before Julia Ward Howe penned "As He died to make men Holy, let us die to make men free," that the North would "go into battle with us singing fanatical hymns like the followers of Cromwell." He also feared carnage if the South's millions of slaves should take advantage of the war to repeat the Dominican massacre. His only practical suggestion for action was that the border states propose an ultimatum that would settle the sectional controversy forever, and if that were rejected, then "let us consider whether we will go with the South or carve out a central Republic containing the glorious conservative belt. . . ." Referring to the chance of acceptance of such an ultimatum as the border states might deliver, Fletcher first wrote, "if this ultimatum is rejected as it will be." He then lined out "will" and inserted "probably will." It was with the same slender hope that led Fletcher to an afterthought addition of "probably" that Nelson stayed in the committee of thirty-three and pushed his plans to plead with his fellow Representatives from the floor.

Just when Nelson had decided that further debate in the committee was useless, and on the very day he had resolved to withdraw from the committee, a member from Massachusetts let in a slender gleam of light by proposing a constitutional amendment that slavery be protected in every state where it then existed unless it be abolished by the consent of that state and every other state in the Union. Sensing some willingness to sacrifice in the interest of compromise in this proposition from a Republican member who was risking the denunciation of his Massachusetts constituents as had Webster in 1850, Nelson stayed with the committee.[20] Ultimately it reported to the floor only one proposed constitutional amendment—the one suggested by the Massachusetts Republican mem-

---

[20] Explained by Nelson in *Congressional Globe*, 36 Cong., 2 Sess., Appendix, 108.

ber—together with a bill to amend the fugitive slave law so as to provide Federal court hearings for those charged with being escaped slaves. It included also a series of resolutions, pleasing to the South, concerned with guaranteeing the inter-state slave trade and slavery in the District of Columbia and with requesting the Northern states to repeal their laws obstructing the enforcement of the fugitive slave act. As to the territorial question, the committee recommended the immediate admission of New Mexico to statehood to close out the problem within the existing limits of the United States. Nelson, believing that the South would not be satisfied with mere resolutions "which may be rescinded at pleasure," submitted a minority report urging the adoption of the proposed ideas in the form of constitutional amendments.[21]

When the House debated the resolutions of the committee of thirty-three, Nelson waited with impatience and some anxiety for his opportunity to speak. After referring to the infrequency of his appearances on the floor, he continued: "I have on many occasions, however, addressed public assemblies; and as a professional man, I have frequently pleaded for the life of my client when he sat pale and trembling behind me, and hung with breathless expectation upon every word that fell from my lips; but never on any occasion have I attempted to address any public assembly under so painful a consciousness of the magnitude of the subject and of my inability to meet it as that which oppresses me now." [22]

Saying that he advocated the most important cause the world had ever known—the life of his country—he prayed that in his efforts he would say nothing that might "be calculated to foment the disturbances that exist in our once happy and peaceful Union." Referring to the lightning rapidity with which events had moved in the previous three months, he avowed that the Congress could have arrested the developments had it not met day after day to discuss any topic other than that which involved "the destiny of our own country and the hopes for free government throughout the world." "What malign influence trammels us," he asked, "that we cannot reach an adjustment in a spirit of conciliation and concession in which the Government was created?" His answer was: "the one is pride of opinion, and the other is party spirit." "I do not pretend to be more exempt from these than other men, but I will in this effort to secure peace and repose to a distracted land, endeavor to relieve myself as far as possible from both."

He next made the point that Congress should not let the news go out to the country that all was hopeless, but should let the people know that some progress had been made and some promising signs existed. In an

---

[21] "Minority Report of the Committee of Thirty-three," in *Congressional Globe*, 36 Cong., 2 Sess. A reprint is in the Nelson Papers.

[22] Nelson's full address is found in the *Congressional Globe*, 36 Cong., 2 Sess., Appendix, 106-11.

attempt to show that a spirit of concession had been uncovered, he pointed to the acceptance by most Southern leaders in Congress of Crittenden's Missouri Compromise line proposal although the Dred Scott Decision gave slave owners the constitutional right to take slaves into any territory, north or south of that line. After extensive justification of the idea of restoring the Missouri Compromise line, he shifted to a catalogue of the reasons for the mass of Southern people thinking that they had good cause for fear and apprehension and should be appeased by firm guarantees. Among his list of causes, he included abolition incitement to slave insurrection, John Brown's raid, mob resistance to enforcement of the fugitive slave law, and Republican attacks on the Supreme Court over the Dred Scott opinions. Returning to signs of hope, Nelson gave generous praise to the Massachusetts Republican who braved the ire of his state in proposing the amendment reported out by the committee, and made reference to concessions and evidences of good will in the other resolutions proposed. Again attempting to stress the necessity for the Republicans' making definitive gestures, he reported the extreme and untrue charges made against the Republican party by Governor Isham G. Harris before the Tennessee legislature.

After further evidences of the dangerous state in the South, even in the border states, he said that secession sentiment was becoming almost impossible to resist unless the Republicans would "come up and meet us in the spirit of compromise of which I have so often spoken." Turning frankly to an appeal to Tennesseans rather than congressmen, he spoke at length on the history of separatist sentiment in South Carolina and pled with his fellow Tennesseans to resent and resist the haughty attempts to coerce them into secession. Particularly did he stress the tax burdens which he said the seceding states were having to assume. He received applause when he exclaimed: "if civil discord is to reign where peace so sweetly smiled before, the men who will have to fight the battles will not be your partisan leaders who desire to be colonels and captains, majors and generals, governors and ministers, but it will be the farmers, the mechanics, and the laboring men of the country. I ask them —and I would to God that my voice could echo and re-echo from one end of my state to the other—are they willing to submit to this to build up a pampered aristocracy in the South?" And to the Republicans he turned and said: "Are you gentlemen of the North disposed to drive us into the mad career of rebellion by brute force? Remember that the Republican party was opposed by a large party in the North; that all the power is not in your hands, and that your laboring men, thrown out of employment and begging for bread, may turn upon you and refuse to fight your battles."

Entering into a series of answers to the rhetorical question, "Why should we destroy our government?" he called to mind many of the leaders and events associated with the founding and growth of the national government and sought in several ways to stir patriotic sentiment, imagining the admonitions of Washington, Jackson, and Henry Clay. As his time ended, he concluded with the warning:

My countrymen, let us heed these warning voices! Let us settle all our controversies in the Union. Oh! trust not to that last delusive argument of the secessionist, that the Government, once dissolved, can be reconstructed. That will never be. The causes which destroy it will forever preclude a reunion. Hate will be intensified and a war of extermination will ensue. It is in vain for either section to calculate upon the cowardice of the other. All are of the same race. All are alike brave, and a war once begun between us, will have no parallel in the contests which history has described. May Almighty God avert it.

It has been said, "agree with thine adversary quickly, whilst thou art in the way with him." If we are governed by this salutory rule, all domestic difficulties will soon pass away from our country, peace will again smile in all our borders, and we will once more enjoy those privileges with which we have so long been blessed, far above every other people.

Both houses of Congress passed by the necessary two-thirds the proposed constitutional amendment concerning permanent protection of slavery and sent it to the states for consideration. This action, together with such indications as the restraint exercised by the Republicans in Congress, who had a majority after withdrawal of the members from Confederate states, in not repealing the laws allowing slavery in the territories and in permitting the territories of Dakota, Colorado, and Nevada to be created without express prohibition of slavery, convinced Nelson that the seceded states should return to the fold. Although the short session came to its end on March 4, 1861, without adopting the Missouri Compromise line demanded by the South, Lincoln's inaugural was couched in carefully chosen language. Two days after the inauguration, Nelson and Horace Maynard, Representative from the Knoxville district, sought out the President to try to add their personal bit to the avoidance of a civil war. Lincoln asked them to return for a private interview the following night and told them that he favored peace and would use his every power to maintain it; that he was not planning to try to collect revenues in Southern ports or even withhold mail facilities; and that he very much hoped the Southern states, after time for reflection, would recede from their position. Nelson and Maynard were both impressed with the President's frankness, and Lincoln seemed pleased at their visit.[23]

With these assurances from Lincoln, Nelson immediately set out for home to combat separation sentiment in Tennessee, satisfied that there was no excuse for a civil war unless the secession leaders were deter-

[23] Nelson describes these visits in a letter to W. G. Brownlow, March 13, 1861, published in the Knoxville *Whig* and copied in the Nashville *Republican Banner*, March 19, 1861. Nelson had been among the Southerners considered by Lincoln for a cabinet post according to James G. Randall, *Lincoln the President: Springfield to Gettysburg*, 2 vols. (New York, 1945), I, 267.

mined to precipitate it as they had already precipitated revolution. He was not counting votes accurately but rather reporting something close to wishful thinking when he concluded that votes in both houses in the last hectic hours demonstrated that a "majority of the Republicans" were favorable to compromise.[24] It is true that some Republicans voted for compromise of non-essential points, but they had displayed remarkable party unity in killing any chance for real concession. And Lincoln, with whose frankness Nelson was so pleased, had done his part to prevent concessions that would have voided any of the Chicago platform on which he had been elected.[25]

For a month after his return, Nelson spent very few days at home. He defended the Union in one or two speeches almost every day to stem the tide of threatening secession sentiment.[26] Then, in early April, Lincoln finally showed his hand in regard to Fort Sumter—or seemed to show it, at least. Impetuous Confederate authorities at Charleston authorized the step; and on April 12, 1861, the fateful firing on Fort Sumter began. On the second day following its surrender, Lincoln's call for 75,000 militia provoked Tennessee's Governor Harris to reply defiantly and issue a call for a special session of the state legislature to meet on April 25. Secession sentiment, now stimulated and augmented in Tennessee, threatened to sweep all before it. Those in the South who had been upholding the Union, and especially those who had considered Lincoln's policy a peaceful one, were now faced with a sobering reappraisal as to the proper object of their loyalty.

---

[24] Nelson to Brownlow, March 13, 1861, in Nashville Republican Banner, March 19, 1861.

[25] Kenneth M. Stampp, And the War Came: The North and the Secession Crisis, 1860-1861 (Baton Rouge, 1950), 123-58, 179-203.

[26] Nelson to Andrew Johnson, April 5, 1861, in Andrew Johnson Papers (Division of Manuscripts, Library of Congress). Hereinafter cited as Johnson Papers. See also the Knoxville Whig, March 30, 1861.

Knoxville 26th April 1861

Present state of the country – Summary

1.

Causes of my attachment to the Union –
1 Boyhood. 2 Declaration. & Farewell Address
3. Ancestors. 4 Old Pensioners. 5 subsequent life

2.

× Government. Law. Anarchy. The
despotism and intolerance of Secession

3.

Revolution for intolerable oppression. –
No cause of Revolution – tho' there
were causes of complaint.
The evil could have been remedied
and was in a fair way of adjustment
One state – S.C. – has done all
the mischief. –
Now and at all times. heretofore
we could have the majority in Congress.
× No analogy to Whig and Tory.

4.

The doctrine of Secession.
1. Quincy on the war bill of 1811.
National Union N° 6 and 7 page 1
2. Hartford Convention. Nat. Un. N° 6 & 7 p 2.

This four page speech outline in Nelson's handwriting is in his papers in the McClung Collection, Lawson McGhee Library, Knoxville. The page references are to his current scrapbook.

Secession continued

3. Washington's Opinion. Scraps. 120.
4. Madison's " " " p. H
5. Jackson – Disunion by armed force
is treason. Nat. Un. N° 6 and 7 p. 9.
6. Clay – An attempt to exercise
such a right should be resisted to the last
extremity. Scraps 65.
7. Treason by the law of Tennesse. Scraps 161 –

5.

Secession is Coercion.
1. No memorial of grievances from
the Southern people. No Southern Convention.
2. South Carolina – the leader. The
Politicians at Washington
1. The purpose long cherished.
2. Buchanan's Treason. Scraps 20, 21,
See old notes, page 3. (3)
3. War of the West
4. Border Conference rejected
5. Virginia Com° refused.Md.
6. Their law of Treason p. 66. p. 95.
7. Montgomery Convention & popular
vote. See notes p. 3.
8 Jeff. Davis threat. Scraps 87 –

9. Sprott and Democracy — Scraps 84.

10. Memphis Avalanche, continued contest p. 132.

11. Treatment of Johnson & Etheridge. Scraps 166.

12. Hanging a Traitor. Scraps 166.

13. Richmond Examiner on Bots, Etheridge
Johnson, Letcher and Summers. Scraps 144.

✗ 14. Contrast this war and its pretexts
with those of the Revolution —

✗ Actual wrongs. Imaginary wrongs.

✗ The fourth of July abolished and yet
they compare themselves to 1776 —

6.

The whole movement wrong because
conducted under false pretences — and
the leaders violated their oath.

1. Misrepresentations of the North.

2. Refusal to abide by Lincoln's election.

3. No reconstruction — getting rights.

4. Secession destroys every bond of
Union in the new Confederacy.

5 The attack on Fort Sumter unnecessary
1 Correspondence with Beauregard and
Anderson. Scraps 166. —

<u>See Over</u>.

2. Virginia Circular. Scraps 164.
3. Pryor's speech ~ ~ ~ 165.

7.

Neutrality and a Border State Convention
1. National Intelligencer. 161 - 164.
2. Tennessee Address. Scraps 154.
3. Kentucky Address. — 156.
4. Crittenden's Opinion ~ 153 - 154.

8.

※ A subjugation of all the Southern States
not intended.
1. Laws under which Lincoln acted. 159.
2. Lincoln's Inaugural. Scraps 124.
3. His address to the Virginia Commissioners
Scraps 160.
4. His Proclamation. Scraps 140.
5. Davis Proclamation. ~ 155.
6. Lincoln's second Proclamation, against
Piracy. Scraps 162.

9.

The Legislature — Secret Session —
Popular Vote — Position of Bell and others.
The French Revolution. Mob Law

11.

Distinction between the Government and
Lincoln.

12.

The Secession leaders violated their oaths
& are not fit leaders for us.

13

Lincoln no power to acknowledge Independence

14.

I would remain in the old Union or form
a Middle Confederacy ~

CHAPTER VIII

Grazing the Edge of Treason

L INCOLN'S CALL FOR TROOPS forced the hand of the border state Unionists, and the resulting decisions split the Tennessee followers of John Bell. Bell, himself, rather quickly completed a transition from standard bearer for Unionism to separationism. When Virginia seceded three days after Lincoln's action, Bell and ten other Tennessee conservatives took the first step toward withdrawal from the Union when they issued a statement commending Governor Harris for refusing to furnish Tennessee troops to aid in coercing the seceding states. They further urged Tennessee to remain neutral unless the Federal government should actually begin a war of subjugation of the South, in which case they approved armed resistance. A conference was suggested to implement the mediation role of the border states. Less than a week later Bell almost classed himself as a separationist before a Nashville mass meeting, but he still opposed an ordinance of secession as needlessly adopting a state of *actual* rebellion. He was particularly anxious that Tennessee and Kentucky pursue identical courses.[1]

Before the April 25 meeting of the Tennessee legislature, the Confederate States of America had been established, and Jefferson Davis had named a commissioner to Tennessee in response to Governor Harris's sending an agent to Montgomery. This session, assuming that the gravity of the crisis justified extraordinary measures, clothed itself with secrecy and took several steps of doubtful constitutionality. A military league was formed with the Confederacy, placing Tennessee forces under the orders of Jefferson Davis—and this while Tennessee was still unquestionably in the Union. Then, omitting the constitutionally required convention rejected by the Tennessee voters the previous February, the legislature undertook to perform the duties of such a convention to the extent of submitting to the people two recommendations to be accepted or rejected on June 8, 1861: a declaration of independence and a proposition to join the Southern Confederacy.

In East Tennessee the leading "Bell" men, Whigs all, responded to these chain-lightning developments with alacrity, and some of the Democrats now joined them. Andrew Johnson was undoubtedly the chief reason for the adherence of some of the Democrats to the Union cause. A fervid admiration of Andrew Jackson and a class-conscious contempt for possessors of inherited wealth combined to align Johnson definitely against the deep South leaders. In the 1861 Senate sessions he denounced

---

[1] Parks, *John Bell*, 396-400.

secession in unbridled terms and left Washington as soon as the special session ended to canvass East Tennessee against withdrawing from the Union in the June 8 referendum.

This situation produced one of the strangest reconciliations of the whole hectic era. Brownlow had long before taken Andrew Johnson as his pet political and personal foe and had almost exceeded his own genius for invective in repeatedly denouncing Johnson as a bastard and atheist. The two men had not spoken to each other for more than fifteen years, so Johnson must has reflected upon the disjointed state of affairs in some amazement when he found himself being highly praised by Brownlow and read of a forger of his name being denounced by Brownlow as a "corrupt liar, low down drunkard, irresponsible vagabond, and infamous coward."[2]

Nelson, who had opposed Andrew Johnson on every political issue for twenty years, but always without breach of comity, now was to have the unusual and stimulating experience of sharing a cause with his most respected former opponent. Nelson and Johnson met late in April and arranged an almost continuous joint canvass of East Tennessee until the June 8 election. They spoke to audiences in almost all of the counties of East Tennessee and in some more than once as excitement rose and denunciation as traitors became more vehement. Both were threatened with assassination, and Johnson had been roughly handled by a Virginia mob when his train stopped on the way back from Washington. As they rode through thickly-wooded passes in the ridges of upper East Tennessee, they never knew when ambush might occur. Nelson was the more influential of the two for the simple reason that a majority of the East Tennesseans were Whigs and had long reserved for Johnson their keenest partisan hatred. But it was the Democratic party that tended to be connected with secession most closely, so that Johnson had the more harrowing experience of trying to appeal to his former Democratic followers against the efforts of Democratic local leaders and national figures.

A friendly observer described the canvass in this manner:

No man in East Tennessee commanded the confidence of the Whigs in so high a degree as Nelson, and no man the Democrats to the extent of Johnson. Both were powerful on the stump; both were earnest and determined, and both were absolutely fearless. . . . Mr. Nelson was exact in his statement of facts, and scrupulously careful, not to suppress or distort anything. He was also bold beyond nearly any man of his day in denouncing what he believed to be wrong. His speeches in this canvass were fair, high-toned, able, argumentative, but at the same time scathing against secession. They were also full of fire and stirring eloquence. . . .

Johnson was always at his best before large popular assemblies. . . . He pleaded for his distracted country with a passionate earnestness that moved

[2] George Fort Milton, *Eve of Conflict; Stephen A. Douglas and the Needless War* (New York, 1934), 103; Coulter, *Brownlow*, 154.

men's hearts as he had never moved them before. It is doubtful whether in all the land such impressive and powerful speeches were made for the Union as were made by these two men. . . .[3]

On April 22, before the meeting of the legislature, Nelson had been met in Knoxville at the railroad station by a large procession marching with the United States flag. That evening he denounced secession and even defended Lincoln's call for troops. After the legislative meeting began, Johnson and Nelson addressed another Knoxville meeting; and at Elizabethton Nelson went so far as to advise railroad bridge burning if "King Harris" [Governor Isham G. Harris] called in troops from other states to overawe East Tennessee.[4] Some friends were now predicting that separation was inevitable and privately urging him to fall in with the movement and try to help give it direction.[5] From Middle Tennessee he heard that Nashville was so excited that some Unionists were being converted by fear to separationism.[6] At Kingsport a dozen secessionists had to be ejected from the building before Nelson and Johnson could speak,[7] and at Jonesboro the two speakers were denied the use of the courthouse by the county court. When Johnson tried to lead off from the street corner, the mob shouted him down with repeated cries of "God Damned Traitor" and accusations of being hired by Lincoln. Nelson was allowed to speak, but occasional groans interrupted him. Rain stopped his speech, however; and when Johnson tried again, the noise of the crowd drove them to the courthouse basement, where they finished while boys poked Confederate flags through the windows. When Nelson and Johnson left the courthouse and started to "Buckhorn" to spend the night, the demonstration was described by one observer as follows:

Such a time has never been since I have lived in the place. . . . When he went to start out to Nelson's they raised the shout, groaned and *booed* him out of town. . . . You never saw such a time. Men on horses ripping up and down the streets, screaming upon the top of their voices, "you damed [*sic*] traitor, you damed traitor."[8]

Nelson clipped an editorial from the Nashville *Union and American* of May 4, 1861, and marked the following passages:

The people of Tennessee have spontaneously rebelled *against the Union.* They are now rushing to arms to resist the Chief Magistrate of "the Union." What do Messers. Johnson and Nelson propose to accomplish by their *Union* meetings?

---

[3] Temple, *Notable Men of Tennessee,* 399-400.
[4] Hamer, *Tennessee,* II, 542, 549.
[5] W. R. Sevier to Nelson (forwarding a letter from James Sevier to W. R. Sevier), April 24, 1861, in Nelson Papers.
[6] John Williams to Nelson, April 27, 1861, in Nelson Papers.
[7] Nelson Scrap Book 13 (1861), page 32, in Nelson Papers.
[8] W. H. Crouch to Landon C. Haynes, May 6, 1861; Nelson Scrap Book 13 (1861), page 33, in Nelson Papers. Part of the Crouch letter is also printed in James W. Patton, *Unionism and Reconstruction in Tennessee,* 53.

Had not Judas betrayed his Savior and Benedict Arnold his country, we
could not have believed in such debasement of human nature.
In their [soldiers dying on the battlefield] last lingering agonies the thoughts
of home will be interrupted by their deep and damning curses of those they
left behind them giving courage and confidence to their enemies.
Let Messers. Johnson and Nelson fully reflect upon the heritage that they are
now preparing for their posterity.[9]

At Blountville, in overwhelming Democratic Sullivan County, the
friends of Union held a meeting at the courthouse and appointed a committee of forty-three to ask Nelson and Johnson not to try to fill their
engagement there because of the real danger of mob violence.[10] This
request they agreed to. But in strongly Unionist Blount County they
were met two miles out of Maryville by an escort of perhaps three
hundred horsemen.[11]

When only ten days remained before the election, Nelson realized that
he could not possibly speak at all the places requesting his attendance
nor reach every East Tennessee community in person. So he spent the
week end at home writing out a full address to the people for publication
in Brownlow's Knoxville *Whig* on the eve of the election. Set in unusually small type, it occupied six of the paper's eight front page columns and two additional columns inside.[12] Having completed this, Nelson set out with Johnson on Monday, May 27, for a whirl-wind conclusion to the campaign.[13] They rode northward over the rugged Clinch
Mountain range to Sneedville, in Hancock County, near the Virginia
border, for a Monday meeting. Tuesday, they rode southwestward down
the Clinch River Valley to Tazewell. Wednesday, they recrossed the
Clinch range to Rutledge, in Grainger County, and then hurried on into
Knoxville for the East Tennessee Convention convening Thursday.

The East Tennessee Convention was the result of a published call
from a group of Union leaders including Brownlow. Twenty-eight
counties responded to the roll call of delegates, and at least four hundred men were present. After the roll call, Nelson was elected president
and spoke for more than an hour.[14] Brownlow was named to the all-
important business committee; and during its absence the convention
was addressed by Thomas D. Arnold, with whom Nelson and Brownlow
had once had a prolonged and critical political feud. Andrew Johnson
was introduced but chose to defer his remarks until Friday, and the
convention adjourned for the day.

At eight the next morning the convention assembled and heard the

[9] Nelson Scrap Book 13 (1861), page 32, in Nelson Papers.
[10] Knoxville *Whig*, May 18, 1861.
[11] Nelson Scrap Book 13 (1861), page 64, in Nelson Papers. The clipping says five
hundred horsemen, but political reports usually exaggerated numbers.
[12] Knoxville *Whig*, June 8, 1861. Undoubtedly this edition was distributed before
the publication date in time to reach the readers before the election on June 8.
[13] Final itinerary given in Knoxville *Whig*, May 25, 1861.
[14] Proceedings of the convention are in Knoxville *Whig*, June 8, 1861.

report worked out by the business committee overnight. After debate and amendment, resolutions were adopted unanimously that praised the freedom of assembly guaranteed in the state constitution, deplored the violation of Federal and state constitutions currently practiced, condemned the secession leaders and avowed that the people were not responsible for the peril facing them, and denounced Tennessee's leadership for needlessly pushing her toward separation. The resolutions declared the proposed election on separation an unconstitutional act of the legislature, described the military convention with the Confederacy and other specific acts of the late legislative session as usurpation, reaffirmed the doctrine of physical resistance to tyranny, and urged defeat of the separation proposition at the polls. It was also expected that the convention should again meet after the election, and the president was empowered to set the date and place.[15] Andrew Johnson then addressed the group for three hours before adjournment.

As soon as the convention was over, Nelson and Johnson began their last circuit before the election, a loop through the northwestern part of East Tennessee.[16] Saturday they rode into the rolling hill country northwest from Knoxville to Clinton, where they spoke to more than two thousand people and inspired some members of the audience to write a Middle Tennessee Unionist leader: "There is no way under Heaven to get East Tennessee out of the Union! We don't intend to go, and so help us God we won't!"[17] On Monday they continued northward along the ever-narrowing valley to Jacksboro, with the unbroken crest of Cumberland Mountain dominating the western horizon. Tuesday, they plunged directly into the Cumberland Plateau mass, climbing steadily along tumbling Turtle Creek and pushing their horses to the limit to reach Huntsville, on top of the plateau. Wednesday was another day of hard riding still further westward across the plateau to Jamestown in Fentress County, where less than a tenth of the land was improved—for every potential vote was deemed critical. Here they turned back southward and eastward to Montgomery on Thursday and then down again from the plateau to Kingston, on the Tennessee River below Knoxville, where they spoke on Friday, June 7, election eve. Brownlow believed rumors of a plot to assassinate Johnson that night on the train from Kingston to Knoxville and sent his son, John Bell Brownlow, to warn Johnson and bring him back to Knoxville in a buggy. When the Brownlow boy arrived, Johnson was speaking and sustaining himself with frequent gulps of whisky punch from a bucket on the floor, while Nelson sat in exhausted sleep on the platform.[18]

[15] Idem.
[16] Knoxville *Whig*, May 25, 1861.
[17] D. K. Young and others to W. B. Campbell, June 3, 1861, Campbell Collection.
[18] Patton, *Unionism and Reconstruction in Tennessee*, 53-54.

In these joint meetings with Andrew Johnson from the shadows of the Smoky Mountains to the top of Cumberland Plateau, Nelson presented his view of the background of the existing crisis and his recommendations for action at the polls and after. He began with an extended discussion of his love of the Union and the assertion that he would not give up the "opinions, the feelings, the attachments" of his whole life "except in a case of extreme oppression, actual, tangible, and otherwise remediless." [19] He then traced the history of Southern extremists from nullification to secession, citing newspapers and orators of that stripe to demonstrate that there had been a long-standing and "diabolical" conspiracy to dissolve the Union. Such quotations as the following were taken from the proceedings of the Charleston Convention which adopted the South Carolina Ordinance of Secession:

It is no spasmodic effort that has come suddenly upon us, but it has been gradually culminating for a long series of years, until at last it has come to that point when we may say the matter is entirely right.

Most of us have had this matter under consideration for the last twenty years. . . .

I have been engaged in this movement ever since I entered political life.

The secession of South Carolina is not an event of a day. It is not anything produced by Mr. Lincoln's election or by the non-execution of the fugitive slave law. It has been a matter which has been gathering head for thirty years.

Nelson then proceeded to a series of quotations from congressional proceedings of the past winter to show that the representatives of the cotton states desired no compromise, with which he contrasted what he considered the willingness of Republicans to compromise, reluctantly, it was true—but, nonetheless, satisfactorily. In this regard he stressed the willingness of Northern legislatures to repeal their personal liberty laws, which were in contravention to the fugitive slave act, and the adoption by the necessary two-thirds in both houses of Congress of a constitutional amendment guaranteeing slavery where it existed—"equivalent to a perpetual guarantee of slavery." This amendment Nelson thought would remove the only real fear of the slaveholders about the territories —a fear that, ultimately, free states would have the three-fourths majority necessary to abolish slavery by constitutional amendment. He also pointed out that new territories were created by Republican votes with laws so drawn as indirectly to protect slavery there and that no action was taken to pack the Supreme Court or otherwise try to destroy the protection afforded by the Dred Scott decision to slave property in the territories.

After discussing at some length the purely abstract nature of the territorial slavery question, he returned to evidences of a compromising spirit by referring to resolutions of a nature satisfactory to the South that

---

[19] Full address may be found in Knoxville *Whig*, June 8, 1861.

passed the House but failed to reach a vote in the Senate. In this analysis of the significance of the compromises adopted by one or both houses of Congress, Nelson was undoubtedly placing the best possible construction on matters; but his point was that the secession leaders wanted no compromise and never waited to see whether any overt act of animosity would come or what the results of another election in the North would be. Actually, the rejection of the Crittenden Compromise by the Republicans was the death of the last hope for adjustment.

Turning to the evidence that secession was not the result of any urgent necessity, he pointed out that the Republicans won by a minority vote and could easily have been beaten at the next election by a fusion of the opposition and that the Republicans had no majority in Congress and could not even have passed an appropriation bill unless the non-Republicans were appeased by a suitable compromise. If the Representatives of the seceding states had remained in Washington, the Republicans would have been powerless to pass any bill injurious to the South. At this point he made a rousing appeal:

And how different the causes which influenced our ancestors to throw off the British yoke from those which have animated the conspirators of the Cotton States. They had many real, actual, positive grievances. . . . They had suffered for years and petitioned and remonstrated in vain. What have we suffered? What wrong has the Government done us? What oppressive law has been enacted?—What deed of tyranny has been done? . . . If, therefore, the Union has been dissolved, it has been for imaginary, not real causes, and the land is to be deluged in blood, not because the people have petitioned and remonstrated to Congress in vain, but because politicians have been deprived of place and patronage by the sovereign edict of the people.

Following up the charge of conspiratorial leadership, Nelson sought to show how little of the separationist action had been initiated by the people. Virginia's secession, which had followed the firing on Fort Sumter and Lincoln's call for troops, he called a deliberate trick. Citing a statement by a Virginian in a speech at Charleston that Virginia would be brought to join the Confederacy by the striking of a blow and the shedding of blood, Nelson denounced the firing on Fort Sumter as a scheme to precipitate Virginia's secession. Saying that Virginia had been dragooned into secession, he sought to show that an effort was being made to do the same to Tennessee. One proof, he maintained, was that the Governor of Virginia had simultaneously asked for three Tennessee regiments and informed Virginia volunteers to stay at home until facilities could be provided for them. From this evidence Nelson drew the conclusion that troops were not needed but that the request was made to try to aid the vote for separation in Tennessee with a martial excitement.

Nelson then aimed charges of unconstitutionality against the actions of the April-May session of the legislature, using about the same terms as the resolutions of the East Tennessee Convention but citing much more detailed information. Sadly referring to John Bell's defection and the public letter Bell and others issued on April 19, followed by Bell's swing toward separation on April 23, Nelson commented: "If they gave you solemn advice on the 19th of April, and on the 23rd of the same month, hauled down their colors and allowed themselves to be misled by a frantic and senseless excitement, but little reliance is to be placed upon them in a crisis like this, 'For, if the trumpet give an uncertain sound, who shall prepare himself to the battle.' " This reference to his former leader and friend was necessitated by an effort Bell made early in June to speak in East Tennessee in behalf of a united front should war come between North and South.[20]

Nelson's next line of attack was a discussion of provisions of the Confederate Constitution that East Tennesseans might find objectionable—referring, of course, to prohibition of both tariff for protection and central government support of transportation facilities. He then turned to the Tennessee Military Act passed by the last legislature and attacked it as unconstitutional and a violation of constitutionally guaranteed civil rights. He condemned the act as granting the governor dictatorial power, as a source of staggering debt to the state, and as a means whereby the state-chartered banks might inflate the currency and destroy economic values. He also attacked as unconstitutional and as an open encouragement to fraud the bill's provisions for absentee soldiers' voting in the June 8, 1861, election.

Turning to a defense of Lincoln, he vigorously affirmed that, if he believed that Lincoln designed to subjugate the South and by force emancipate the slaves, he would advise resistance as readily as any Southern man, "at all hazards and to the last extremity." But his study of Lincoln's actions had convinced him that no violations of the Constitution had occurred or were likely to occur. In considerable detail he defended Lincoln in the matter of the forts retained in the South. In his closing remarks, Nelson took the following position:

But it is said this is a war between the North and the South, and we are compelled to take sides. I do not so regard it. It is a war between the Government of the United States and rebellious citizens who have committed treason against the Government. Neither is it a war between Lincoln and the South. It is a war between the Constitution and those who have violated it. . . .

Free men of Tennessee! If you are allowed to vote on the 8th of June, it is yet in your power to arrest the despotism of "King Harris," and retrieve the blunders of a misguided Legislature. It is yet in your power to prevent a war in our midst; to save the lives of our citizens; to preserve our cities, towns, and villages, and to secure the blessings which Heaven has promised to the peacemaker. It may be yet in your power to rescue the Union itself, and to

[20] Parks, *John Bell*, 402–04.

preserve the stars and stripes as a priceless legacy to posterity. If a fair election is held, and Tennessee is voted out of the Union, it behooves us all to act together to avoid a civil war among ourselves. If the election is carried by force or fraud, then let every friend of the Union throughout the State cry, "every man to his tents, O Israel!" Should that dreadful alternative be forced upon you,

> "Snatch from the ashes of your sires
> The embers of their former fires
> And he, who in the strife expires,
> Will add to theirs a name of fear,
> That tyranny will quake to hear."

As the returns began to come in from East Tennessee, Nelson, Johnson, Brownlow, and the other Unionist leaders had reason to be elated. Only five counties in East Tennessee, all strong or overwhelmingly Democratic counties, voted for disunion.[21] While the section did not yield a 25,000 majority as Nelson had hoped, it did vote more than two to one against leaving the Union, 32,923 to 14,780. It was evident in studying the returns that almost all of the Whigs had been held in the Union camp and that a substantial percentage of the Democrats had also voted for the Union. Even Nelson and Johnson's trip up to the Cumberland Plateau had been fruitful: Scott County turned out more than a third more Unionist votes than it had in the February referendum, and Fentress County was changed from an evenly divided vote in the February election to a Union triumph of 651 to 128.

Returns from Middle and West Tennessee were appalling, however, 58,265 to 8,198 and 29,127 to 6,117 respectively for disunion. And to add insult to injury, military camps reported 2,741 for disunion to none for the Union. State-wide election returns added to more than a fifty-seven thousand majority for independence and almost as many for union with the Confederacy. Pondering the news of intimidation and fraud and studying the election returns from Middle and West Tennessee, Nelson reached the conclusion that the election had been carried by force and fraud.

The overwhelming majorities against disunion in the February election had seemingly melted away. In the fifteen counties showing less than one hundred Unionist votes each, a comparison of February Union votes and general Whig voting strength (which Nelson believed must be mostly Unionist if not intimidated) with the pitiful Unionist showing indicating the following:[22]

---

[21] All election returns taken from *The Tribune Almanac . . . 1838-1868.*
[22] *Idem.*

County	Approx. Whig voting strength	Union votes in February, 1861	Union votes in June, 1861
Lincoln	450	815	none
Humphreys	250	327	none
Franklin	300	206	none
Hickman	175	298	3
Shelby (Memphis)	1,800	197	5
Giles	1,200	550	11
Warren	350	452	12
Tipton	375	147	16
Robertson	1,200	332	17
Coffee	300	698	26
Williamson	1,600	1,684	28
Obion	500	328	64
Sumner	775	770	69
Dickson	375	490	72
Rutherford	1,475	1,529	73
Totals	11,125	8,823	386

Over eighty-eight hundred Unionists in February reduced to less than four hundred in June, in these fifteen counties where more than eleven thousand Whig voters lived, indicated force and fraud to Nelson's mind. Fresh from the loud cheers of thousands of East Tennessee loyalists, conscious only of the overwhelming Unionism of East Tennessee Whigs, he could not conceive of eleven thousand Whigs anywhere going to the polls and voluntarily casting only 3½ per cent of their votes for the Union. Furthermore, in Davidson County, including the capital city of Nashville, more than three thousand former Whigs contrasted sharply with the four hundred and two Union votes.

It was not possible that the bulk of the former Whigs had stayed away from the polls because the total vote of Tennessee was ten thousand more than had been cast in the exciting presidential election of 1860. Despite the difficulty the Confederates would have had in trying to coerce many thousands of positive votes, Nelson reached the conclusion that secret balloting had been denied and Unionists in Middle and West Tennessee made fearful for their lives and the safety of family and property. He assumed that pro-secession poll managers checked off the voters against registration lists to discourage non-voting. News of violent interference with efforts to make Unionist speeches had come from across the plateau, and Nelson had some realization of the intimidating effects of mob psychology from the treatment he and Johnson had received at Jonesboro and other places as well as from the fact that his friends had persuaded him not to come to Sullivan County to speak.

As soon as the results of the election were known, Nelson exercised his authority as president of the East Tennessee Convention to issue a call for it to reassemble a week later, June 17, at Greeneville. Threats against his life, and against Johnson, Brownlow, and other militant Union leaders, suggested inconvenience, if not actual danger, in meeting again in Knoxville.[23]

Pending the assembling of the delegates, Nelson wrote out his angry "declaration of grievances," which the convention would adopt as written, and a set of radical resolutions which proved to be much more controversial.[24] The declaration claimed that the recent election had been a free one in no part of the state except East Tennessee, specifically charging that Union speeches were not permitted, Union papers were not allowed to circulate, and constitutional guarantees of secret ballot were disregarded as pro-secession poll officials marked and exposed Union votes to frighten and coerce the voters. The five Union votes in Memphis, where 5,613 votes were cast, was cited as one proof of the charge. Knowledge of East Tennessee Union strength was kept from the people of the rest of the state by suppression of proceedings of the Knoxville session of the East Tennessee Convention continued the declaration. Condemnation of absentee voting by soldiers and citation of newspaper dispatches that quoted secessionists as saying that they would hold possession of the state even if in the minority were followed by the charges that the vote was officially tabulated and announced by a "Disunion Governor, whose existence depends upon the success of secession," and that no provision was made for an examination of the vote by disinterested persons or for a legal contesting of the election. It was declared that the results did not represent the will of the people—that had an election been held all over the state as it was in East Tennessee the decision would have been for the Union.

Then followed a hint of revolution against state authorities: ". . . but, if this view is erroneous, we have the same—(and, as we think, a much better,) right to remain in the Government of the United States, than the other divisions of Tennessee have to secede from it." The remainder of the declaration was a bill of particulars against secession, similar to Nelson's speeches over East Tennessee, which ended:

It has involved the Southern States in a war whose success is hopeless, and which must ultimately tend to the ruin of the people.

Its bigoted, overbearing and intolerant spirit has already subjected the people of East Tennessee to many petty grievances; our people have been insulted; our flags have been fired upon and torn down; our houses have been rudely entered; our families subjected to insult; our peaceable meetings interrupted; our women and children shot at by a merciless soldiery; our towns pillaged; our citizens robbed, and some of them assassinated and murdered.

No effort has been spared to deter the Union men of East Tennessee from the expression of their free thoughts. The penalties of treason have been threatened against them, and murder and assassination have been openly

---

[23] Patton, *Unionism and Reconstruction in Tennessee*, 24.
[24] The declaration was published in the Nashville *Republican Banner*, June 28, 1861.

encouraged by leading secession journals. As secession has been thus over-bearing and intolerant while in the minority in East Tennessee, nothing better can be expected of the pretended majority than wild, unconstitutional and oppressive legislation; an utter contempt and disregard of law. . . .

The resolutions Nelson drafted to accompany the declaration an-nounced that the Union counties of East Tennessee, and all other Union counties in the state which saw fit to co-operate with them, would, in the period of revolution, be the legal government of Tennessee and should proceed to exercise the powers and functions of the state gov-ernment. They further promised that, for the sake of peace, this "legiti-mate" Union government of Tennessee should not try to prevent for-mation of volunteer companies among them or deny the use of the railroad to military forces unless their rights were actually invaded.[25] When the convention met at Greeneville with thirty counties repre-sented and a somewhat reduced representation, Nelson's document became the occasion for a spirited struggle in the business committee and on the floor. On the fourth day more moderate counsel prevailed under the leadership of Oliver P. Temple, Horace Maynard, and some of the less well-known Union leaders—but only over the opposition of Nelson and Andrew Johnson's son, Robert, who fought to the last for the more radical stand.[26] Friends of Andrew Johnson had already per-suaded him to leave for Washington to seek aid from Lincoln for East Tennessee.

Nelson's declaration of grievances was adopted and followed by reso-lutions to the following effect: the people of East Tennessee desired to avoid civil war in their section; the action of the legislature providing for the separation election was unconstitutional and not binding on the people of East Tennessee; East Tennessee prayed the legislature of the state to grant separate statehood; and finally, claiming the right to de-termine their own destiny regardless of whether separate statehood was granted, the convention provided in detail for a convention to meet at Kingston at the call of Nelson to effect a separate state organization.[27]

The declaration and resolutions were published in the Knoxville *Reg-ister* of July 4, 1861, and castigated under the heading "Declaration of Falsehoods!" It was asserted that "We, the people of East Tennessee," called no meeting, that the elections in Middle and West Tennessee were free and that no Union paper there even charged to the contrary, and that open ticket voting was defensible. The Nashville *Republican Ban-ner* of June 28, 1861, also printed the convention action and commented unfavorably. Its editor ineptly argued that the elections had been free on the grounds that only five votes in Memphis proved no intimidation —else how could so pitiful a minority dare vote in the face of the over-

---

[25] Nelson described his resolutions in the Knoxville *Whig*, August 24, 1861.
[26] Temple, *Notable Men of Tennessee*, 102-04.
[27] The resolutions were printed in the Nashville *Republican Banner*, June 28, 1861.

whelming majority. This hardly served to disabuse Nelson's mind of the conviction that the election had not been a fair one. There was undoubtedly pressure in all parts of the state where one faction was in great majority, and in many of the counties of Middle and West Tennessee it was dangerous to vote for the Union. A Union meeting at Paris, Tennessee, was broken up by disunionists and one Union man was killed in the disorder. There were also reasonably reliable reports of soldiers from outside Tennessee voting in the election.[28] But Nelson's claim that a free election would have produced a Union victory was ill-advised in the face of the size of the separation vote and may be understood only in the light of East Tennessee's relative isolation from the fervor of the rest of the state.

The petition for separate statehood was duly presented to the legislature with reference to the fact that separate status was not a new idea, but few hoped for favorable action. Meanwhile, a new opportunity for resistance opened in connection with the regular state elections scheduled for early August, 1861. Nelson in the first congressional district, Horace Maynard in the second, George W. Bridges in the third, and Andrew J. Clements in the fourth (Cumberland Plateau) district announced for election to the Congress of the United States—opposed by candidates for the Congress of the Confederate States of America.[29] This was defiance in action rather than simply talk, and the fact that the Confederate authorities permitted the election contest to be completed may be explained by the hope of a Confederate victory's easing the situation in East Tennessee. During this canvass news of the Federal rout at the battle of First Bull Run chilled the hopes of East Tennessee Unionists that Lincoln could rescue them militarily. In the face of this news, Nelson carried his district by about two-thirds as great a majority as Unionism had carried it in June—this being a majority of more than five thousand and so decisive that neither of his opponents would seek a seat in the Confederate Congress.[30] In the second district Horace Maynard had the same success. In the third and fourth districts both candidates claimed victory and sought seats in their respective congresses.[31]

Nelson was not in Tennessee when the results were made known, however. He had learned from what he considered reliable authority that a warrant for his arrest had been issued to take effect the day of, or immediately after, the election—perhaps if it became evident that he was elected. So he laid plans to escape, as did Maynard and Bridges.

---

[28] Patton, *Unionism and Reconstruction in Tennessee*, 20-21. For evidence that the voting in this election set a pattern which was voluntarily followed in many post-Reconstruction elections see Daniel M. Robison, *Bob Taylor and the Agrarian Revolt in Tennessee* (Chapel Hill, 1935), 9, 70, 96, 147, 175, 185, 186, and 203.

[29] *Ibid.*, 28-29.

[30] Jonesboro *Express*, August 16, 1861, carried the returns.

[31] Patton, *Unionism and Reconstruction in Tennessee*, 29.

Having issued the call for the East Tennessee Convention meeting at Kingston to convene on August 31, 1861,[32] he left home on the morning of the election with his sixteen-year-old son, David. His object was to reach Barbourville, Kentucky, and await the election returns. If elected, he intended to go on to Washington and serve in the United States Congress. If defeated, he would return home and "decline any action against the popular will." [33]

Nelson took precautions to avoid detection, staying away from the direct and easy route through Cumberland Gap to Barbourville. Instead, he planned a night ride from Rogersville, in Hawkins County, directly across the mountains. In Rogersville, he noticed the suspicious glances of Confederate sympathizers; and he was fully aware that as president of the East Tennessee Convention and avowed candidate for the United States Congress he was marked as perhaps no other East Tennessean as titular head of a rebellious movement against the Confederacy. But returning home would accomplish nothing; only the mountains offered escape.

On the evening of August 4, with his son and two employed guides who knew the mountain passes, Nelson waited with growing excitement and impatience for darkness to cloak their flight. As darkness enfolded they slipped along the winding valley northward to the foot of the massive escarpment of the Clinch Mountains, being careful not to wind the horses before the hard climb began. The effort of the horses as they made their way ever higher along the steep and winding trail up the face of the mountain was agonizingly slow. Finally, the crest was reached and the mounts were allowed to rest before the tedious descent began. The cool, moist air and silence were in sharp contrast with the raucous strife down in the ocean of darkness behind them.

But time was precious, and again they moved along behind the guide, twisting and almost looping as the trail dropped along the sides of the mountain folds. Then they were leveling off again, and soon the sound of Clinch River rushing along its rocky bed could be heard. At midnight they reached Kyle's Ford and felt the shock of mountain-cold water as the horses splashed across. But now the air seemed colder, for the friendly soil of East Tennessee was ending. Across the western tip of Confederate Virginia lay the safety of Kentucky, but it was twenty miles away and beyond rugged Wallen Ridge. Only five hours remained to get at least past the vicinity of Jonesville and within striking distance of their objective before dawn should expose them to curious and probably hostile eyes.

After the horses drank at the ford, the riders hurried them along the side of a winding valley until the guide announced the Virginia line. In

---

[32] Knoxville *Whig*, August 3, 1861.
[33] *Ibid*, August 24, 1861, carried Nelson's full explanation of the episode.

only a few more minutes they were conscious of rising ground as they approached the pass over Wallen Ridge. Then, in a confusion of hoof-beats and hoarse cries, the flight was ended. Thirty horsemen surrounded them, and the leader called out that they were under arrest. Nelson and the guides were relieved of their pistols but were not tied after Nelson gave his word not to try to escape. Under guard of ten of his captors Nelson pushed on over Wallen Ridge and down Powell River Valley toward the Confederate army post at Cumberland Gap—a prisoner.[34]

---

[34] Described by Nelson in *idem.* This report by Nelson is also found in *The War of the Rebellion: A Compilation of the Official Records of the Union and Confederate Armies*, 128 vols. (Washington, 1880–1901), Series II, Volume I, 825. Hereinafter cited as *Rebellion Record*. The news story on Nelson's arrest appeared in the Knoxville *Whig*, August 10, 1861.

CHAPTER IX

The Last Link Is Broken

A S THE MORNING SUN dispelled the mists and revealed the unbroken face of Cumberland Mountain to the northwest, Nelson and his guards wearily made their way toward Cumberland Gap. Hour after hour passed while they rode along the foot of the mountain, which tantalized him with its monumental demarcation of the Kentucky border and safety. He had, many weeks before, recognized the dangers involved in his course of action and hence suffered no shocked regrets. His pride would not allow him to inquire of his captors the charge against him—or later even of Colonel F. M. Walker, into whose custody he was delivered at Cumberland Gap.[1] Silently he speculated upon his own fate and what precipitate action his friends in East Tennessee might take when they learned of his capture. Particularly was he anxious that no harm befall his son.

After a few hours of exhausted sleep at Cumberland Gap, Nelson was told that he was to be sent back along the same route and then on eastward to Abingdon, Virginia, more than a hundred miles away on a road crossing two mountain ranges and never more than a few miles from the Tennessee border. Nelson knew that friends might attempt to rescue him, and the sixty-man guard re-enforced that opinion. He was correct in assuming that it was a possibility; for as the trip was begun, Felix K. Zollicoffer at Knoxville telegraphed Abingdon that a rescue might be attempted and reported that Nelson's friends were using menacing language.[2] However, more moderate counsel prevailed, and no violence was attempted in his behalf. As the almost symbolic mass of Cumberland Mountain receded to the west and finally disappeared, Nelson probably wondered if he would ever again see his beloved highlands.

Arrival at Abingdon brought quickly a sense of relief—both as to his personal fate and the danger of dire consequences for East Tennesseans as a result of hasty action. In the first place, he was met at Abingdon by John Baxter, one of the ardent East Tennessee Unionists who had been at the East Tennessee Convention. Baxter, an outstanding lawyer, had volunteered his services to Nelson as counsel in Richmond; and the Confederate military authorities had permitted him to join Nelson—a permission in itself encouraging. Also at Abingdon he was met by Dr. Jeptha

[1] Nelson's report in Knoxville *Whig*, August 24, 1861.
[2] Zollicoffer to Editors of the Abingdon (Virginia) *Virginian*, August 6, 1861, in *Rebellion Record*, Series II, Volume I, 825.

Fowlkes, a peace commissioner from the Confederacy to East Tennessee. Dr. Fowlkes manifested a zealous interest in quieting East Tennessee and in obtaining Nelson's release on honorable terms in order that his confinement might not further incite East Tennessee Union men. He showed Nelson a letter to the peace commissioners from the Confederate Commanding General of the Department of Tennessee, Major General Leonidas Polk. It was written in a spirit of magnanimity toward East Tennesseans and proposed to respect their feelings and assure them that the presence of troops was solely to protect the mountain passes against invasion by Federal troops. Irritating language and offensive bearing of troops toward East Tennesseans was specifically prohibited, and an obviously heartfelt desire to avoid any injury or even offense characterized the letter. Its contents affected Nelson deeply and shook his former conviction that East Tennesseans were marked for military compulsion to support a cause they opposed. Fearing that any admission of changing opinion would be mistaken as an effort to gain release by appeasement, Nelson did not let Dr. Fowlkes or the Richmond authorities know of his reaction.[3]

On the train ride from Abingdon to Richmond, Saturday, August 10, 1861, several members of the Tennessee delegation to the Confederate Congress talked with Nelson and went out of their way to offer assistance to him and to the people of East Tennessee. In Richmond he was treated with great kindness and visited by many leading Confederates. Governor Zebulon B. Vance of North Carolina, Nelson's prewar acquaintance, and others urged him to take his seat in the Confederate Congress —but this Nelson would not consider.[4] He was anxious, however, for more than personal reasons, to secure his release as soon as possible. He feared that at any time his friends would arrest Confederate leaders as hostages and that Confederate counter arrests would lead to the horrors of civil war in East Tennessee.

Some recent developments now brought his problem into clearer focus. The newspaper reports of the August election throughout Tennessee revealed that an increased majority over the June vote had adopted the permanent constitution of the Confederacy. This tended to weaken his belief that the majority of Tennesseans in a free election would not vote for disunion. General Polk's letter had convinced him that East Tennesseans would not be subjected to military tyranny or interference beyond the needs of defense unless local rebellion against Confederate authority compelled it. He was also assured by Confederate leaders that no test oaths or compulsory draft laws would be adopted. He read of the confiscation laws passed or contemplated by both Federal and Confederate governments and reached the conclusion that "the

[3] Nelson's report in Knoxville *Whig*, August 24, 1861.
[4] Temple, *Notable Men of Tennessee*, 176.

mutual hatred which [had] grown up between the antagonist sections of the Union" had shattered the Union forever and that it was both politic and wise to submit to a result which seemed inevitable—"however we may deplore it." But the most conclusive argument was the recent Federal defeat at Bull Run, rendering it improbable that any help could reach East Tennessee from the North in the foreseeable future.[5] This stark fact, together with the impressiveness of preparations and confidence (indeed, overconfidence) in Richmond, probably convinced Nelson that the Confederacy was a *de facto* government—regardless of *de jure* considerations. And citizens were, in English jurisprudence, exonerated from any blame in obeying *de facto* governments.

Newspaper reports were urging punishment for Nelson; and such editorials, falling into East Tennessee Unionist hands, might precipitate the action Nelson feared. The Memphis *Appeal* editorialized that the government should make an example of this "brawling traitor," that the time for leniency was past, and that Nelson should get ten years in prison.[6] The Richmond *Whig* on Monday morning commented:

We hear generally that his conduct has been rebellious and defiant, and unworthy of a patriot. But we also hear that he has been a man of fair repute in the past, and one who is likely to respect his word when pledged. If he will give that pledge, let him go; if not, and his treason is overt and incontestible, hang him; if doubtful, send him with a flag of truce, and make a present of him to Old Abe.[7]

Having made his decision to seek release, Nelson drafted an informal proposition and asked for a response to it. In this first draft he supposed that he was a prisoner of war and could be paroled upon a promise not to take up arms or counsel or abet any hostile act. He added, however, "unless in the actual necessary defense of my own person or property, when wrongfully assailed." [8] He then listed five express conditions, reserving to himself the right to write or speak in vindication of his past conduct and exempting himself from any civil or criminal indictment in Confederate or Tennessee courts. No change of mind is evidenced in this draft, which was not considered acceptable by Confederate authorities. A second draft dropped the reserved right to fight in defense of person or property and all of the "express conditions" of the first draft. The word was much more conciliatory, and instead of reference to status as "prisoner of war" he referred to a charge of "treason" and disavowed any act of treason. Still no evidence of a change of opinion was included. In the third, and final, draft he made that concession in an added paragraph:

---

[5] Nelson's report in Knoxville *Whig*, August 24, 1861.
[6] Memphis *Appeal*, August 14, 1861.
[7] Richmond *Whig*, August 12, 1861.
[8] The first two drafts of this letter to Jefferson Davis are in the Nelson Papers under date of August 12, 1861. The final form is published in the Knoxville *Whig*, August 24, 1861, and also in the *Rebellion Record*, Series II, Volume I, 826.

In view of the increased majority in the election which has just taken place in Tennessee, I shall feel it my duty, as a citizen of that State, to submit to her late action, and shall religiously abstain from any further words or acts of condemnation or opposition to her Government.[9]

This letter was considered satisfactory in Jefferson Davis's office; and the President of the Confederacy signed a letter to Nelson the following day referring to Nelson's promise as a citizen of Tennessee to submit to her late action and "religiously abstain" from further condemnation of her government, stating that his government desired only peace throughout its territory and made no inquiries into former political opinions and informing Nelson that his release had been ordered together with the release of his party.

The day after Nelson departed from Richmond, the editor of the *Enquirer* of that city wrote that he hoped that the generous course of the Confederate government toward Nelson would promote quiet in East Tennessee and that Nelson would "probably issue an address to his people before long." [10] Nelson stated categorically that no terms or conditions, "express or implied, public or private," attended his release beyond the letters between himself and Jefferson Davis. It was so out of character for Nelson to make a false statement in such a situation that it should not be deduced that Nelson promised to issue an address. Either the *Enquirer* editor knew him well enough to guess that he would feel compelled to "vindicate" his action before the people, or, after his release, Nelson mentioned to some friend that he would issue such an address. Arriving home in Jonesboro on Thursday, August 15, Nelson hastened to Knoxville and wrote out his full explanation of events and the reasons for his action. Then, disavowing any promise to Confederate authorities that he would use his influence for the Confederacy, he did advise his friends to abstain from further opposition to the Confederate or Tennessee governments.[11]

Brownlow printed Nelson's explanation on the front page of the following week's paper and approved Nelson's acceptance of the situation because "as a prisoner he could have done nothing and would have suffered in private affairs also." [12] The Knoxville *Register* of August 29 poked fun at the position Nelson assumed, saying that it resembled Anthony's speech in *Julius Caesar* and adding that it reminded the editor of a famous orator's remark: "it is sorta so and sorta not so, but a little more sorta not so than sorta so." A week later, perhaps after a suggestion from Confederate officials that Nelson could be of great service to them if he would, the *Register* became serious and printed the address with the comment: "Mr. Nelson's character and standing in this commu-

[9] *Rebellion Record*, Series II, Volume I, 826.
[10] Richmond *Enquirer*, August 15, 1861.
[11] Knoxville *Whig*, August 24, 1861.
[12] *Idem*.

nity, and before the country, forbid us to doubt that he will fail to redeem to the fullest the pledge he so fairly and freely gave."

One Knoxville Confederate, whom Nelson had assisted with political recommendations to John Bell, confided to his diary:

The lately liberated traitor T. A. R. Nelson has been in town several days. He is not much seen in the daylight, but he passed me on the street last night going into his hotel, the Lamar House. This house has recently changed proprietors, and has become black republican in the hands of the Smiths, a hen-pecked yankee and his wife.

Nelson, before his arrest, put a call in the "Whig" for the assembling of a Convention at Kingston for the purpose of erecting East Tennessee into a separate state, or rather of claiming to be *the state, a la the Wheeling Convention.* That call has not been revoked. He was liberated at Richmond on promising acquiescence in the Southern Vote of Tennessee. But until he revokes his proclamation, I will not believe in his good faith. I put a piece in the Register embodying this idea.[13]

The diarist recorded the same day a strong condemnation of General Zollicoffer for threatening and arresting "little leaders" while "the deluding villains . . . go on unmolested." He headed his list of "villains" with the name of Nelson. On October 12, 1861, he returned to the same topic while commenting upon the trial of Unionists in Knoxville for sabotage and sedition: "Yet my sense of justice revolted at *one* feature. The miserable victims were the *sincere dupes* of such dishonest knaves as Johnson, Nelson & Co. . . . If the proceedings had been against these few leading *knaves,* & had been pushed to severe, nay even capital, punishment, then justice would have been attained, and the minds of their followers would have been disabused ere long." By July 5 of the next year, 1862, he was so bitter that he made the following entry:

Indeed there was never, since the world began, such a shameless piece of cowardice acted out among men as that perpetrated by these infamous leaders of East Tennessee toryism. In their speeches and writings they counseled the people to rebel against the Confederate authorities, and resorted to the most dishonest artifices to persuade them thereto: yet these leaders *themselves* merely "grazed the edge of treason" and carefully made cats paws of the poor deluded people by thrusting them forward to do what these cowardly leaders would not do.

Regardless of the interpretations placed upon his actions, Nelson considered that he had been perfectly consistent. Throughout the summer he had urged the seizure of the railroad before Confederate troops could do so and, after that was refused in the Greeneville session of the East Tennessee Convention and troops were in possession of the railroad, non-resistance unless "assured of undoubted aid from the Government of

---

[13] Diary of W. G. McAdoo, Sr., 1857-1868, August 18, 1861. The original of this diary belongs to Brice McAdoo Clagett and is deposited with Mrs. Clayton Platt of Ambler, Pennsylvania. For this study a copy was used that was loaned to the writer by Dr. Stanley J. Folmsbee of the University of Tennessee, Knoxville.

the United States." Now that Federal aid was seemingly hopeless, permanent non-resistance was a logical conclusion.

A few days after Nelson returned to Jonesboro from Knoxville, where he had issued his address to the people of East Tennessee, he was visited by A. M. Lea, a Confederate brigade commissary. They talked about conditions and prospects in the area at great length, and Lea left with the impression that Nelson would eventually come out openly for the Southern cause. Lea also obtained aid from Nelson in enlisting Confederate volunteers.[14] On August 26, 1861, several Union leaders from various counties met in Knoxville at Lea's invitation and endorsed Nelson's address and called upon their friends in Kentucky and elsewhere to return home and submit to "the powers that be."Lea proposed publishing a handbill with Nelson's address, his friends' endorsement, an appeal by Lea to his friends and relatives, and "General Zollicoffer's general order holding out the olive branch." [15] Whatever the sanguine hopes of Lea, Nelson did not acknowledge allegiance to the Confederate government of Tennessee by voting in the November 6 Confederate election.[16]

Two days later the extreme Unionists, evidently expecting a rescuing Federal army to rush in on the signal and rejecting Nelson's warning not to initiate resistance unless "assured of undoubted aid from the Government of the United States," attempted to burn nine railroad bridges between Stevenson, Alabama, and Bristol, Tennessee-Virginia. Five of the bridges were successfully burned, but General Buell did not order his forces in Kentucky to hurry into East Tennessee. Instead, he continued to mature his plans for the capture of Nashville and central and western Tennessee. Confederate General Zollicoffer, on the other hand, reacted more vigorously by withdrawing the "olive branch." Harsh repression of Unionism, disarming of Unionists, and martial law in Knoxville were his answers.

Now Nelson's worst fears became reality, for in the words of one student of the Civil War in East Tennessee:

In order to stamp out future trouble the Confederacy now felt it necessary to treat the East Tennesseans with the suspicion and harshness that war always imposes upon those who have it within their power to hinder victory. Squads of soldiers were sent out into every district to break up Unionist gatherings, to disarm the populace, and to arrest the leaders.[17]

In the resulting confusion, brigands and self-appointed patriots made a shambles of East Tennessee:

Vigilante committees prowled over the country, armed to the teeth, arresting

[14] A. M. Lea to A. T. Bledsoe, August 26, 1861, in *Rebellion Record*, Series II, Volume I, 827.
[15] *Idem.*
[16] A. G. Graham to Jefferson Davis, November 12, 1861, in *Rebellion Record*, Series I, Volume IV, 239.
[17] Coulter, *Brownlow*, 171.

men on suspicion of hostility to the new government, and shooting others down. The Unionists then, despairing at length of relief from the North and regarding their houses and lives in danger, formed themselves into secret "bushwhacking" societies, shot Confederates from ambush and destroyed their property. This in turn maddened the Confederates and provoked them to savage retaliation. A civil and guerrilla war was thus begun, the horrors of which almost defy description.[18]

For almost a year after the outbreak of this terror, Nelson endured keen distress, doubtlessly asking himself over and over again how it could have been avoided. He had foreseen accurately the consequences of hasty uprising and had privately and publicly advised against it from the day Confederate troops arrived in East Tennessee. But, somehow, the forces he had helped to unleash and had not been able to control had brought his land and his people to perhaps the worst plight of any large group in the nation. The savage hatred growing between neighbors and former friends and the bitter schism within families were as bad as the physical suffering and destruction. It was growing evident that, whatever the outcome, scars would remain as long as a single participant was alive; and it was probable that one party or the other would be exterminated or banished. When one of the Unionist generals of East Tennessee arrested the men of Lee County, Virginia, who had captured Nelson in August, 1861, he wanted to hang them—simply for having taken into custody a man who was released in a few days. In reporting the episode to the United States Secretary of War, General George W. Morgan included a request that East Tennessee troops be used elsewhere than in their home country—so great was the danger of atrocities.[19]

During this harrowing year, Nelson refused to answer political questions because he considered himself pledged not to maintain his views.[20] He resented fiercely any persecution of Union men, but evidently did not blame the officially constituted Confederate authorities and accepted passes for himself and his family to travel freely in East Tennessee.[21] Meanwhile, he observed with growing certainty of mind the unconstitutional acts Lincoln committed in trying to save the Union—particularly the calling out of an army without congressional authorization and the suspension of the writ of *habeas corpus*. The military success of the Confederacy was also impressive by the fall of 1862. Lee had relieved Richmond in the Seven Day's Battle, outflanked and shattered the Federal army at Second Bull Run, and crossed the Potomac into Maryland.

---

[18] Patton, *Unionism and Reconstruction in Tennessee,* 63.

[19] Morgan to E. M. Stanton, June 27, 1862, in *Rebellion Record,* Series I, Volume XVI, 1009-10.

[20] R. M. Barton to Nelson, September 13, 1862, in Nelson Papers, reveals that Nelson had refused to answer a political question in a previous letter because he considered himself pledged not to maintain his views.

[21] *Idem.* A pass in the Nelson Papers under date of September 24, 1862, is accompanied by a personal note signed, "Your friend, John E. Toole, Col."

Although he was unable to defeat McClellan at Antietam Creek, he had withdrawn safely across the Potomac and stood seemingly impenetrable between Richmond and a badly injured Federal army. General Bragg had somewhat countered the loss of Middle and West Tennessee by slipping through East Tennessee into Kentucky and forcing the Federals to fall back precipitately to meet him at Perryville. Nelson, isolated at Jonesboro, could hardly have been expected to appraise all the hidden factors accurately and predict the downfall of the Confederacy. On the contrary, in the fall of 1862 the destruction of the Confederacy appeared impossible.

When General Samuel Jones was placed in command of the district of East Tennessee in September, 1862, he found many Unionists, including Nelson, expressing the opinion that all hope of preserving the Union was gone and that it was the duty of all who remained in the Confederacy to support it—with arms if necessary—to conclude the frightful war.[22] General Jones immediately wrote Nelson a highly complimentary letter asking for an interview to inform himself of conditions in order to further the interests of "our country." [23] He knew none of the Union men of East Tennessee personally and selected Nelson as the most influential, perhaps because of his presidency of the East Tennessee Convention.[24]

Before Nelson reached Knoxville for this meeting with General Jones, the news of Lincoln's Emancipation Proclamation had arrived. This cast an entirely new light on the existing conflict. The East Tennessee Unionists had never been abolitionists. Brownlow had said in the 1860 election contest that he would be ready to join the Southern states in revolution if Lincoln should advocate even interference with the interstate slave trade and if Congress should pass and the Supreme Court uphold such hostile legislation. After Lincoln's election Brownlow had declared in May, 1861, that if Lincoln contemplated the abolition of slavery, he would join the South and fight Lincoln to the death.[25]

Andrew Johnson had also defended slavery and had denied the right of the Lincoln administration to touch it. Throughout the tumultuous spring of 1861 the position of the Unionists of East Tennessee had been based in part upon the assumption that Lincoln could not and did not wish to try to interfere with slavery in the South. In the United States Senate, Johnson had blamed the abolitionists for the country's troubles and denounced them as enemies of the nation. But Johnson, appointed by Lincoln as military governor of Tennessee after the Confederate troops were cleared from Middle and West Tennessee, and earnestly

---

[22] Samuel Jones to George W. Randolph, Secretary of War, C.S.A., September 24, 1862, in *Rebellion Record*, Series I, Volume XVI, Part II, 668-69.
[23] Jones to Nelson, September 25, 1862, in Nelson Papers.
[24] Jones to George W. Randolph, October 4, 1862, in *Rebellion Record*, Series I, Volume XVI, Part II, 908-09.
[25] Coulter, *Brownlow*, 137-38.

trying to sustain his chief's policy in 1862, stated in Nashville on July 4, 1862, nearly three months before the Emancipation Proclamation:

I am for this government above all earthly possessions, and if it perish, I do not want to survive it. I am for it, though slavery be struck from existence and Africa swept from the balance of the world. I believe, indeed, that the Union is the only protection of slavery—its sole guarantee; but if you persist in forcing this issue of slavery against the Government, I say in the face of Heaven, give me my Government and let the negro go! [26]

Nelson's attitude toward slavery did not alter. He had said in speeches and published addresses in the spring of 1861 that if he believed it to be the object of the North to subjugate the South and emancipate slaves in violation of the Constitution, he would go as far as the farthest in advocating the utmost resistance. Although he could not know immediately what his former colleagues, Brownlow and Johnson, would do in response to the proclamation, he almost certainly had a good idea. Brownlow had been expelled from the Confederacy and was currently touring the North denouncing secession in venomous terms to wildly cheering, and paying, audiences in almost every major city in the North. Of this tour and its remarkable reception Brownlow's biographer says:

Brownlow had undoubtedly become a radical and he had arrived at that position through his contact with the people of the North and through his inherent disposition to go to extremes. He shot venom and spleen and fire and brimstone at the Southerners, he told how they should be hanged, drawn, and quartered .... in the excitement of a speech he lost all sense of proportions and largely the limits of good taste. But these things made a good show and afforded rare entertainment for the commonality of the North. The Parson mistook their applause as a meaning of complete agreement with his policy of extermination for the Southerners.[27]

By the time of Lincoln's proclamation Brownlow had so whipped himself into fury that he never faltered in his stride. And Johnson was obviously not going to weaken the chance of Union victory by turning against Lincoln because of the slavery question.

Willing to strike out alone, if necessary, Nelson discussed the proclamation and related problems extensively with General Jones and then sat down in the general's office and wrote out an address to the people for Jones to have published.[28] It appeared in the Knoxville *Register* of October 5, 1862, and was reprinted in other papers and as a handbill.

The address began with a reference to Nelson's frequently stated declaration that he would advocate resistance to unconstitutional emancipation of slavery, and it continued with a quotation of the essence of

---

[26] Lloyd Paul Stryker, *Andrew Johnson: A Study in Courage* (New York, 1930), 103.

[27] Coulter, *Brownlow*, 234.

[28] Samuel Jones to George W. Randolph, October 4, 1862, in *Rebellion Record,* Series I, Volume XVI, Part II, 908-09.

A Brady photograph of William G. Brownlow, Nelson's close friend and
political ally until 1862. Provided by the Library of Congress.

Lincoln's Emancipation Proclamation. He then made reference to his warning that slave insurrection might follow the outbreak of a civil war and reaffirmed his opinion that secession was impolitic and unconstitutional. Nevertheless, he maintained, one violation of the Constitution did not justify violation by the other side. The right of revolution was another matter—a right he had sustained in Congress and in other speeches. Although love of Union and confidence that it was the best government in the world had controlled his opinions in the past, this proclamation of Lincoln's was judged the most barbarous and atrocious act of the Civil War. After some detailed attack on the proclamation, he inquired:

The Union men of East Tennessee are not now and never have been committed to the doctrines of incendriaism [sic] and murder to which Mr. Lincoln's proclamation leads. What, then, is the path of duty in the trying circumstances which surround us? Is it to belie all our past professions and to sustain Mr. Lincoln's administration, right or wrong? Is it to justify a man, whom we had no agency in elevating to power, not only in abandoning the Constitution of the United States, but in repudiating the Chicago platform, his inaugural address and messages to Congress in which the absolute right to slavery in the States where it exists was distinctly and unequivocally conceded? Or is it, in view of his many violations of the Constitution, and this crowning act of usurpation, to join that side which at present affords the only earthly hope of successful resistance?

Nelson then turned his attention to the persecutions of Union people and declared that the Confederate supreme command in East Tennessee was not aware of them and had not authorized them. He pled with the persecuted not to let their sense of personal wrong blind them to the dangers from Lincoln's government. After expressing a hope that Northern citizens might overthrow the revolutionary Lincoln government (perhaps in the 1862 by-elections) and open the way for a healing of the schism in the Union, he launched upon his extended peroration:

But, if through fear, or any other cause, Mr. Lincoln's infamous proclamation is sustained, then we have no Union to hope for, no Constitution to struggle for, no magnificent and unbroken heritage to maintain, no peace to expect, save such, as with the blessing of providence, we may conquer....
    It is almost unnecessary to declare to you that I adhered to the Union amidst good report and evil report, suffering and danger, while it was in my power to support it, and that, when my efforts were paralysed [sic] and my voice silenced by causes beyond my control, I have cherished the hope that all might yet be well; but "the last link is broken" that bound me to a government for which my ancestors fought, and whatever may be the course of others, I shall feel it my duty to encourage the most persevering and determined resistance against the tyrants and usurpers of the Federal administration who have blasted our hopes and are cruelly seeking to destroy the last vestige of freedom among us. If you would save yourselves from a species of carnage unexampled in the history of North America, but unequivocally invited in Mr. Lincoln's proclamation, let every man who is able to fight buckle on his armor, and, without awaiting the slow and tedious process of

conscription, at once volunteer to aid in the struggle against him. The race is not always to the swift nor the battle to the strong, and it cannot, in the nature of things, be possible that a just God will prosper the efforts of a man or a government which has hypocritically pretended to wage war in behalf of the Constitution, but now throws off the mask and sets it utterly at defiance. No despot in Europe would dare to exercise the powers which Mr. Lincoln, in less than two brief years, has boldly usurped. He has suspended the writ of *habeas corpus* in regard to all persons who have been or may be imprisoned by military authority, and thus destroyed a right essential to the liberty of the citizen. . . . He has called armies into the field, without authority, according to his own acknowledgement, and has become a military Dictator. He now claims the prerogative to abolish slavery without our consent; and, if he can thus take our negroes, why may he not take our lands and every thing else we possess, and reduce us to a state of vassalage to which no parallel can be found save in the history of the Middle Ages.

General Jones wrote the Confederate Secretary of War of the address and commented upon its strong Union tone, saying that he thought Nelson would have modified it if he had asked, but that both thought it would appeal to Union men better in its existing form.[29] In all probability the general had misunderstood Nelson about amending the address. Undoubtedly Nelson would have taken advice on inconsequential aspects of the draft, but Jones did not know his man if he thought that he could have caused Nelson to delete the essence of his Unionism. Jones intended to make the most of Nelson's support and wrote the editor of the Athens, Tennessee, *Post* to copy the address and comment in such a way as to please Nelson and encourage others to follow.[30] He tried hard to get Nelson to go on a speaking tour but was not successful.[31] At one time he wrote Richmond optimistically that he thought that Nelson and John Netherland, "who are the most influential men in East Tennessee," would take to the stump.[32]

In trying to make the most of former Union leadership, General Jones ran afoul of partisan interests. In disgust, he wrote that the Southern men in East Tennessee were small politicians who did not want influential Union men to change their course and get into competition with them and that their denunciatory articles caused much mischief. He told the editor of the Knoxville *Register* in decided terms not to pub-

---

[29] *Idem.*

[30] Samuel Jones to Editor of Athens *Post*, October 4, 1862, in *Rebellion Record*, Series I, Volume XVI, Part II, 907-08.

[31] Jones to Nelson, October 17, 1862, in *Rebellion Record*, Series I, Volume XVI, Part II, 957-58.

[32] Jones to George W. Randolph, October 14, 1862, in *Rebellion Record*, Series I, Volume XVI, Part II, 945-46. Verton M. Queener, "The Origin of the Republican Party in East Tennessee," in East Tennessee Historical Society's *Publications*, No. 13 (1941), 77-78, states that the following leading Unionists openly denounced the Emancipation Proclamation: John Baxter, William B. Carter, T. A. R. Nelson, John Netherland, and James G. Spears. The latter was dismissed from the army by Lincoln because of his bitterness over the proclamation.

lish such articles, and he wrote another editor that this was no time to permit party feelings to drive away any who could serve the cause.[33]

The Knoxville Confederate, W. G. McAdoo, Sr., who had written into his diary such strong criticism of Nelson, Johnson, & Co., illustrated General Jones's problem with his comments on this development. About rumors that such a "card" was to be published he wrote: ". . . I hear it hinted that these arch traitors are about to embrace the eleventh hour opportunity. . . . I have no longer any faith in their 'cards,' their oaths, or anything else. They hate the Southern Government too intensely to ever become its friends." [34] After favorable editorial comment on Nelson's address appeared in the *Register*, McAdoo charged that the *Register* was completely "given over to the 'Union' party," remarking caustically about the editor's apology for outrages by Southern men on Unionists. He continued, "the Register censures as unpatriotic those leading Southern men who do not applaud in every particular Nelson's address; and yet the address distinctly favors *reconstruction!*" He reasoned from the appearance of things that an attempt was being made "to build up the Union Party on the platform of Nelson's 'address,' with the idea of *reconstruction* as a basis, and with the leading active principles of *hostility to Secessionists*, and *original Southern men*." [35]

Nelson received some congratulatory messages, but declined either to go on a speaking tour or to accept a colonel's or brigadier general's commission to raise troops.[36] A letter from H. L. McClung expressed pleasure that they were again on the same ground, offered congratulations "from political as well as personal considerations," and recalled:

> I went through with the same struggle you have experienced. Old party ties—a belief that our difficulties might have been averted—that they were brought upon us by a party with which I had never acted—a party who preferred a disruption of the Union to a loss of office. I hesitated, long hesitated. But, when convinced that it was narrowing down to a sectional strife, that I had to take sides either with the South or North, I could no longer hesitate. . . .[37]

Two other problems arose in connection with the address. One concerned the charge of forgery that Unionists made and that was dispelled only with difficulty.[38] The other was more personal. Nelson's seventeen-

---

[33] *Idem.;* Jones to Editor of Athens *Post*, October 4, 1862, in *Rebellion Record*, Series I, Volume XVI, Part II, 907-08.

[34] Diary of W. G. McAdoo, October 3, 1862.

[35] *Ibid.*, October 11, 1862.

[36] C. W. Charlton to Nelson, October 5, 1862; petition from ninety-four citizens of Greeneville to *id.*, October 6, 1862; H. L. McClung to *id.*, October 7, 1862; General E. Kirby Smith to *id.*, November 17, 1862, in Nelson Papers.

[37] H. L. McClung to Nelson, October 7, 1862, in Nelson Papers.

[38] Samuel Jones to Nelson, October 17, 1862, in *Rebellion Record*, Series I, Volume XVI, Part II, 957-58.

year-old son, David, against his father's wishes and while his father was away from home, had gathered together about seventy members of a company of militia he had commanded in 1861 and tried to slip through the Confederate lines to join the Federal army at Cumberland Gap. He was apprehended and sent to Madison, Georgia, where he was imprisoned at the time of his father's address.[39] Nelson knew that he was liable to charges of seeking to buy his son's release by deserting to the Confederates, but a delay in the address would lose all of the impact of immediate reaction to the Emancipation Proclamation. Not a word was spoken between Nelson and General Jones about the boy during the interview in which Nelson wrote the paper, and none of Nelson's friends mentioned the matter to Jones. Nonetheless, there were a few who made the charge, and Jones wrote Nelson:

It is due to you that I should state that neither you nor anyone ever intimated to me that you desired the release of your son, nor did I intimate any promise or intention of releasing him. I took it for granted that you did desire it, but I had too just an appreciation of your character to suppose for one moment that your action on so important a matter would be influenced by that motive. I have heard that your son was young and indiscreet. . . . I have released a number of prisoners besides your son, and I released him because I supposed it would be more gratifying to you and because I judged that the boy would be more likely to become a more loyal and useful citizen if brought within your influence than if left in prison with persons older and more culpable than himself. If you think the insinuations against your motives worthy of notice you are at liberty to make such use of this note as you may think proper.[40]

Just what General Jones thought his affirmation would achieve among men who chose to doubt Nelson's honor after thirty years of unsurpassed reputation for integrity is difficult to understand. If a corrupt bargain had been made, Jones would have had both personal and political reasons for denying it fully as strong as Nelson's.

General Jones was mistaken in the confidence he expressed in David's becoming a loyal Confederate citizen. Colonel John E. Toole had actually asked Nelson to inquire of David which Jonesboro people imprisoned at Madison, Georgia, could be trusted on release and Nelson sent a list of such people with David's comments on each.[41] But no sooner was David free than he went to Richmond and somehow managed to get through the Confederate lines to the home of relatives in Lambertsville, New Jersey. On October 22, 1862, he addressed a letter to President Lincoln

---

[39] David Nelson to "Hon Sir," October 22, 1862, in Papers of Abraham Lincoln (Division of Manuscripts, Library of Congress). Internal evidence makes it clear that this letter was addressed to Lincoln.

[40] Jones to Nelson, October 17, 1862, in *Rebellion Record*, Series II, Volume IV, 922.

[41] Nelson to Toole, October 16, 1862, in *Rebellion Record*, Series II, Volume IV, 919.

asking for some appointment in the Federal army. "My father," he continued, "you are probably aware has at last given up all hope & gone over body & soul to Jeff Davis. This is very mortifying to me." David particularly hoped to be sent as an officer to Cumberland Gap where he expected to find the members of his party who had succeeding in escaping from East Tennessee.[42] Lincoln wrote Andrew Johnson, Military Governor of Tennessee: "David Nelson, son of the M. C. [Member of Congress] of your State, regrets his father's final defection, and asks me for a situation. Do you know him? Could he be of service to you or to Tennessee in any capacity in which I could send him?" [43] Just what David did during 1863 is obscure, but by 1864 he was a lieutenant in the Federal army stationed at Cumberland Gap.[44]

Meanwhile, as the months passed following his address, Nelson was forced to observe the failure of his predictions. No slave insurrections produced "a species of carnage unexampled in the history of North America," and Confederate military success soon turned to steadily mounting disaster. As the battle zone swept into East Tennessee, Confederate authorities, high and low, hardened their hearts to civilian interests; and the Confederate Congress adopted progressively more drastic measures to stave off defeat. Instead of the slaughter's ceasing, it came closer home. East Tennessee was to find that its former sufferings were but prelude. Caught in this vortex of real civil war, Nelson dwelt with mental anguish and tortured searchings of his soul.

---

[42] David Nelson to Lincoln, October 22, 1862, in Papers of Abraham Lincoln (Division of Manuscripts, Library of Congress).

[43] Lincoln to Johnson, October 31, 1862, in *Rebellion Record*, Series I, Volume XVI, Part II, 658.

[44] A Table of Organization in *Rebellion Record*, Series I, Volume XXXIX, Part II, 71.

CHAPTER X

With Burning Words

N ELSON'S PLIGHT DURING the bewildering developments of the Civil War years was probably typical of a large and generally misunderstood group in the border states and of some even further south. The definitiveness of war tends to foster the fallacy of perfect polarization, and the middle groups finding comfort in neither camp seldom are seen in clear focus. John Bell's biographer said of him: "Under the pressure of such times, he was a pathetic figure. Strong in intellect but slow in reaching decisions, and deliberate and cautious in action, he could never be a leader in a crisis." [1] But Bell lived in Middle Tennessee where overwhelming separation sentiment swiftly developed after Lincoln's call for troops; and he knew that the disastrous defeat of Unionism in the June 8, 1861, election was not the result of force or fraud as Nelson convinced himself it was. Had Nelson lived where Bell did and seen what Bell saw, his own policy of submission to an honest expression of popular will (firmly advanced in every speech he made prior to that election) would probably have led him along the path of accommodation followed by most of the Whig leaders in the South.

Andrew Johnson left East Tennessee in August, 1861, and thereafter experienced no moderating or mitigating influences upon his rampant Unionism. His shouts to the galleries of the United States Senate that he would arrest and hang secessionists if they were convicted of treason aroused applause hardly calculated to raise doubts in his mind. [2] And his appointment as military governor of Federally occupied Tennessee gave direction, purpose, and active outlets to his Unionism. Always behind the Federal lines, he was conscious of the North's growing strength and its probable ultimate success. Able to observe at first hand the disintegration of slavery in the path of Union armies, he was weaned away from any Armageddon stand on what seemed to him almost as theoretical a question as slavery in New Mexico had been.

Brownlow's biographer thinks he might quite characteristically have gone over to the disunion side and probably would have done so had separation in Tennessee come in one quick contest. [3] But by the time separation was voted, Brownlow was committed deeply to Unionism; and before he had time to be affected by developments unfavorable to his cause, he was expelled to the North by Confederate authorities. Thereafter, in his rabid denunciation of Southerners before cheering Northern

---

[1] Parks, *John Bell*, 396-97.

[2] *Congressional Globe*, 36 Cong., 2 Sess., 1354.

[3] Coulter, *Brownlow*, 152.

audiences in almost every major city in that section, he convinced himself beyond any turning back.

Many East Tennessee Unionists joined the Federal military forces in the summer and fall of 1861, thereby surrendering their wills to a type of allegiance that discourages even the thought of reconsidering. Had Nelson been free to do so, he might well have raised and led a regiment or brigade in the Union cause—and in so doing closed the door upon judgment of events as they developed. But his capture in August, 1861, and subsequent parole imposed immobilizing terms upon him. Had he been less keen in his observation, less able to discern the significance of his information, or less well informed, he might have maintained an uncritical Unionism typical of many plain people of East Tennessee. Had he been free to escape to Kentucky, his position behind the Federal lines might have impressed upon him the same considerations that dominated the thinking of Andrew Johnson. But Nelson was doomed by the accidents of residence and early capture and parole to live out the conflict in the twilight zone that would not yield to any scrutiny whether it was sunrise or sunset for the Union. No peaceful awaiting of the issue was possible, and it was often a tantalizing thought that his judgment and prediction might bring an end sooner to the suffering and peril of those he had helped lead into their plight. Refugees and East Tennesseans in the Federal army only heard about the suffering of their relatives and neighbors; Nelson knew it through his own eyes and ears, and this knowledge sometimes drove him to an ill-considered action in the desperate hope for alleviation.

During the year following his 1862 address advising co-operation with the Confederates, Nelson was undergong a trying reversal of his pro-Confederate position. Prohibited from pro-Union activity by the terms of his parole and from pro-Confederate activity by his slowly reviving hope for reconstruction of the Union, he calmed his restlessness by making notes of his observations, and of numerous episodes reported to him, for incorporation in poetic form. Before the entry of Union troops in force into East Tennessee in the fall of 1863, he had composed two poems of more than four hundred lines each with copious explanatory notes. He arranged for these to be published anonymously in a sixty-four page book at Philadelphia in 1864.[4] One of the poems, "Secession," was published in Brownlow's Knoxville *Whig and Rebel Ventilator* after the paper was re-established, but without the notes and still anonymously.[5] These writings constitute the only index to his reviving hope of Union

---

[4] [Thomas Amis Rogers Nelson], *Secession; or, Prose in Rhyme, and East Tennessee, a Poem* (Philadelphia, 1864). This small book contained the poems in about forty pages and detailed explanatory notes in nineteen pages. The following pages are based upon the text of the poems and the notes.

[5] Knoxville *Whig*, February 13, 1864.

success and growing hatred of secession, but they reveal much that he was thinking about and musing over during this year of decision on the battle fronts.

The inconsistencies of secession leadership Nelson found a fruitful topic. He contrasted their prewar chants of peaceable secession with their martial spirit and their former suggestion of reconstructing the Union with their current denunciation as traitors of all who "would past alliances renew." He considered them "cunning knaves" to stress defense of slavery as the cause of the war at home while courting English aid on the basis that the war was over free trade—and even promising a plan for gradual abolition of slavery as a price for English assistance. He ridiculed the collapse of the "King Cotton" thesis and criticized sharply the failure to use cotton as a "specie basis" for paper money in order to control inflation as had been promised. He described as "sour grapes" the references to foreign aid, after such aid appeared impossible to procure, as of no service to the Confederacy—when there had formerly been a long series of articles in Southern papers promising victory through foreign intervention. Summing up the opportunist policy of Confederate propagandists, he wrote:

> With Protean shape, chameleon hue,
> Forever changing, ever new—
> A thing of magic and of might,
> Ne'er warped to wrong, but always right!

Nelson found much to mull over in the optimistic line of the Confederate leaders as contrasted with the harsh realities of the war:

> Who hath not heard that WASHINGTON,
> With all its wealth, would soon be won?
> That one brave bee, of Southern hive,
> From Northern swarms, could vanquish five?
> That craven Yankees would not fight,
> And, seeing us, must take to flight?
> That war *their* fields might desolate,
> But dare not visit Southern State?
> Tho', if it came, then glory's blaze
> Should burn it out in sixty days?
> While Southern men need have no fears,
> As none might fight but Volunteers?

> Who doth not know that Washington
> Has not been reached, will ne'er be won;
> That one live Yankee is as much
> As Southern knight may safely touch;
> And that to tread on Northern soil
> Somehow produces strange recoil?
> Who hath not seen the fierce conscription—
> In all its moods, beyond description—
> Compel the twelve months' Volunteers,
> Against their will, to serve three years?

> Hunt Union sympathizers down,
> And, handcuffed, bring them into town?
> Who doth not feel that War, defied,
> Has sadly humbled Southern pride,
> When conquering legions come at will,
> Our lands and harbors all to fill?
> Who now can Northern courage doubt
> When promised victory proves a rout?

In following up this point, he mentioned a long series of Confederate defeats and mocked the Confederate pre-battle boasts of "impregnable" and their post mortems that none of the places were "fit to hold." Also mentioned was the contrast between the brave promises made when Lee invaded Pennsylvania and the lame excuses when driven out:

> If, with a routed army, LEE,
> O'er swollen streams, is forced to flee,
> He never purposed to remain;
> His object was—*to save his train.* . . .

Another aspect of the war impressed Nelson—the fact that those who had so eloquently stirred up the people to war and who would "spill their last and reddest drop" often hired substitutes or at least sought officers' commissions so that "with gilded coats and brazen spurs, they might the soldier's duties shun, and snatch the fame that he had won!" Here, Nelson was revealing considerable ignorance of the casualty rate among even high ranking officers in both armies. Especially did he resent the preachers—whose business he said was to declare "on earth peace, good will towards men"—praying for war and prophesying that the South would slay Yankees like cattle and then, "when the fiery tide was turning, . . . besetting heaven that war should cease." In disgust he added, "As if the JUST would deign to hear prayers meant alone for human ear."

The rigors of a blockaded land under the stress of war oppressed him, and he laid the many inconveniences and sufferings at the door of secession leaders. He resented keenly the inflated paper currency that was forced upon people in payment for their precious goods. Impressment of food and horses at arbitrary prices far below market value he deplored. He mentioned that corn was established for impressment payment at two dollars a bushel when it was selling on the open market for five dollars and that other commodities were priced in proportion. Poultry, honey, leather, and even bedclothes were impressed or simply seized without the offer of payment in the nearly worthless Confederate currency. As a result of the seizure of sixty per cent of the leather by government officials, thousands of women and children had to go barefooted through the winter "while some young stripling, whom it suits, struts, high and dry, in seven-leagued boots."

War shortages were also directly felt in East Tennessee at an early date. Mercantile stores soon closed, pins and needles could not be had, and there was no material for clothing. Nelson wrote of his wife's disgust when tears appeared in her last petticoat. Newspapers almost disappeared, sometimes being printed on wrapping paper. Martial law required the use of passes and so put into the hands of military officials a power to oppress. Some denied Union men passes to go for salt. The conscription age was raised by state law for the militia to fifty-five, working hardships on those who could not afford substitutes and must leave families without protection. Heavy taxation, including the ten per cent tax in kind on all agricultural goods, became a nuisance as well as an oppression. Many farmers were critically injured by the complete destruction of their fences as firewood, a fact well known to Nelson. And news of the death of young men on distant battlefields was constantly casting families into despair.

As the months of war wore on, Nelson's list of presumed "outrages" on Unionists by Confederate authorities or unauthorized gangs grew long. The hanging of the railroad bridge burners of 1861 by order of drumhead court-martial he declared murder for which all involved could be tried after the war. He legalistically maintained that if the bridge burners were in the service of the United States, they were prisoners of war, and that if they acted on their own initiative, they were guilty of only a penitentiary offense under the state law. He considered valid the numerous report of theft of Union men's goods by Confederate soldiers as well as the legalized theft by application of the confiscation laws. The expulsion of wives and children of Unionists refugees to Kentucky or other parts of the North occasioned much suffering and was duly noted by Nelson. Many Unionists were imprisoned without charge or knowledge of accuser, and the writ of *habeas corpus* was effectively nullified when the Confederate military authorities refused to acknowledge state judge writs and insisted on a Confederate government court writ. Since the Confederate district judge was supposed to be at Nashville, long since captured by the Federal forces, but was actually wandering with the Confederate army, no one in East Tennessee could obtain an effective writ. Nelson, with his worship for the legal rights of a defendant, found this intolerable. Unionists were disarmed by Confederate order and left at the mercy of brigands, and their houses were frequently entered by Confederate soldiers without warrants of any kind.

In referring to one type of outrage, he wrote:

> Could helpless woman's shrieks be heard
> Beyond the dells where crimes occurred;
> Could childhood's fruitless cries for life
> Arise above War's din and strife. . . .

The note to these lines explained that the outrages to which women residing in remote mountain settlements had been subjected could not, "with propriety, be described." He continued by describing a Madison County, North Carolina, incident in which Union families, denied salt, had broken into the warehouse and taken their supplies. Confederate troops were sent and committed "every species of indignity and outrage to the Union population, male and female." The troops took some prisoners, ostensibly to Knoxville, but actually out in the laurel thickets to be shot. "Among the persons thus murdered, was a boy between twelve and fifteen years of age, who was only wounded at the first fire, but was shot a second time, and killed while piteously begging to be taken to his mother."

Attempts by Unionists to avoid conscription into the Confederate army led to many touching episodes that came to Nelson's attention. Refugees were continually attempting flight northward, and many were captured and imprisoned. Others sought to hide in the mountain laurel thickets, only to be hunted out by hired bands of Cherokee Indians. Nelson commented: "England, in her wars with America, received and deserved the execration of the world for her barbarity in employing the Savages; and the Southern Confederacy will become equally odious."

The names of many East Tennesseans who were considered martyrs to Unionism were widely known. Nelson tells of one Unionist in Federal uniform who was wounded and then shot in cold blood when discovered by the Confederates. A civilian in Hawkins County, ignorant of the disarming law, resisted the attempt to take his gun and was killed in his own house. And a Dunkard preacher of Sullivan County was murdered by soldiers because he refused to give up his horse to them. Nelson also collected stories of indignities and injuries suffered by Unionists arrested in East Tennessee and held in Alabama and Georgia. He recorded the refusal of a jailor to let the ministers among the prisoners hold services or even pray at the bedside of a dying Unionist. Brutality in trying to catch draft-dodgers was also a common occurrence. Nelson catalogued instances of near strangulation inflicted by hanging old men and even women in seeking to extort information.

For those responsible, Nelson had little feelings of charity in 1863. Of the leaders of secession he wrote in conclusion to his poem on that subject:

What hissing curse, or crushing blast,
Shall be o'er perjured traitors cast,
Who swore their country to sustain,
But gladly give that country pain?
Who can atone for all the blood

That deluges, like angry flood,
And fills a land with groans and tears,
That happiest stood among her peers?
. . . .
Where'er they go, let withering scorn
Against their coming quickly warn;

> Whate'er they say, let shy distrust,
> In doubt, deny their statements just;
> Whate'er they do, let jealous eyes
> Their best performances despise;
> From their vile presence turn away,
> Trust not the miscreants who betray;
> Do not their callous conscience mock
> With oaths that cannot bind or shock;
> Withhold the honors they may seek
> With brazen front or bearing meek;
> Imbue your children with a dread
> Of all who in Rebellion led;
> And, while its gay, deluded fair,
> And misled votaries you spare,
> Let every proud, detested name
> Be "damned to everlasting fame!"

Throughout these poetic releases from his tension, Nelson repeatedly returned to the theme of love of his "secluded land, of gentle hills and mountains grand" and expressed his acute nostalgia for the days before the war. It was in these months that he composed his song of praise of East Tennessee in the opening passages of the poem by that title.[6] But the tone changed abruptly as he contemplated her current condition:

> Thy fields are waste, thy towns are dull,
> Thy trade destroyed, thy prisons full;
> Thy bravest men away are driven,
> The only exiles under heaven,
> The ties all rent that bind to earth,
> And nothing now can move to mirth.

And at another point he exclaimed: "Oh! Union, born in throes and blood, well nurtured by the wise and good, what wickedness has sought thy life, 'mid civil broils and party strife!" Casting into poetic form an idea he had used in his conciliation speech in Congress, he asked whether the country's dead heroes could look down and exert a power to lull the storm and followed the question with a series of negations—naming each time a national hero and describing what each would do if he had the power. After dealing in this fashion with Washington, Jackson, and Webster, he turned to his political idol, Henry Clay:

> It cannot be—or matchless CLAY
> The veil that hides would tear away,
> And his tall form erect display
> Arrayed in dazzling robe of white,
> And, flashing with angelic light,
> Upon an arching rainbow stand,
> Viewed by a torn and bleeding land;
> And, with an eloquence new-born,
> A maddened people loudly warn;

---

[6] Quoted in Chapter V.

> Bid War's infernal carnage cease,
> And million's voices cry for peace!

Federal military aid was not forthcoming until September, 1863, when Burnside occupied East Tennessee in force. However, conditions were made worse for Unionists during this wait by false alarms. Nelson commented that four movements of a partial character were made into the area and exerted a disastrous influence on Union men. Each time, believing that an army sufficient to hold the area was advancing, they became imprudent in their "expressions of satisfaction, and, as a consequence, were arrested and treated with greater rigor than ever." So when Burnside's army approached, there was difficulty in believing that rescue was real—a feeling Nelson portrayed in this passage:

> And is it not a fitful dream,
> That o'er our darkness bright may gleam,
> Then leave us, all our cries unheard,
> Heart sick and faint, from hope deferred?

One Greeneville man wrote Nelson a letter when it appeared that Union forces would be withdrawn from Upper East Tennessee, pleading that Nelson use all his influence to prevent it. "You know or can imagine what the fate of our country will be if the rebel forces are allowed to come in upon us again." [7]

Nelson probably best expressed his purpose in writing the poems in the passage:

> Oh! could the truthful muse display
> The terrors of *our* night and day,
> All that has sprung from rage and fear,
> All we have felt and witnessed here;
> With burning words, compare, contrast,
> The dismal present with the past—
> Show all that has been done or meant
> By one bad, bold experiment—
> . . . .
> *Our* people would not be alone
> Their long loved flag to claim and own—
> The very Rebels, in disgust,
> Their heartless leaders would distrust;
> With shouts of gladness, rush to view
> The emblem of their safety, too,
> And, cursing their delusion, vow
> To raise it as their standard now!

Between October, 1862, when Nelson issued his address denouncing the Lincoln Emancipation Proclamation, and September, 1863, when he had completed his poems, he veered as far from the conservative course as ever in his lifetime. At the one extreme was his injunction to

---

[7] J. A. Galbraith to Nelson, September 26, 1863, in Nelson Papers.

Southern men, "let every man who is able to fight buckle on his armor"; and at the other was his imprecation on secessionist leaders, "let every proud, detested name, be 'damned to everlasting fame!' " These expressions within a single year bear witness to the wrenching pressure East Tennessee's plight imposed upon him, and it seems reasonable to assume that the extremity of the latter statement was almost an act of penance for the former. When the time came that proscription of ex-Confederate leaders was an avowed policy of his life-long friend, Brownlow, Nelson was among his most stubborn opponents.

Although Nelson painted the return of United States troops in the most glowing terms while anticipating their arrival, the sad facts of military occupation by friend or foe caught him by surprise. Before the "deliverers" had been in East Tennessee three months, Nelson was writing to General S. P. Carter of the United States Army that he could not get home to Jonesboro and was staying with a friend, Gaines McMillan, who would hand Carter the letter. McMillan was going to Knoxville to request a guard for his property. Being a Union man, he had furnished all he could spare to the army, but soldiers had taken all of his oats and threatened to break open his smokehouse. They had insulted his family in his absence, and Nelson had with great difficulty restrained them by persuasions and entreaties from seizing all the family's provisions. The family was being annoyed daily by Federal troops. Nelson continued that he had supposed Andrew Johnson and Horace Maynard had had the interests of East Tennessee in mind and would have used their influence with Lincoln to have the army instructed that they were coming among friends, not enemies. But, as it turned out, Nelson said, the Union army was more destructive to Union men than the Confederate army ever was. "Our fences are burned, our horses are taken, our people are stripped in many instances of the very last vestiges of subsistence, our means to make a crop next year are being rapidly destroyed. . . ." He also complained that the certificates, when given for produce taken, were often for far less than the actual value. General Carter was urged, as he loved East Tennessee and as he would "preserve the Union party from ruin," to exert a prompt influence.[8]

The year 1864 brought a new personal anxiety to Nelson because David had entered the Federal army and was involved in repeated actions of considerable danger. David was a lieutenant in command of a light artillery company stationed at Cumberland Gap in May, 1864; but by the fall of that year he had joined the staff of Brigadier General Alvan C. Gillem with a cavalry division. He served as an aide-de-camp in the final campaigns of the war.[9] During October David was involved in sharp actions, and the following month participated in serious reverses

---

[8] Nelson to S. P. Carter, December 26, 1863, in *Rebellion Record*, Series I, Volume XXXI, Part III, 507-08.

[9] *Rebellion Record*, Series I, Volume XXXIX, Part I, 846.

in which many casualties were sustained.[10] In December General Gillem's forces conducted a sweep of 461 miles through upper East Tennessee and were in frequent contact with Confederate detachments.[11] In early 1865 the division was back in Knoxville, where David could tell his father of his campaigns; but in March he was off again for a vigorous action through the mountains as far as Henderson, North Carolina, and back to Greeneville, Tennessee.[12] In every report, General Gillem had cited his staff for gallantry, efficiency, coolness, and daring under fire. When he became commanding officer of the District of East Tennessee for occupation purposes, on July 4, 1865, David, by then a captain, was still his aide-de-camp.[13]

While David was on active duty, his father's thoughts were drawn to postwar plans. The defeat of the Confederacy was not conclusive, yet her enemies had every reason to be jubilant. Already there were those looking beyond the hard fighting still to be done, in both the political and military arena, before the conflict should end. Reconstruction would pose many and difficult problems, and Nelson was still president of the East Tennessee Convention with power to call it into session.

Nelson had expressed hope for a reconstruction of the Union when he issued his address in 1862 denouncing Lincoln's Emancipation Proclamation, asking "if the light of freedom is not utterly extinguished in the North, may we not hope that a spirit of resistance will be aroused in that section, which, combined with the efforts of the South, will hurl Mr. Lincoln from power, and even yet restore peace and harmony to our distracted and divided country?"[14] No revolutionary outburst in the North against Lincoln had materialized, but now a constitutional oppor-

---

[10] Ibid., Series I, Volume XXXIX, Part I, 844-46, 890-92.

[11] Ibid., Series I, Volume XLV, Part I, 819-24.

[12] Ibid., Series I, Volume XLIX, Part II, 13, and Part I, 330-37.

[13] It is probable that David's older brothers, Alexander and Stuart, as well as his next younger brother, Thomas A. R., Jr., were involved in military service. Their names do not appear in the index to the Rebellion Record, and the Nelson Papers contain no items throwing light on this matter, but an interesting (although without source citation) reference appears in Carl Sandburg, Abraham Lincoln: The War Years (New York, 1939), III, 495: "The army service records of the four sons of a Tennessee Union Democrat, Thomas A. R. Nelson, were reviewed by Lincoln when the father applied for the release of a son held in a Northern prison. Two of his sons, the father stated, were serving with Union armies. Another son had from choice gone into the Confederate Army, served twelve months, and been discharged. A fourth son, the father represented, had been practically forced into Confederate service, though he had always favored the Union side. In behalf of this fourth son, who had now spent several months in prison, the father asked a discharge. Lincoln endorsed the application: 'Hon. Mr. Nelson, of Tennessee, is a man of mark, and one whom I would like to have obliged.' The boy took the oath of Union allegiance and was released." Sandburg's source was probably an article by Leslie J. Perry, "Appeals to Lincoln's Clemency," in The Century Magazine, LI (1895), 253. This article refers only to a Mr. Nelson, without initials or address, as the author of the letter. The letter itself is not in the Lincoln materials used by the editors of Lincoln's writings and presumably is not extant.

[14] Knoxville Register, October 5, 1862, published the address.

tunity to remove him was soon to be offered in the presidential election of 1864. Nelson's awareness of the Whig watchword "conservative" was sharpened by the receipt in January of a letter from an anti-administration Unionist expressing the fear that the country's prospects were growing darker every day because of radicalism. "I pray you & our friends, while you aid the powers that be to suppress this rebellion, that you fail not to warn our people to remain steadfast in their conservative principles. The destructives cannot save this nation, & if our people go with them we will only help on the general ruin which is certain to come unless the radicals are overthrown." [15]

The next national administration would be faced with the fundamental questions involved in restoring the Union, and Nelson became convinced that the former Whigs of Tennessee should attempt to make their weight felt in the election of a President to succeed Lincoln who would bring the war to the quickest possible conclusion and re-establish the Union with the least confusion and delay. Another session of the East Tennessee Convention was apparently needed to ascertain the views of the people and to arrange for unity of action if possible. Nelson's letter to Jefferson Davis upon which he was released in 1861 had pledged him not to aid the Federal government in the military struggle or oppose the Tennessee Confederate government.[16] The question of violation of this pledge was involved in his issuing a call for the East Tennessee Convention to reconvene, but the military control of the state by the Federal army virtually eliminated the matter of not opposing the Confederate authorities in the state. Also, Military Governor Andrew Johnson had called for election of county officers under the terms of Lincoln's proclamation of amnesty and reconstruction of December 8, 1863. Concluding that his parole terms did not deny him the right to participate in the reorganization of his own state government after Confederate military forces had been expelled, Nelson issued the convention call for a meeting in Knoxville on April 12, 1864.

William G. McAdoo, the Confederate diarist, considered Nelson's action a violation of the compact with Jefferson Davis, and he reported that a man from Rogersville said that Nelson's action was the result of loss of personal property to Confederate cavalry.[17] Not only was this judgment assuming a pettiness of reason for taking a step seriously involving interpretations of personal honor, it was also made without the knowledge that Nelson had recently complained that the Federal forces were more destructive than the Confederates had ever been.[18]

When the convention assembled, Nelson had an opportunity to dis-

---

[15] W. B. Carter to Nelson, January 19, 1864, in Nelson Papers.

[16] Knoxville *Whig*, August 24, 1861, published the letter.

[17] Diary of William G. McAdoo, March 1, 1864.

[18] Nelson to S. P. Carter, December 26, 1863, in *Rebellion Record*, Series I, Volume XXXI, Part III, 507-08.

A photograph of Andrew Johnson, made in 1866 by Alexander Gardner. Nelson was President Johnson's only personal selection for defense counsel in the Impeachment trial. Photograph was provided by the Library of Congress.

cover how the leaders of the group viewed his course during the troubled years since their last gathering. He was pleased to learn that a majority of the Union leaders of 1861 still held him in the same high esteem as when they elected him their president and still concurred in his view of the proper course of action.[19] They agreed that Lincoln's administration ought to be opposed and defeated at the polls and that ex-Confederates should not be politically proscribed in the reconstructed governments. At this date, the conservative leaders of East Tennessee were not aware that Lincoln, himself, was parting company with the radical leaders of his own administration on the subject of reconstruction policy.

Not all the former convention leaders concurred, however. Andrew Johnson defended Lincoln's administration and his own stringent policy of disfranchisement of Confederate sympathizers in the local elections he had authorized for the preceding March. Brownlow, whose normal proclivity to leap to extreme positions had been strongly re-enforced by his triumphant tour of the North during the war, now displayed a bloodthirsty desire to wreak vengeance on returning Confederates and proscribe them politically. Johnson and Brownlow were joined by a new group of leaders who had risen to positions of prominence in the Union army and were imbued with a martial hatred of foes still in arms against them. After four days of angry debate one of Andrew Johnson's personal friends, probably at Johnson's suggestion that only harm could come from further bitter exchanges, moved adjournment *sine die*. The motion carried, and East Tennessee Union leaders abandoned efforts to restore the unity of 1861.

Nelson, John Baxter, John Netherland, William B. Carter, John M. Fleming, and most of the prominent prewar Whig Unionist leaders of East Tennessee decided to support the Democratic party's peace platform and General McClellan against Lincoln. This was an anomalous situation when Whigs supported the Democratic party while life-long Democratic Andrew Johnson accepted the vice-presidential nomination on the Union ticket headed by Republican Lincoln. However, within East Tennessee, the Whigs found it a familiar experience to be opposing Johnson. The primary reason for this decision by Nelson was the promise in the Democratic platform to end the war by compromise concessions—a plan Nelson had long hoped to see materialize because it would provide an early end to the fighting and would avoid the temptation to persecute a helpless opponent inherent in unconditional surrender.

Andrew Jackson Fletcher, who had been a refugee in the North during the war, was deeply alarmed by the course of East Tennessee Union-

[19] Temple, *Notable Men of Tennessee*, 92, 120, 165, 407-08. It is of paramount significance that Temple, himself a Radical during Reconstruction, conceded that "a majority of the Union leaders of East Tennessee" opposed the Lincoln administration in 1864. The following account of the April convention is based on Temple.

ists in supporting McClellan. He wrote one of East Tennessee's Lincoln supporters, Oliver P. Temple:

All I ask and desire of my friends in East Tennessee is that they will not identify themselves with this infamous party. . . . Their only hope of present success is the failure of the present [military] campaign. Consequently their faces are bright at every disaster and sad at every success of the union army. . . . They discourage enlistments in every conceivable way. . . . They hate and denounce the East Tennesseans who refused to take sides with the South in this war. In one short sentence *they are traitors with all the instincts of rebels without the rebel's courage.* . . .

McClellan is not the representative man of the party. He is no politician—no statesman. He has but one simple idea and that is to restore his lost reputation. He thinks that a verdict of the American people at the ballot box will do that—Hence he is willing to be elected president by *any* party and on *any* platform. . . .

. . . I have already told you that the Copperheads loath and despise the East Tennessee Unionist as a traitor and a tory to his section. Now let me tell you that the union people of the North hate and despise the Copperheads far beyond their hatred for the rebels in the south. There is no limit to the admiration and sympathy of the Unionists in the North for the true unionist of East Tennessee. But when ever it appears that the East Tennesseans or a majority of them have joined the Copperheads every vestige of that sympathy will expire. . . . Hated with a deadly hatred by rebels,—scorned by Copperheads, and despised by unionists north, the East Tennesseans after years of glorious sacrifices and sufferings, by a last act of folly will cease to enjoy the sympathy or respect of any party. . . . I knew that Nelson & Baxter & Spears were honest, noble generous and brave and I tell you *I wept* over the view every where taken of them. I loved them all—I knew that they had suffered and to see them at one breath destroy all the rich fruits of their sufferings was more than I could bear. . . .

Baxter is an honest, bold candid man that can get into error and get out of it like a man—He will survive this unfortunate step. Because he will be found denouncing the northern wing of the rebellion in less than six months.— [This was an incorrect prediction, as Baxter remained an outspoken Conservative and opponent of Radicalism in Tennessee and the North.] But poor Nelson! equally honest, generous and brave he is so obstinate that he has never been able to see any error he has ever committed. All the powers of Earth could not get him to modify any thing he may have written or spoken thirty years ago.[20]

In his next letter to Temple, Fletcher reported that in a speech before the Evansville, Indiana, Union League he had tried to "draw a distinction between what was here called 'the Nelson party in East Tennessee' and the Copperhead-peace-party of the north." But in rebuttal to his speech he was reminded of speeches in the April, 1864, meeting of the Knoxville Convention and of Nelson's published address of October, 1862, in which he had urged resistance to the death to Lincoln—"let every man who is able to fight buckle on his armor."[21]

---

[20] Fletcher to Temple, July 22, 1864, in Oliver P. Temple Papers.
[21] *Id.* to *id.*, October 17, 1864, in Oliver P. Temple Papers.

Political organization for a McClellan campaign in Tennessee was established by a gathering at Nashville of the anti-Lincoln forces—principally former Whigs. This convention nominated a slate of electoral candidates and placed William B. Campbell (former Whig governor) and Nelson on the ticket as electors-at-large for the state. Nelson did not wish to become actively involved and had not consented to serve. Furthermore, Andrew Johnson, acting in his capacity as military governor, substantially eliminated the chances of a McClellan victory in Tennessee by approving the recommendation of a Radical state convention to add clauses to the test oath for voters which included: "I will cordially oppose all armistices or negotiations for peace with rebels in arms." Since negotiations with rebels in arms was exactly what the Democratic party platform called for, this clause disfranchised any McClellan supporter. A protest petition to Lincoln was signed (in printed form) by the McClellan electors, including Nelson.[22] Lincoln refused to set aside the Tennessee supplementary clauses, and the McClellan movement was legally paralyzed.

Meanwhile Nelson had declined the nomination with a published explanation that for several months he had been resolved to withdraw from active politics and had entered into two professional partnerships —one with John Netherland. He continued:

. . . While I have not hesitated, in private conversations, to express my opinions as to the Presidential contest, I have carefully abstained from all efforts to disseminate them, either upon the stump or through the press. Although I have been wantonly and unjustly assailed and misrepresented in the public prints, my desire to remain in private life has remained so strong that I have not even exercised the ordinary right of self-defense. There are thousands of living witnesses who know that I have often defended the cause of the American Constitution and Union at the risk of my life, and have suffered captivity, exile and the loss of property in its behalf. That cause is as dear to me now as it ever was, and I have lived in vain for fifty-two years in East Tennessee if I cannot submit to a season of calumny and vituperation. A period of civil war is not favorable, either to free discussion or calm deliberation; but, hoping that the terrible contest in which we are engaged must soon terminate in complete triumph, I will, should it become necessary, at a proper time and under proper circumstances, vindicate my political conduct and opinions, and show that my record is as consistent as that of any public man in the state.[23]

Nelson's hope that war would soon end was to be fulfilled, but what was to follow could hardly be described as a period favorable to free discussion or calm deliberation. And Nelson would find how impossible of realization was his desire to remain in private life.

---

[22] Printed copy of petition may be found in the Nelson Papers under date of 1864 (at the beginning of 1864 materials).

[23] Knoxville *Whig*, October 12, 1864.

CHAPTER XI

The Observer's Role

NELSON'S WITHDRAWAL FROM ACTIVE POLITICS limited him to an observer's role while civil government was restored in Tennessee. Before the conclusion of the war Tennessee Unionists had been sharply divided by differences of opinion concerning Lincoln's policies and the treatment to be meted out to Confederates. The term "Radical" was freely accepted by the congressional group desiring to punish "rebels" and exclude them from political power in the restored South, and the Tennessee faction led by Brownlow considered themselves allied with that party. The term "Conservative" was the one most often employed to describe the party in Tennessee (as throughout the South) with which Nelson was affiliated.

Although these terms were in use as political distinctions, it must be realized that they were relative terms. There came to be a Radical view and a Conservative view on each major issue, and some Tennessee leaders occasionally crossed the line. Furthermore, the process of separation was not clear and sudden. Brownlow and his followers, who finally constituted the core of the Tennessee Radical party, were essentially a residual group after repeated losses of support. The process of shrinking may be said to have begun with the first election on the question of separation, that of February, 1861. In that election an overwhelming majority of Tennessee voters had been Unionist. Lincoln's call for troops reduced the Unionists to a minority in the June, 1861, plebiscite. Among the Unionists of June were many who accepted the verdict of the state and actively or passively supported the Confederacy. During the war others from among the remaining active Union group cooled or rebelled because of Lincoln's policies, and in the 1864 election such a large number of Unionists favored McClellan that Andrew Johnson considered it necessary to disfranchise them by the test oath clause concerning opposition to armistice or compromise. Now that the war was ending, reconstruction issues were applying pressure on the remaining nucleus of "unswerving Unionists." [1]

The Radical group to which Brownlow adhered in 1865 commanded the support of only a fragment of the state's former voters—none of the ex-Confederates and a questionable portion of the Unionists. But it was this group which took the first successful steps toward reconstituting civil government in the state. They called a convention to meet in

---

[1] Thomas B. Alexander, *Political Reconstruction in Tennessee* (Nashville, 1950), 39.

Nashville on January 9, 1865, which took steps that were to be the subject of controversy until the Radical party could be overthrown in Tennessee. Many of the more cautious members of this group considered that their task was solely to provide machinery for the election of a constitutional convention and insisted that to take any further steps would be unconstitutional. But the Radical leaders feared that in the election of a convention, after a thorough public canvassing of the issues, the Conservative faction would win a majority of the seats. Consequently, they wrangled until a large number of the delegates had gone home in disgust and, with Andrew Johnson's aid, then pushed their program through.[2]

The convention submitted to the people, in a February 22 referendum, a state constitutional amendment abolishing slavery and a long schedule of items declaring null and void the Tennessee Declaration of Independence of 1861, repudiating all acts of the Confederate legislature of the state, granting to the first legislature to assemble under the revised constitution the power to determine the qualifications for voting, and providing for the election on March 4, 1865, of a governor and legislature. The members of the convention also resolved themselves into a political party convention and nominated Brownlow for the governorship and a slate of candidates for the legislature, over half of whom were members of the convention. It was necessary to provide that the legislative elections would be by general ticket over the entire state rather than in the customary district arrangement because many of the counties were still so disrupted that no elections could be held. Johnson issued a proclamation formally authorizing the elections called for by the convention before he left for Washington to be inaugurated as Vice-President.[3]

After this January convention had completed its work and Johnson had given its decision the force of law by proclamation, the reaction of the qualified voters remained to be seen. No Confederate sympathizers could take the oath required of voters, nor could any who still had even a slim hope for a compromise conclusion to the war. The Unionists who could vote were not all prepared to follow the lead of the convention majority and elect a vindictive man governor with an unpredictable legislature. Many doubted the legality or propriety of the action taken, and the crucial question was how much recognition would be accorded the election. Passive resistance was the strategy of those opposing the re-establishment of civil government on such a basis and under such auspices as the convention had proposed. If no large vote turned out, it was hoped that this convention's action would prove to be just another in the series of abortive attempts begun by Andrew Johnson in 1862.

---

[2] *Ibid.*, 18-30.

[3] For complete schedule see Joint Committee on Reconstruction, *Report*, 39 Cong., 1 Sess., 6-7.

Then a more cautious and conservative effort might be possible in restoring Tennessee to civil rule.[4]

In following the policy of passive resistance the Conservative papers
ignored the approaching elections editorially and published only paid
election notices. The proponents of the convention's proposals were
fully aware of this approach and conducted a vigorous campaign to get
out the votes, pleading for 60,000 or even 100,000. On February 22 only
25,293 favorable votes were cast on the constitutional amendment and
the schedule, and the success of the Conservative boycott was demonstrated by only 48 votes against the proposals. Nevertheless, this total
met the ten per cent requirement of Lincoln's reconstruction proclamation of December 8, 1863; and Johnson promptly proclaimed the amend-
mend operative and authorized the organization of civil government
thereunder. On March 4, Brownlow and the legislative slate received
about 23,000 votes and took control of the state government.[5]

There was no doubt as to the attitude of the newly-installed governor, for Brownlow had launched a campaign to arouse hatred of Confederates as soon as he was able to return to Knoxville and reopen the
Whig office, in November of 1863. After many of Brownlow's articles
had incited a severe spirit of vengeance, he commented in typical style
on January 11, 1865, that some

. . . peace loving, constitutional, conservative, fence-riding, half-Union, half
rebel, half horse and half alligator men, of East Tennessee, complain at the
severity of the articles written by the editor of this paper, and ascribe to
their influence the murder of many of the rebels who have been welcomed
with bloody hands to hospitable graves, since the Federal occupation of this
end of the State. If we have been instrumental, by our speeches or editorials,
in bringing to a violent death any one or more of the God-forsaken and hell
deserving persecutors of Union families in East Tennessee, we thank God
most devoutly—shall take encouragement from the past and do more of the
same sort of work! [6]

Partly because of the circulation of the Knoxville *Whig* throughout
East Tennessee, the naturally difficult problems of aroused passions
after a civil war were critically inflamed. As a result of the many pressures on East Tennesseans during the war, a crop of bitterness was ripe
by its close. As Confederate soldiers began to return to their homes in
East Tennessee, many found themselves unwelcome. A wave of mur-

---

[4] Alexander, *Political Reconstruction in Tennessee*, 33.
[5] *Ibid.*, 34-48. The Nashville *Dispatch* and the Nashville *Daily Press* are examples of
Conservative papers that ignored the election. Brownlow's Knoxville *Whig* and the
Nashville *Daily Union* sought feverishly to bring out the voters. For Johnson's
proclamation see Joint Committee on Reconstruction, *Report*, 39 Cong., 1 Sess., 8-9.
The most nearly complete election returns for these two elections are found in the
Tennessee *House Journal*, Brownlow Assembly, 1 Sess., 16. This General Assembly
does not have a number in the regular series and is officially known as the Brownlow
Assembly.
[6] Knoxville *Whig*, January 11, 1865.

ders, whippings, and threats drove a substantial portion of the ex-Confederate population out of East Tennessee by the end of 1865. Thus, the end of war brought no peace to East Tennessee, and Nelson was deluged by letters from distraught people. It must have been a source of deep sorrow to him that his life-long friend was the callous chief instigator of the reign of terror. When almost one hundred citizens petitioned Governor Brownlow to issue a proclamation urging all citizens to refrain from acts of lawlessness and personal violence, he issued a rabble-rousing proclamation couched in language calculated to increase the hatred for returning Confederates and strengthen the wave of vindictive outrages.[7]

Considering Nelson something of a titular head of East Tennessee Conservatism despite his public disavowal of willingness to engage in political activity, people in all walks of life wrote or visited him seeking aid during this dreadful postwar year. Some beseeched him to aid in getting husbands out of prison to save their children from privation. One refugee in South Carolina wrote repeatedly to learn if he dared return, reporting in one letter that many refugees from East Tennessee were in South Carolina and that one had told him that "men have been beaten down lately in the streets of Jonesboro, and others of the most reputable character tied up and whipped, from which I incline to think that it must be the settled purpose of the whole population to expel the last one of the few remaining southern party from the country."[8] From Rogersville came a plea for aid from a mother who reported that boys of pro-Southern families were not allowed to go to school by a mob ruling the town.[9] From Newport came a report from a tanyard owner that he was being driven from the state by a mob of intoxicated men whose sole charge against him was that his house had been used by Confederate authorities to administer oaths. He did not think he could salvage any of the value from his property under the circumstances.[10] Many of Nelson's clients, indicted for treason by Radical grand juries, reported that they could not return to Knoxville for their trials because of the danger of assassination.[11]

During the summer of 1865 Nelson received a request that he establish a paper in Knoxville to counteract Brownlow's *Whig*. It must have been a strange idea to Nelson that he should engage in a journalistic combat with Brownlow. The letter read:

---

[7] Alexander, *Political Reconstruction in Tennessee*, 57-61. For the full text of Brownlow's proclamation see the Knoxville *Whig*, June 7, 1865; and for his own private comment on it see Brownlow to O. P. Temple, May 30, 1865, in Oliver P. Temple Papers.

[8] O. R. Broyles to Nelson, January 22, 1866, in Nelson Papers.

[9] Mrs. Joseph B. Heiskell to Nelson, July 26, 1865, in Nelson Papers.

[10] Robert S. Roadman to Nelson, August 20, 1865, in Nelson Papers.

[11] Numerous such reports may be found in the Nelson Papers scattered through the 1865 materials.

The voice of the people, both Conservative and Southern, is clamorous in
its demand for the establishment of a journal at Knoxville that shall have for
its purpose the restoration of civil quiet; justice to all parties and the oblitera-
tion, so far as possible, of all prejudices engendered by the past bloody
struggle. The broad Conservative ground taken by yourself during the war;
the magnanimity you have manifested toward returning paroled Confederates—the . . . tenacity with which you have clung to the law and words of
the old Constitution naturally causes the conservative and law abiding masses
to turn an anxious eye toward you for the desired restoration.

The increased hostility towards the returning Confederates and their
sympathizers is alarming and can't be attributed to any other source than the
influence arising from the circulation of a certain journal in this country.
The circulation of a journal advocating a lenient policy would palliate these
differences and restore the former equilibrium of society. As it is, anarchy
reigns throughout the country. Not a day passes but what some "rebel" re-
ceives his 400 lashes or its equivalent—the contents of a minnie rifle.—Even
those whose names have not been associated with the Armies of this or any
adjacent department share the same brutal fate, etc.—

. . . .

You are aware of the effect of the circulation of—on the public mind! It
is most murderous to the interests of society. The rabble have it as their guide
and text book; and as they see no other journal conclude that it is the only
one published on the Continent and a true exponent of the old Union doctrines. . . .[12]

Nelson continued to keep out of active politics as the Radical party
clamped its grip on the state. The legislature passed the measure defining
the electorate, which it had been empowered to do in the schedule ac-
companying the constitutional amendment adopted in February. This
act excluded almost every ex-Confederate and kept the state government in the possession of Unionists. The act also reserved the legislature's
right to amend this bill should it not be found sufficiently restrictive.
The August congressional elections were the first test of the attitudes
of the electorate established under this law. The candidates who sought
election to Congress were generally men of prominence in ante-bellum
Tennessee, and all who came even close to victory were Whigs. It would
appear that Democratic leaders who were not disfranchised under the
proscriptive legislation of the Brownlow Assembly recognized that the
Unionists were preponderantly former Whigs who would support none
but Whigs.[13] The results of this election were disconcerting to Brownlow and the extreme Radicals because more than half of the votes were
cast for candidates disapproving his program.[14] Therefore, when the legislature convened in the fall a more stringent disfranchising measure
was proposed and became the most controversial issue.

By mid-spring of 1866 two concurrent developments aroused vigor-

---

[12] Bird G. Manard to Nelson, July 28, 1865, in Nelson Papers.
[13] Thomas B. Alexander, "Whiggery and Reconstruction in Tennessee," in *Journal
of Southern History*, XVI (1950), 294. For the text of the franchise law see *Acts* of
Tennessee, Brownlow Assembly, 1 Sess., 32-36.
[14] Alexander, *Political Reconstruction in Tennessee*, 93.

ous political activity and ended Nelson's brief retirement from the political arena. Within Tennessee a violent struggle over the passage of the new franchise bill reached a dramatic deadlock when the Conservative members of the legislature resigned and prevented a quorum. Special elections were called, and the Radicals won four seats in nineteen contests, one of those almost a farcical election. This gave the Radicals a bare quorum, and they passed the bill which virtually surrendered elections into the governor's hands. The governor now was to appoint every registration commissioner, and the commissioner was to be the judge of conflicting testimony concerning the past loyalty of applicants for registration. Conservatives denounced the measure as unconstitutional and opened a vigorous anti-Brownlow campaign. In the national capital Andrew Johnson was finally showing a tendency to break with the congressional Radicals who had been so delighted with him as a successor to the assassinated Lincoln. When Johnson vetoed the Freedmen's Bureau Bill, Brownlow instantly dug up the hatchet he and Johnson had buried in only a shallow grave when they joined forces for Unionism in 1861. The political enmity between these two East Tennessee party leaders flared again in all its old intensity, and Tennessee Conservatives were encouraged by this evidence of support from the President.

Nelson was now prepared to come out into the open in defense of his ante-bellum political opponent against his former political colleague and friend. Alvan C. Gillem, under whom David Nelson had served, wrote President Johnson on June 29, 1866: "As you no doubt anticipated, the Governor of this state heads a most bitter party in opposition to you. . . . The Radical party in this state contains but a small fraction of the original Union party. . . . Among your most active supporters is to be found nineteen-twentieths of the ability of the Union men of the state. Netherland, Nelson (T. A. R.), Kyle, Temple, East, Houston, Francis B. Fogg and a host of others. . . ." [15]

The immediate cause for Nelson's return to public affairs was, strangely enough, an objective on which he and Brownlow agreed—separate statehood for East Tennessee. When the franchise bill was stalled in the legislature, Brownlow encouraged a renewed agitation for separate statehood. Nelson was present at the convention which met at Knoxville in May, 1866, and was appointed by its president, Oliver P. Temple, to the committee on resolutions. Resolutions were forwarded to the legislature praying separate status, and Nelson made a full-fledged address favoring the proposal.[16] Nothing came of the matter, and some have judged the statehood movement to have been merely a club used by Brownlow to try to push the franchise bill through to final passage. Nelson, however, was certainly in earnest about the proposal.

---

[15] Gillem to Johnson, June 29, 1866, Johnson Papers.
[16] Knoxville *Whig*, May 2 and 9, 1866.

The subject of statehood for East Tennessee was the last upon which Nelson and Brownlow could stand together. In July, 1866, Nelson was chairman and the chief speaker at a Knoxville Conservative meeting denouncing the Radical legislature and voting resolutions of confidence in Andrew Johnson. In this address Nelson said that he had always fought Andrew Johnson politically and had been fearful of his course when he became President, but that he was delighted at Johnson's change and his position. Nelson also expressed opposition to the idea of mass punishment of ex-Confederates and condemned the Radical attempt to make pocket boroughs of the Southern states by dominating the Negro vote and disfranchising ex-Confederates.[17] Brownlow's *Whig* commented contemptuously about the meeting but did have a word of praise for Nelson's speech.[18]

The year 1866 was to be the critical year for Andrew Johnson and his Conservative plan of Reconstruction because the congressional by-elections would determine whether he could control Congress or even maintain enough support to prevent the overriding of his veto. Conservatives throughout the country sought to muster support for Johnson and Conservative candidates for Congress, and a convention was called to meet in Philadelphia in mid-August, 1866. Nelson attended this pro-Johnson convention and was elected vice-president for Tennessee.[19] Upon his return home, he was urgently requested to speak in the Conservative cause. From his one-time home, Elizabethton, came a request from a Conservative meeting to address them on Chancery Court meeting day. "Radicalism is not engulfing everything here to the extent I feared," wrote the secretary of the meeting, "and the people are very anxious to hear the other side. . . . If we can have our views presented here, in a proper light *soon enough*, we can make a good divide in old Carter [County] yet."[20] Edmund Cooper, an ante-bellum Whig leader and active Conservative in southern Middle Tennessee, wrote Nelson from Bedford County asking for help there. "In no county of middle Tennessee are we so hard pressed as in this and hence the anxiety of our friends to have a demonstration worthy of our cause. The radical course now taken by Hon. W. H. Wisener renders the movement important, and in aid of it I need your services. . . ."[21]

The flurry of Conservative political activity culminated in Tennessee with a mass meeting in Nashville on September 13 to endorse Johnson's restoration policy and the actions of the Philadelphia convention. The call sent out for this Nashville meeting summarized the purpose of the

---

[17] Knoxville *Commercial*, July 27, 1866.
[18] Knoxville *Whig*, August 1, 1866.
[19] Newspaper clippings concerning the Philadelphia convention may be found in the Nelson Scrap Book for 1864–1866, under dates August 13, 14, and 15, 1866, in Nelson Papers.
[20] A. Jobe to Nelson, August 22, 1866, in Nelson Papers.
[21] Edmund Cooper to Nelson, August 27, 1866, in Nelson Papers.

whole movement. "A great popular demonstration at the Capital of Tennessee, in support and endorsement of the action of the Philadelphia National Convention will carry its weight of influence where it is needed most." It would encourage "the earnest men who are fighting the battle of the Union and the Constitution at the North." [22] This Conservative effort was actively participated in by Johnson, himself, who made his fateful "swing around the circle" of Northern cities speaking in behalf of Conservative candidates.[23] But the Radicals were too clever for Johnson and discredited him and his cause in an effective campaign of personal smear and "bloody shirt waving." The results were disastrous for the Conservatives, for a Congress was elected that would enact into law over the President's veto the entire Radical Reconstruction program.

Brownlow's administration in Tennessee was steadily losing supporters as a result of its radical course of proscription, and the fall session of the legislature was asked to enact further discriminatory legislation against ex-Confederates. The real security of Brownlow's faction, however, was jeopardized by the continuous defection of former followers among the Unionists, and the governor frankly admitted in January that the Radicals would lose the state elections of 1867 with the existing electorate of Union men in the state. He, therefore, reversed his own former position and overrode the general attitude of Unionist East Tennessee by pressing through the legislature a Negro suffrage bill.[24]

The high tide of Radicalism in Tennessee was reached in the furiously contested election of 1867. This was the first opportunity for the voters of the entire state to express their opinion of Governor Brownlow and his administration. A new legislature and representatives to Congress were to be elected also. Both parties organized in ante-bellum fashion, and every implement of political warfare was revived or expanded to meet the occasion. Nominating conventions met locally to select candidates for Congress and for the legislature. State conventions named the gubernatorial candidates. The Radical party, calling themselves the Republican Union party, nominated Brownlow to succeed himself and adopted resolutions affirming the general Radical policies, praising the congressional Radicals, and condemning President Johnson.[25]

---

[22] A copy of the printed invitation to the meeting is in the Nelson Papers under date of September, 1866.

[23] An unusual analysis of Andrew Johnson's efforts in 1866 may be found in a series of articles by Gregg Phifer: "Andrew Johnson Versus the Press in 1866," in East Tennessee Historical Society's *Publications*, No. 25 (1953); "Andrew Johnson Takes a Trip," in *Tennessee Historical Quarterly*, XI (1952), 3-22; "Andrew Johnson Argues a Case," in *ibid.*, 148-70; "Andrew Johnson Delivers his Argument," *ibid.*, 212-34; "Andrew Johnson Loses His Battle," *ibid.*, 291-328. The basic treatment of 1866 politics is Howard K. Beale, *The Critical Year: A Study of Andrew Johnson and Reconstruction* (New York, 1930).

[24] Alexander, *Political Reconstruction in Tennessee*, 122-31. Brownlow's statement that Negro voters were necessary to prevent the state from passing "into disloyal hands" was made in a message to the Tennessee General Assembly dated January 14, 1867.

[25] Alexander, *Political Reconstruction in Tennessee*, 141.

The Conservatives adopted the name Conservative Union party and denied that they represented a revival of the Democratic party. Former Democrats took a back seat at the Conservative state convention out of anxiety not to alienate the Whig-Unionist-Conservative group in the state who could vote. Every man mentioned for the gubernatorial nomination was a prominent Whig—William B. Campbell and Edmund Cooper of Middle Tennessee, Emerson Etheridge of West Tennessee, and Nelson and John Netherland of East Tennessee. Etheridge was nominated by Cooper and accepted by the convention, which adopted resolutions favoring universal suffrage for white men, acceptance of Negro suffrage as adopted by the Radical legislature (perhaps in an attempt to court Negro votes in the forthcoming election), and Johnson's policies.[26]

The only hope of the Conservatives was to divide the Negro vote and carry the election with a majority of the white votes. Nelson considered this a forlorn hope and did not make any effort to campaign in behalf of the Conservative candidates. The Union League was organized throughout the state by the Radicals to arouse Negro hatred and fear of Conservatives. A catechism employed to indoctrinate Negro voters included the following items:

Question. With what party should the colored man vote?
Answer. The Union Republican party.
Q. Why should the colored man vote with that party?
A. Because that party has made him free and given him the right to vote.
Q. To which party do the friends of the colored man in Congress belong?
A. To the Republican party.
Q. What is a Democrat?
A. A member of that party which before the rebellion sustained every legislative act demanded by the slaveholders. . . .
Q. Is it known by any other name?
A. It is known as Conservative, Copperhead and rebel. Under each name it is still the same enemy of freedom and the rights of man.
Q. Would the Democrats make slaves of the colored people again if they could?
A. It is fair to presume they would, for they have opposed their freedom by every means in their power, and have always labored to extend slavery.[27]

Brownlow, fearing that the Negro vote might not be held in line even by the efforts of the Union League chapters, exercised his recently granted power to call into active service a state guard. These troops served a very useful purpose in encouraging Radical party campaign progress, but the contest was marred by violence at several places re-

---

[26] Ibid., 141-42.
[27] Walter L. Fleming, ed., West Virginia University Documents Relating to Reconstruction (Morgantown, West Virginia, 1904), No. 3, contains the official ritual, constitutions, catechisms, and certain other documents pertaining to the Union League in the South during Reconstruction. The catechism is found on pages 28-33 of this publication, and is also found in Walter L. Fleming, ed., Documentary History of Reconstruction, 2 vols. (Cleveland, 1906-07), II, 13-19.

sulting in a number of deaths. The Negroes were effectively indoctri-
nated and regimented, being voted under careful scrutiny of Radical
leaders. Not only was the governor and every congressman chosen from
the Radical party, but also every member of the state senate and all but
three members of the lower house of the legislature. Etheridge had
taken the extreme position that Brownlow's regime was unconstitutional
and ought to be overthrown by revolutionary action. He, therefore,
received far fewer votes in East Tennessee than a moderate Conservative
such as Cooper or Nelson would have polled.[28]

The only public participation by Nelson was the endorsement of a
published statement to the effect that the disfranchisement act was unconstitutional and that election judges might disregard the law if they
personally considered it unconstitutional. This was a feeble gesture since
Brownlow appointed the election commissioners, but it brought a blast
from the Knoxville *Whig* in which Brownlow denounced the signers in
his usual terms—except for Nelson. Brownlow merely expressed surprise
that so good a lawyer as Nelson should take that position.[29]

With the Brownlow Radicals in full control of every department of
the state government for another two years, Nelson kept to his growing
legal practice and awaited developments—and they were not long in
coming. After a fruitless year-long search for grounds on which to
impeach President Johnson, the congressional Radicals at last found
their excuse in the President's removal of Secretary of War Edwin M.
Stanton and brought their campaign to a successful conclusion on February 24, 1868, with the passage of the articles of impeachment. Attorney General Henry Stanbery resigned his cabinet position to head
Johnson's defense. Other nationally famous lawyers were retained, including Benjamin R. Curtis of Massachusetts, former Associate Justice
of the United States Supreme Court, Jeremiah S. Black, former Attorney General and Secretary of State, and William M. Evarts, acknowledged leader of the New York bar. Nevertheless, Johnson was toying
secretly with a desire to speak in his own defense and justify his entire
career, for he knew that none of the aforementioned could or would
appeal to the people rather than the Senate. He was later to declare to
his counsel that he would not care for conviction by the Senate if he
stood acquitted by the people of the nation.[30] For that aspect of the
defense he chose the man whom he had personal reasons to respect as
colleague and foe, Thomas A. R. Nelson.

[28] Alexander, *Political Reconstruction in Tennessee*, 146-62. A very revealing episode concerning the regimentation of Negro voters at Columbia, Tennessee, on election day, written by a Radical sympathetic with Negro suffrage, may be found in a
typewritten manuscript entitled The Southern Unionist, by Samuel M. Arnell, Jr.,
based on a manuscript left by his father. Professor Stanley J. Folmsbee of the University of Tennessee allowed the writer to see the manuscript.
[29] Knoxville *Whig*, January 9, 1867.
[30] "Notes of Colonel W. G. Moore, Private Secretary to President Johnson, 1866-
1868," *American Historical Review*, XIX (1913-14), 123 and 132.

CHAPTER XII

A Mirror of the Man

JOHNSON'S CALL OFFERED Nelson an opportunity to combine his two favorite professions, counselor and conservative politician, and to employ his talents against the most serious salient the Radicals had yet driven into the Conservative position. He hurried to Washington and entered into a series of daily conferences with the President and other members of his counsel.[1] Although it did not at first appear that his services were really needed, Nelson set to work with characteristic thoroughness studying congressional actions since the war and other matters relevant to the case, allowing himself only four or five hours sleep a night.[2] In the pre-trial consultations he concurred fully with the other counsel that Johnson should make no personal appearances before the Senate.[3] When the trial began, it was agreed between opposing counsel that the number of summation addresses would be limited. Under the arrangement Nelson was not to deliver a major address. With this decision he was fully in agreement because he could write out for the record the appeal to public opinion Johnson wanted—an appeal which the counsel doubted would affect the votes of the Senators.

When the Senate heard the charges against Johnson on March 13, 1868, the President was represented by Stanbery, Curtis, and Nelson, who asked forty days to prepare the President's answer. The House managers opposed such a delay, and the Senate, in secret session, decided to grant nine days. Then a debate ensued as to the date for the actual beginning of the trial after Johnson's response. Again the managers pressed for immediate trial, Benjamin Butler delivering an extensive speech on the subject. Nelson replied to Butler by pointing out that some of the charges would involve inquiry "running back to the very foundation of the government" and investigations which he perceived to be "almost interminable." "Now what do we ask for the President of the United States? . . . Simply that he shall be allowed time for his defense . . . the same opportunity which you would give to the meanest criminal that ever was arraigned before the bar of justice. . . ." The Senate decided, however, that after the managers had replied to the President's answer the trial would proceed immediately.[4]

---

[1] "Notes of Colonel W. G. Moore, Private Secretary to President Johnson, 1866-1868," *loc. cit.*, 125-27.

[2] Nelson to Lizzie (youngest daughter), April 5, 1868, copy in Nelson Papers. The original is in the possession of Mrs. James H. Stewart of Knoxville, Tennessee.

[3] "Notes of Colonel W. G. Moore, Private Secretary to President Johnson, 1866-1868," *loc. cit.*, 127.

[4] Stryker, *Andrew Johnson*, 603-09.

President Johnson was so aroused by the gratuitous assaults upon his character made by the House managers in opposing the defense requests for more time that he privately declared that, if his defense was not conducted according to his idea of suitability, he would appear before the Senate in person and defend himself.[5] This feeling of Johnson's was buttressed when Alexander H. Stephens called to urge Johnson to make his own defense, saying: "No one can do it as well as yourself, and I believe your safety demands it." [6] During the days when the response to the charges was being prepared, counsel was with the President a good portion of every day; and on Sunday afternoon, March 22, the day before the reply was due in the Senate, they had again to dissuade Johnson from appearing personally before the Senate the following day.[7]

During this hectic week an unexpected difficulty arose. Jeremiah Black, one of the counsel, was attorney for United States citizens who claimed ownership of Alta Vela, a small guano island, off the coast of Haiti, which the Dominican Republic had seized. Black demanded the dispatch of a naval vessel to protect American interests, but Secretary of State William H. Seward refused—citing Black's own decision when Secretary of State in 1857 to reject an American private claim to another Caribbean island, Cayo Verde. Black asked the President to review Seward's decision. At this point in the case J. W. Shaffer, another attorney for the Alta Vela claimants, obtained from Benjamin Butler a written legal opinion in favor of the claim. Shaffer obtained endorsements on this claim from other members of the House prosecution. The idea seems to have been to assure President Johnson that he could act in this case without antagonizing his political enemies. The plan did not work, however, and Black felt compelled to resign from the defense counsel to better pursue his clients' interests. The Radicals claimed that Black had withdrawn because Johnson's case was hopeless.[8]

---

[5] "Notes of Colonel W. G. Moore, Private Secretary to President Johnson, 1866-1868," *loc. cit.*, 123.

[6] *Ibid.*, 125.

[7] *Ibid.*, 127.

[8] Stryker, *Andrew Johnson*, 612-614; George Fort Milton, *The Age of Hate: Andrew Johnson and the Radicals* (New York, 1930), 534-39; William N. Brigance, "Jeremiah Black and Andrew Johnson," in *Mississippi Valley Historical Review*, XIX (1932-33), 205-18; William A. Dunning, "More Light on Andrew Johnson," in *American Historical Review*, XI (1905-06). Stryker advances an interpretation, based on a recollection by E. C. Reeves, which places Jeremiah Black in a very bad light. Milton, while more cautious, accepts much of the same material. Brigance, on the other hand, vigorously defends Black and attacks the recollection by Reeves as completely in error. Dunning, writing before the Reeves recollection was written, concludes that nothing in the existing documents suggests anything morally discreditable to anyone concerned. The subject is a very difficult one to be dogmatic about, but Nelson's later claims about the dating of the signatures of the House managers seems to be sustained. And even Brigance concedes that the signatures of the House managers were at least indirectly related to the trial. It is not unreasonable to guess that Andrew Johnson suspected improper pressure, and Johnson may have conveyed that impression to Nelson and other members of the counsel.

When the President's answer was filed on Monday, March 23, 1868, Evarts asked for thirty days to prepare for trial. Again the managers opposed, and seven days were allowed. In this debate Stanbery said that since March 13 "every moment has been occupied with the pleadings; not an instant lost, not a counsel absent. We have refused all other occupations; we have devoted ourselves exclusively to this day and night, and I am obliged to say two days sacred to other duty. . . . We have been so pressed with this duty that we have not had an opportunity of asking the President 'What witnesses will you have?' " [9]

On the day the President's response was filed, the Washington *Star* carried a description of Johnson's counsel, describing them as differing much in bearing and in personal appearance but all bearing the impress of men of ability. Stanbery was pictured as distinguished-looking, tall, graceful, and "with a countenance indicative of thought and sagacity." Curtis was short, of compact figure and bull-doggish expression, somewhat resembling Johnson. Evarts was a "lawyer-like looking person," thin and small, with features suggesting quickness and acuteness of thought. William Groesbeck of Ohio had just appeared as a replacement for Jeremiah Black, and his appearance indicated force and self-possession. Nelson's career in Tennessee was briefly described, and the report continued:

As Military Governor of Tennessee, Mr. Johnson was pretty severe in his denunciation of the political course of Mr. Nelson, and it is noted now as a curious reverse of circumstances that Mr. Nelson should now appear before the Senate as one of Mr. Johnson's advocates. The conceded ability of Mr. Nelson among those by whom he is best known, had doubtless caused his retention by the President as one of his counsel. In appearance Mr. Nelson is rather solid than brilliant; and the peculiarly deliberate manner in which he enunciates his words, while drawing upon his head the blessings of the reporters, tends to make his speaking monotonous and tiresome.

Judging from externals, Messrs. Stanbery and Evarts will do the scalpel work of the trial, and Messrs. Nelson and Curtis the sledge-hammer business.[10]

After some difficulty the President's counsel obtained an adjournment until Thursday of the following week to give them time to arrange their presentation of defense. Friday night Nelson had reached what he considered the snapping point of his nerves from long-continued overwork and inadequate sleep, so he attended a play. Saturday night he accompanied one of Tennessee's Senators to a dancing school recital where he observed more than two hundred children dance. Afterward, he attended a circus and enjoyed the animals and acts enormously. On Sunday, he found the time to write an elaborate and detailed description of the dance recital and circus in a letter to his eleven-year-old daugh-

---

[9] Stryker, *Andrew Johnson*, 617.
[10] Copied from the Washington *Star* by the Nashville *Republican Banner*, March 28, 1868.

The defense counsel is in the foreground, and Nelson is probably at
the extreme left of this group.

A sketch of the Impeachment scene by Theodore R. Davis, originally published in *Harper's Weekly*, April 11, 1868.

ter, Lizzie. "I enjoyed the whole performance very much and wished that Lizzie and Mollie had been at my side to enjoy it too. Your affectionate father. P. S. Tell your ma that the Impeachment testimony closed on the part of the House Managers yesterday evening. . . . I think they made a very poor case." [11]

The opening address for Johnson was made by Curtis the following Thursday, and then the long procession of witnesses for the defense were questioned. Sickness kept Stanbery away much of the time, but the Senate would not recess the trial until he was well. Nelson took notes for the purpose of writing his defense of Johnson for the record; but as the trial approached its conclusion, the House managers requested the Senate to allow more summation addresses. This caused Nelson and Groesbeck to deliver their final arguments before the Senate instead of submitting them later in writing. Nelson explained that they had not prepared written arguments and asked permission for them to speak extemporaneously.[12] He would not have spoken even when all the managers decided to had not the President outlined certain points and specifically asked him to present them.[13] These "certain points" were, of course, the complete defense of Johnson's career and the answer to the innumerable irrelevant attacks upon his character injected improperly by the managers into the record. The other members of the counsel refused to answer these irrelevancies that were portraying the President in vile terms before the American people. They were striving to keep the case within the specified charges and win acquittal. But Johnson, as he had said, was more interested in acquittal before the people. Only one day before he took the floor, Nelson was assigned his task—to talk to the American people rather than the Senators confronting him.

On April 23, after the first closing address for the prosecution was completed, Nelson began as the first member of the defense counsel to present the summation arguments.[14] In his opening passages he explained that many things had been said to draw as insulting a picture as possible of the heart and mind of the President while almost nothing had been said to vindicate him against those charges. He then asked the rhetorical question, "Who is Andrew Johnson?"—using it as a springboard to launch himself into a biographical sketch. He traced Johnson's rise from poverty to the United States Senate through almost every political office the people had to bestow. Johnson's Unionism in 1860-1861 was then stressed as was his role as the sole Senator from a Confederate state to remain in the Senate defending the Union. His subsequent career was explained as a faithful pursuing of the objects of the war as stated in the congressional resolutions of 1861, which maintained that the war was

[11] Nelson to Lizzie, April 5, 1868, copy in Nelson Papers.
[12] *Trial of Andrew Johnson*, 3 vols. (Washington, 1868), I, 534-35.
[13] New York *Times*, April 25, 1868.
[14] *Trial of Andrew Johnson*, II, 118-87, is the text of the address.

"not prosecuted on our part in any spirit of oppression, nor for any purpose of conquest or subjugation, nor for the purpose of overthrowing the rights or established institutions of those States, but to defend and maintain the supremacy of the Constitution and all laws made in pursuance thereof, and to preserve the Union with all the dignity, equality, and rights of the several States unimpaired. . . ." This resolution, said Nelson, was adopted almost unanimously in both houses of Congress, and it was the key to the President's actions.

When Nelson reached the point at which he and Johnson had parted company, Lincoln's Emancipation Proclamation, his candidness would not compromise even by slurring over the point. Instead, he stated: "In the progress of the war he felt that it was necessary for him to yield the question of slavery so far as he had any influence in the State or section of country in which he resided. He did yield, and he went as far as the farthest to proclaim emancipation in the State over which he had been placed as military governor; but in all other respects he has endeavored to carry out the terms of this resolution. . . ." [15]

In dealing with Johnson's presidency, Nelson maintained that he was following in Lincoln's footsteps and that he had acted in good faith throughout the controversy with Congress. Nelson then turned to the question, previously debated, as to whether the Senate was a court, limited by court procedure, or a legislative body judging its own limitations. He cited arguments from English history and by the framers of the United States Constitution to sustain his position that the Senate in impeachment trials was a court—offering rebuttals to the managers' precedents drawn from English history.

In dealing with a statement made by Manager Butler that "common fame and current history" might be relied on to prove the President's course of administration, Nelson exclaimed:

"Common fame" you are to resort to! Is it possible that we have come to this? Is it possible that this great impeachment trial has reached so "lame and impotent a conclusion" as this, that the honorable manager is driven to the necessity of insisting before you that common fame is to be regarded as evidence by senators? I hope it will not grate harshly upon your ears when I repeat the old and familiar adage that "common fame is a common liar." Are the senators of the United States to try the Chief Executive Magistrate upon rumor, the most dangerous, the most uncertain, the most unreliable, the most fatal and destructive proof that ever was offered under the sun? Why, the glory and boast of the English law and of the American Constitution are that we have certain fixed principles of law, fixed principles of evidence that are to guide, to govern, to control in the investigation of causes; and one of the beauties, one of the greatest perfections of the system of American jurisprudence is that when you go into a court of justice nothing scarcely is taken by intent. There sits the judge; there are the jury; here are the witnesses who are called upon to testify; they are not allowed to give in evidence any rumor

---

[15] *Ibid.*, II, 124.

that may have been afloat in the country; they are compelled to speak of facts within their own knowledge. The case is investigated slowly, cautiously, deliberately. The truth is arrived at, not by any hasty conclusion, but it is arrived at upon solemn trial and upon patient and faithful investigation; and when the result is attained it commands the confidence of the country, it secures the approbation of the world, and that result is acquiesced in by the citizen; and if it be in a higher court it passes into the history of law and goes down to posterity as a precedent to be followed in all time to come; and, herein, senators, is the great security of the liberty that the American people enjoy." [16]

He continued to attack Butler's efforts to tie outside pressures and considerations into the trial, discussing at great length Butler's references to the "public pulse."

When Nelson had discussed further the nature of the Senate as a court and had finally turned to the content of the case by discussing the meaning of the terms "crime" and "misdemeanor" in their constitutional usage, the hour of four had arrived. Senator Yates interrupted to suggest that, if Nelson desired, the Senate might adjourn. Nelson indicated that he was fatigued, but that he would continue if the court wished. Yates then moved adjournment, and the motion was carried. Long before this time, the galleries were almost empty and most of the Senators had departed. [17] Nelson understood fully that he was not making a strong impression on his audience within the Senate chamber, but he was also aware that he was carrying out the instructions of his client.

At eleven the following morning, he took up again the nature of crime and continued on that topic for some time. Then he introduced an explosive ingredient. Two of the managers had made damaging remarks and insinuations concerning the reason Black had resigned as the President's counsel. Nelson now exposed the Alta Vela affair from the President's viewpoint but carefully avoided imputing to the four House managers an improper scheme.

After reciting several statements by Stanton to prove that the Secretary of War had held a good opinion of Johnson until the impeachment began, he launched into a discussion of the articles of impeachment one by one. In the process he took up the subject of General Lorenzo Thomas's attempt to replace Stanton as Secretary of War—which had comic-opera aspects—and for a time brought the audience under the sort of control Nelson was accustomed to maintaining from the stump. He portrayed the episode in comic-seriousness and provoked repeated bursts of laughter. Thomas had been made a laughing-stock in the questioning of witnesses, so the audience was already prepared to be amused by anything concerning him. After consuming the entire session and speaking more than seven hours in the two sessions together, Nelson concluded with an emotional appeal for justice:

---

[16] *Ibid.*, II, 135.
[17] Philadelphia *Press*, April 24, 1868.

And when the day shall come—and may it be far distant—when each of you shall "shuffle off this mortal coil," may no thorn be planted in the pillow of death to embitter your recollection of the scene that is being enacted now; and when the time shall come, as come it may, in some future age, when your own spirits shall flit among the hoary columns and chambers of this edifice, may each of you be then enabled to exclaim—Here I faithfully discharged the highest duty on earth; here I nobly discarded all passion, prejudice, and feeling; here I did my duty and my whole duty regardless of consequences; and here I find my own name inscribed in letters of gold, flashing and shining, upon the immortal roll where names of all just men and true patriots are recorded! [18]

Nelson's address was not well received by the press. The vigorously Radical Philadelphia *Press*, clamoring for the conviction of the President, ridiculed what its editor called "the national conundrum: Who is Andrew Johnson?" "The Southwestern lawyer, whose fame is 'right smart' out in Tennessee, we are afraid has not answered the inquiry, although he has substantially reproduced, through several loose and rambling columns, the famous autobiography of the ex-alderman. . . .Curiously enough, but characteristically, Andrew Johnson has managed by the introduction of this melodramatic attorney to deface the record and humiliate afresh the country. He cannot even be tried without disgrace. . . ." [19]

When the second day's portion of the speech was concluded, the same paper had a bit more moderate comment to make:

It is admitted that, having extricated himself from the difficulty incurred by his own act in answering the difficult conundrum proposed at the commencement of his speech, his arguments to-day were more pointed than those advanced by him yesterday. Notwithstanding this, he has not retrieved his lost reputation, except with the few who are aware of the fact that he is cramped by the requirements of his client, that just such a speech should be delivered at this juncture of the trial; in other words, it is gradually becoming apparent that the notes from which he speaks were prepared by the President himself, and consequently it cannot be expected that he should attain even ordinary dignity or brilliancy in his effort. [20]

The Washington *Evening Star* commented that Nelson had spoken with unmistakable earnestness and had succeeded in making some good points, but that he was tedious and his style was of the "stump school of oratory." [21] The New York *Times* advised at the end of the first day that Nelson's speech would make refreshing reading after the legal arguments heard from other speakers. But at the conclusion of his speech the *Times* condemned it as an appeal to feeling rather than judgment and

---

[18] *Trial of Andrew Johnson*, II, 187.
[19] Philadelphia *Press*, April 24, 1868.
[20] *Ibid.*, April 25, 1868.
[21] Washington *Star*, April 24, 1868.

more properly addressed to a jury than a court.[22] The *Times* also reported that Nelson's effort was looked upon as the President's own view of the case.

A somewhat friendlier comment appeared in the New York *Herald* on April 24: "Mr. Nelson's style showed little artistic finish, and his arguments were thrown around with a magnificent indifference as to point and arrangement. Some of his rhetorical flights were marvelously giddy, yet sustained without accident. On the whole his speech, which has not yet been finished, was a great impassioned appeal to defend the President without strict regard to time and place, the rules of logic, or the nicer distinctions in grammar and philology. It was the speech of a lifetime friend of the President, and if it were not as courtly, as scholarly and as unimpassioned as it might have been, it had the merit of being the sincere expression of the speaker's mind. . . ." The following day the *Herald* reported that portions of Nelson's speech were received with "evident approbation" and that it was "particularly impressive in the peroration." Editorially, the comment was that Nelson's defense was "well conceived" and would stand "as a fair example of earnest, honest eloquence." It evidently came from the heart, concluded the editorial, and carried the sympathy of the reader.

The best clue, however, to the reception among the people with whom Andrew Johnson was most concerned and to whom the address was most directly aimed—the voters of Tennessee—was not to be found in the reactions of the Northern press. Brownlow's Knoxville *Whig* had its comment to make on April 29. Brownlow knew as well as any man what would impress the voters of Tennessee; and although he was currently engaged in his most untrammeled campaign of villification of Johnson, he wrote: "We have had a friend to sit by our side and read us the entire speech. We pronounce it able, eloquent and argumentative, fully sustaining the reputation of the orator as an advocate and speaker. True, we are on the other side of the question, and confidently expect to announce in our next issue the conviction of the President, and the inauguration of his successor; but this does not blind us to the merits of Mr. Nelson's speech." If Brownlow ever gave credit to any opponent other than Nelson, the evidence has never come to light.

Twenty-five years afterward, an admirer of Nelson wrote that the address was "a mirror of the man as an advocate, and recalls vividly to mind his speeches before our Supreme Court [of Tennessee] and the juries of East Tennessee. Whatever of strength, whatever of weakness he had, is herein well displayed, and nowhere have I found so good an illustration of Colonel Nelson's combined powers of elaborate legal argument and of lofty, impassioned eloquence."[23]

Nelson's own judgment was expressed a month after the occasion:

---

[22] New York *Times*, April 24 and 25, 1868.
[23] Ingersoll, "Biographical Sketch of Thomas A. R. Nelson," *loc. cit.*

I had for weeks labored under the impression that, under the rules of court and the arrangements of counsel, I would not be permitted to address the Senate, and . . . the rule was not altered until the day before I commenced the address, when I had no sufficient time within which to arrange my crude notes and memoranda, or to condense the argument, as lawyers and public speakers are often enabled to do, by thought or reflection. Weary and fatigued after I had spoken, it was out of my power to make corrections, and I left it to the Senate reporter to make, as I believe he most faithfully did, a *verbatim* report of the speech just as it was delivered. In looking over it, I can perceive many places in which I might have applied the pruning hand of correction, and have ample reason to regret that it is not half so good a speech as I would have wished to make in so great a cause. It was intended, however, just as much for the people, the great common arbiter, as for the Senate; and while I am sensible that it falls below the exquisite standard of sublimated criticism, I flatter myself with the belief that the abuse and ridicule which have been heaped upon it by Mr. [Thaddeus] Stevens and others will cause it to be generally read and understood by the common people *now*, and that it may, even *hereafter*, survive the carefully prepared written address and the jejune platitudes and chronic denunciations of Mr. Stevens himself.[24]

Nelson was not again involved actively on the floor of the Senate for four days, during which closing arguments proceeded. But on April 28, after the conclusion of one of the managers' arguments, Nelson was advised by Butler that after the recess he was to read a statement concerning the Alta Vela case. Butler's statement was an attempt to claim that he had signed the opinion that military assistance should be used to protect American claims to Alta Vela before the President committed the act which brought impeachment. On the basis of that claim as to dates, Butler attacked Nelson strenuously for injecting an irrelevancy into the trial for the purpose of "insinuating calumny" on the part of the managers. He also said that Nelson's statement contained "every element of falsehood" and referred to him as the "veriest tyro in the law in the most benighted portion of the Southern country."[25]

This was the stump speech combat at which Nelson was far more experienced than in the formal arguments before an impeachment court, but it was expressed in terms of personal insult and imputations of dishonor that Nelson's East Tennessee opponents knew better than to use. Not even Andrew Johnson, himself, who was considered without peer in the rough and tumble debates on the Tennessee hustings, had ever dared breach comity with Nelson. As soon as Butler concluded, Nelson was on his feet, his gray eyes flashing, but he was possessed of the cold calm of righteous indignation. He began quietly by saying that the Alta Vela matter was entirely relevant and had been introduced by Manager Boutwell in his address immediately prior to Nelson's. He further demonstrated that the newspapers hostile to the President had done their best to prejudice the opinion of the public and the Senators by repeated in-

[24] Knoxville *Whig*, May 27, 1868.
[25] *Trial of Andrew Johnson*, II, 263-65.

sinuations that Black resigned because he considered the case hopeless. Nelson injected the comment that had he been leading the defense he would have met and answered every irrelevant slur cast upon the President by each of the managers. He disclaimed any intention of making an assault upon the managers and then reached Mr. Butler:

> While I treated them with civility, while I treated them with kindness, and, as I think, with very great forbearance, the honorable gentleman to-day has made imputations upon me which I hurl back with indignation and with scorn —undeserved imputations. I treated the gentleman on the other side with courtesy and kindness. He has rewarded me with insult and outrage in the presence of the American Senate. It will be for you, senators, to judge whose demeanor is most proper before you, that of the honorable gentleman who foully and falsely charges me with insinuating calumny, or my course in vindicating the President of the United States in the discharge of my professional duty here. So far as any question that the gentleman desires to make of a personal character with me is concerned, this is not the place to make it. Let him make it elsewhere if he desires to do it.[26]

Senator Yates called Nelson to order for the last remark, to which he replied that he did not wish to make use of improper language but that he hoped he would be pardoned for "repelling the strong remarks made by the gentleman on the other side." He then went into the dates of the letters involved, saying that he had had them in his possession when he first referred to the matter and that he had sent for them again and would ask permission to read them the following day. Someone asked what the point was, and Nelson launched into a specific explanation of why Andrew Johnson had refused to do as Black had asked him, going further than in his original references to the matter by accusing Black directly of acting "improperly, under those circumstances, in withdrawing his services from the President of the United States." [27]

After further statements in proof that the letters were signed after impeachment proceedings had begun and that they had been used in an attempt at blackmailing the President to act, he concluded by repeating that he would ask permission to introduce the letters the following day. Butler's comment, "I trust not until they are shown not to have been mutilated," brought an outraged exclamation of "Sir!" from Nelson. When Manager Logan said that he was certain he had not signed the letter after impeachment was "thought of," Nelson responded: "I will say with great pleasure that I had no design to misrepresent any gentleman concerned in the cause; and in order that the matter may be decided I will have the letter brought here. . . . If it shows I am mistaken, I will bring it here in fairness to the Senate; and if it shows that I am right I will bring it again in fairness to the Senate. That is all the gentleman can ask, I am sure. I may possibly be mistaken." [28]

[26] *Ibid.*, II, 266.
[27] *Ibid.*, II, 267-68.
[28] *Ibid.*, II, 268.

The following day every effort was made to muzzle Nelson and prevent the introduction of the letters. As Nelson rose with the letters in his hand, Senator Charles Sumner interrupted him with an order that he be censured by the Senate for disorderly words "apparently intended to provoke a duel or to signify a willingness to fight a duel." Sumner repeatedly interposed objection as Nelson sought the floor until not even the conviction-bent Senate majority could longer stomach the unsportsmanlike behavior. On motion of Senator Trumbull that Nelson should have permission to respond to Butler's statement of the preceding day, ignoring Butler's attempt to modify the motion so that the letters could not be read, a majority agreed on voice vote.[29]

Nelson began by saying that he intended no offense to the Senate and hoped that he would be allowed to defend himself if any action was to be taken on Senator Sumner's censure order. When he attempted to read the letters, Butler objected that they were "not genuine nor proved." Senator Davis challenged Butler's right to make objection after the Senate had granted the privilege of making an explanation to Nelson. This problem was obviated by Senator Howard's objection to the reading of the letters. Senator Hendricks, after an attempt to move on to other business was ruled out of order, moved that Nelson be allowed to read as much of the letters as would indicate date. Again the Senate majority agreed, but repeated badgering hampered even this limited permission. However, Nelson doggedly persisted over all objections until he had forced into the record the fact that the letters had only one date, that of March 9, 1868, after impeachment was under way.[30]

The following day, April 30, the first order of business was Sumner's motion of censure. A motion to lay it on the table was made, and Sumner asked for a recorded vote. The first Senator whose name was called asked that he be allowed to propose a question before voting—had Nelson intended to challenge Butler to a duel? Nelson obviously wanted no Senatorial vote of censure blemishing the legal reputation he held on such an exalted plane, but to avoid it even at the cost of secret compromise with himself as to his intentions was a price he would not pay.

It is a very difficult question for me to answer. . . . When the gentleman read his remarks to the Senate I regarded them as charging me with dishonorable conduct before the Senate, and in the heat of the discussion I made use of language which was intended to signify that I hurled back the gentleman's charge upon him, and that I would answer that charge in any way in which the gentleman desired to call me to account for it. I cannot say I had particularly the idea of a duel in my mind, as I am not a duelist by profession; but, nevertheless, my idea was that I would answer the gentleman in any way in which he chose to call upon me for it. I did not intend to claim any exemption on account of age or any exemption on account of other things that are appar-

[29] *Ibid.*, II, 280-81.
[30] *Ibid.*, II, 281-83.

ent to the Senate. That was all that I meant to signify, and I hope the Senate will recollect the circumstances under which this thing was done. . . .[31]

The motion was then laid on the table by a vote of thirty-five to ten. Even Butler had expressed a wish that the matter be dropped.

Nelson had not seen the end of Alta Vela. Thaddeus Stevens had been one of the House managers to sign the letter giving a favorable opinion on the American Alta Vela claims, and Nelson's attack as it stood in cold print in the record of the trial was damaging. A few days later Stevens opened an attack on Nelson on the floor of the House of Representatives and in the newspapers, repeating the charge that he had entered irrelevant material into the record for the purpose of assailing the motives of counsel for the prosecution. He denounced Nelson as dishonorable and a violator of elementary legal ethics, using the same line of attack as Butler, which had been countered by Nelson in the record. Nelson answered in his usual fashion with an extended newspaper "card," in which he gave the complete history of the affair and showed from the court record that both Butler and Boutwell had made insulting references to Black's resignation to discredit the President before Nelson mentioned the subject. He also pointed out that he had deposited the letters with the Senate clerk and that Butler procured them from the clerk—and had not subsequently denied their genuineness or the date of them, which made him out in error and established that they were signed after impeachment began.

Turning to Stevens's attack on his legal ethics, Nelson said that he would be glad to have his standing in the profession compared with that of Stevens's. In this connection he commented that he was at the moment retained by Andrew Johnson and by Governor Brownlow of Tennessee in a case to which the state was a party—"two distinguished citizens whose opinions differ as widely as the poles, and both of whom have known me personally ever since the commencement of my professional career." He also commented that in a long career he had generally found that when his opponent was prolific in his praises, little of importance had been said, but that "when he resorted to satire, ridicule and abuse, I had invariably uttered something that had made an impression." His parting comment was that he would be obliged to Stevens and "his newspaper associates in criticism and vituperation for a few more advertisements of the same sort; and, with a view to the interests of my distinguished client, I earnestly invite them to renew their efforts, as often as possible, to disturb his safe anchorage at Alta Vela." This was published in the Washington *National Intelligencer*, the Knoxville *Whig*, and probably other papers, at least in Tennessee.[32] The intriguing thing about its publication in Brownlow's *Whig* was that the editor, having fervently hoped and worked for conviction, filled almost half his front page with Nelson's

---

[31] *Ibid.*, II, 307.

[32] Washington *National Intelligencer*, May 11, 1868.

card. Brownlow could not refrain from taking pride in the role of his home-town friend—a reflection of the little-known private personality of the bellicose editor.

When Nelson had made his first appearance on a floor of Congress, in December of 1859, and had been aroused to some sharp exchanges by Pryor, the Virginia fire-eater, one newspaper correspondent had written his paper that the two men got a little sharper than either bargained for. "We find comfort, however, in the thought that its severity tends only to keep people from 'waking up the wrong passenger.' Nelson was waked up through mistake. If it be agreeable to him, he will be allowed to slumber through the present Congress." [33] Perhaps Nelson's last appearance in Congress conviced Butler and Stevens that they, too, had made the mistake of "waking up the wrong passenger."

Meanwhile, the suspenseful trial wore on. Evarts made the principal closing argument for the President in a fourteen-hour effort. Stanbery was too sick to be present for the last two weeks, but appeared to make a short and pointed closing:

But if, senators, as I cannot believe, but as has been boldly said with almost official sanction, your votes have been canvassed and the doom of the President is sealed, then let that judgment not be pronounced in this Senate chamber; not here where our Camillus in the hour of greatest peril, single-handed, met and baffled the enemies of the republic; not here where he stood faithful among the faithless, not here where he fought the good fight for the Union and the Constitution. . . . No, not here, seek out rather the darkest and gloomiest chamber in the subterranean recesses of this Capitol, where the cheerful light of day never enters. There erect the altar and immolate the victim.[34]

Finally, in the seventh weary week of actual trial, the case was closed on Wednesday, May 6. But the decision was not yet to come. For almost two weeks the Senate debated in closed session, and the Radical leaders conspired and intimidated to try to prevent the necessary seven Republican Senators from joining the Democrats to win acquittal. Saturday, May 16, was the long-awaited day. The vote was taken on the eleventh article of impeachment, which was deemed by the Radicals their best opportunity for conviction; and Nelson heard, with exulting heart, the Chief Justice intone "the President is therefore acquitted on this article." The President's bodyguard ran the length of Pennsylvania Avenue to the White House with the news. Nelson and Stanbery rushed from the Senate Chamber to a waiting carriage and drove careening down the avenue to the White House. As they dashed from the carriage up the steps, Nelson's lameness did not prevent him from outrunning the panting Stanbery and bursting into Johnson's study "reeking with perspiration and hot with glee." [35]

---

[33] Louisville *Courier*, December 12, 1859.
[34] Stryker, *Andrew Johnson*, 701.
[35] Milton, *Age of Hate*, 611-12.

The other articles were not voted on until ten days later, after the Republican National Convention had met; but the efforts of the Radicals to win even one of the bolting Senators were unavailing, and acquittal was voted on the other articles presented. Stanbery, Evarts, and Nelson were at the counsel table to hear the final tension-snapping words.

When Johnson had been acquitted by the recorded margin of one vote, with perhaps three votes in reserve had they been needed, Nelson departed immediately for home. On the train ride to Knoxville, he may well have pondered whether his presence on the President's counsel had actually helped. But in so close a vote as that, where acquittal depended upon "seven Republican Senators with consciences," [36] too many factors were imponderable. Senator Joseph S. Fowler, of Tennessee, was a good example. He had been elected Senator by Brownlow's Radical legislature and had had an unbroken record of supporting the congressional Radicals. He had voted to repeal the President's amnesty power, to pass the Radical Reconstruction bill over Johnson's veto, and to pass over presidential veto the tenure of office act—for the violation of which Johnson was impeached. He had also voted to repass the District of Columbia Negro suffrage bill over Johnson's veto and had announced the adoption of Negro suffrage in Tennessee as the "greatest victory since the rebellion commenced." But it was on the impeachment of the President that he chose to make his first break with the Radicals.[37] His enigmatic vote for acquittal was one of the seven Republican votes. As Nelson so often said in defense of his rule of "abundant caution," "No man on earth can tell what will happen to strike most forcibly the mind of a jury, or which point in the case the court will go off on." [38]

But there was to be little time to contemplate Johnson's past tribulations, for the President's future was immediately to demand Nelson's attention.

---

[36] Stryker, *Andrew Johnson*, 732.

[37] Alexander, *Political Reconstruction in Tennessee*, 132-33, 175. For Fowler's comments on the trial see manuscript Autobiography of Joseph Fowler, in Joseph Smith Fowler Papers (Division of Manuscripts, Library of Congress).

[38] Ingersoll, "Biographical Sketch of Thomas A. R. Nelson," *loc. cit.*

CHAPTER XIII

Unraveling Brownlowism

NELSON'S STAY IN Knoxville was brief because he was persuaded to attend the Democratic National Convention which convened in New York on July 4, 1868. The Republicans had already nominated Grant, but no one aspirant appeared in the lead as the Democratic meeting approached. Andrew Johnson wanted the nomination and believed that he might be able to capture it. Nelson had always admired Johnson's personal qualities, and three months of observing the President under terrible stress had raised Nelson's estimate of Johnson to one of true greatness. All of the defense counsel were deeply impressed. Curtis wrote his uncle during the trial: "My respect for the moral qualities of the man is greatly enhanced by my knowledge of him. . . ." [1] Stanbery told the Senate that Johnson had stood firm as a rock against all temptation to abuse his powers. "I have seen him endure day after day provocations such as few men have ever been called upon to meet. No man could have met them with more sublime patience. . . . The Constitution is as safe in his hands from violence as it was in the hands of Washington. But if, Senators, you condemn him, if you strip him of the robes of his office . . . mark the prophecy: The strong arms of the people will be about him. They will find a way to raise him from any depths to which you may consign him, and we shall live to see him redeemed, and to hear the majestic voice of the people, 'Well done, faithful servant; you shall have your reward!' " [2]

After almost three months in Washington, Nelson wished to remain in Knoxville with Mary and the children. Anne Elizabeth's children were all grown now; her youngest, Anne Helen, was about to celebrate her nineteenth birthday. Mary's eldest, Charles, was already fifteen. Even the baby, Lizzie, was ten. Soon there would be no children at home, and he loved children about him in his hours of relaxation and gaity. [3] Furthermore his practice needed his strict attention. But, whatever the personal sacrifice or professional loss, he could not deny a renewed call to serve Johnson.

In the absence of a national Conservative party to resist the Radical Republicans, Nelson had decided to recognize the necessity of compro-

[1] Stryker, *Andrew Johnson,* 652.

[2] *Ibid.,* 700-01.

[3] Joshua W. Caldwell, *Sketches of the Bench and Bar of Tennessee* (Knoxville, 1898), 282-86.

A portrait of Mary Jones, the second Mrs. Nelson, painted by Samuel Shaver. It is owned by Mrs. Charles M. Austin of Washington, D.C., and is in the possession of Mrs. J. W. Johnson, Jr., of Lookout Mountain, Tennessee. The children of Mary Jones Nelson were Charles (b. 1853), Mary (b. 1854), Valentine Sevier (b. 1855), Selden (b. 1857), and Lizzie (b. probably 1858).

mise and concession in political action and give his support to the Democratic party as the only organization effectively opposing radicalism.[4] His reluctance to attend the Democratic National Convention was overcome when it appeared Johnson needed his help. One of the Conservative leaders of Memphis, upon hearing that Nelson had doubts about going to New York, urged: "The nomination *may* depend on the vote of Tennessee and I feel certain that the vote of Tennessee will depend on your presence . . . and a full representation from East Tennessee." [5]

Nelson was selected chairman of the Tennessee delegation and chosen to place Johnson's name in nomination. He made an earnest effort to show that Johnson was the obvious man for the platform adopted and that his heroism and sacrifice would appeal to the people as would the qualities of no other candidate. The delegates and spectators interrupted him frequently to cheer his praise of Johnson and broke into a pandemonium of long-continued demonstration at the conclusion of his nominating speech. Appreciative cheers were not necessarily votes, however. Johnson was never in the lead, and his vote dropped steadily as the balloting continued. After a deadlock appeared inevitable, Horatio Seymour, the permanent chairman of the convention, was nominated over his positive declination.[6] That night Gideon Welles confided to his diary: "I do not consider the nomination a fortunate one for success or for results. Seymour has intellect but not courage. His partyism predominates over patriotism. His nomination has been effected by duplicity, deceit, cunning management, and sharp scheming." [7]

Nelson left New York in disgust and saw the ocean for the first time by returning to Knoxville via Norfolk, Virginia. Upon reaching home he discovered that it had been advertised without his knowledge that he would address a meeting at Knoxville the following Saturday. He refused to attend this or other meetings, in Virginia and Georgia, to which he had been invited. In writing Johnson about these refusals he said:

This may be, and I fear is, wrong; but feeling as I do that you have been treated with the greatest ingratitude by the very party which owes its continued existence to your firmness; that, having made the most gallant fight that ever was made in behalf of the Constitution, you deserved, above and beyond all other men, the position of leader; and that you were sacrificed, not by the people but by disappointed office hunters—I have no heart to turn round, so soon, and sing hosannas in favor of a proceeding which was utterly contrary to my judgement and feelings. At least, as I stand in the relation of counsel and nominated you as chairman of the Tennessee delegation, I have felt that it would not be becoming in me to say anything in public until I should see some evidence of your course. My action might, possibly, be mis-

[4] Nashville *Republican Banner*, February 23, 1872, carried Nelson's explanation of his collaboration with the Democratic party in 1868.

[5] John W. Leftwich to Nelson, June 22, 1868, in Nelson Papers.

[6] Nashville *Republican Banner*, July 7, 8, and 9, 1868, carried convention news with special reference to the Tennessee delegation.

[7] Stryker, *Andrew Johnson*, 747.

construed as reflecting your sentiments, altho' the public would have no right so to construe it, and, as I do not know them, I prefer to remain silent. . . .[8]

In concluding this letter Nelson made a comment that might be considered banter were it not for the seriousness with which both Nelson and Johnson viewed the matter. Rather, the remark should be taken as an indication of how deeply the Conservatives felt that the impeachment had so obviously been an attempt at political lynching that it in no way reflected upon Johnson except as a near martyr in defense of constitutionalism. "After all, I do not know but that, as far as you are personally concerned, it may be best that your political career should terminate with your present administration. You have made already a splendid name for history and some unforseen contingency might mar it in the next few years."

Nelson refused all invitations to participate in the ill-fated Seymour contest against Grant. He busied himself with the complicated questions arising from war dislocations, such as the struggle between the Methodist groups for possession of church property. In one case he described the Southern Methodist withdrawal from the mother group as an "entering wedge in the great rebellion" and declared that there was no use for such an organization as the Southern Methodist church.[9] In another case, political antagonism did not prevent Governor Brownlow from retaining Nelson together with a famous Radical lawyer to represent the State of Tennessee before the United States Supreme Court.[10]

The spring of 1869 brought renewed demands upon Nelson in the political arena—this time in the form of petitions that he seek election to the state supreme court. The Radical party regime in Tennessee continued to exist only because Brownlow had appointed Radical judges to the state supreme court in the reorganization of Tennessee. Conservative attempts to have declared unconstitutional the restrictive franchise legislation and other Radical measures had been generally unsuccessful in this Radical court, and it was clearly understood by both Radicals and Conservatives that the supreme court of the state was the key to control of the state government. Hence, the judicial elections to be held on May 27, 1869, were a source of anxiety to the Radicals and of hope to the Conservatives.

In March Nelson received a request from the spokesman for an East Tennessee group that he run for the state supreme bench. The letter suggested that the Radicals might have multiple candidates in the field and that "it has seemed to us that independent candidates, of established legal character and known integrity, acceptable to the profession and to the intelligent people, might, by combined effort, be elected." [11] A peti-

---

[8] Nelson to Johnson, July 21, 1868, Johnson Papers.
[9] Knoxville *Whig*, December 9, 1868.
[10] Brownlow to Nelson, November 9, 1868, in Nelson Papers.
[11] W. F. Cooper to Nelson, March 10, 1869, in Nelson Papers.

tion from Middle Tennessee soon reached him with the names of fifty-eight professional men and firms—saying that without regard to party, profession, or business, the signers earnestly appealed to him to become a candidate for the supreme court. "Your good name among all the people would go far towards abolishing party and sectional lines" the petitioners avowed.[12] Thirty-two members of the East Tennessee bar also petitioned him in flattering terms to seek the office.[13] After serious reflection on the greatly increased burden carried by the court since the war, Nelson agreed to announce as a candidate. But he maintained that the nature of the office was such that he would not conduct a canvass.[14]

Although Brownlow had had himself elected to the United States Senate by his legislature and had turned the governorship over to De-Witt C. Senter, the Radical control of election laws was not relaxed, and the Negro vote was kept largely intact for Radical candidates. Hence Nelson was defeated along with other challengers. Nelson's personal reputation was so highly esteemed, however, that even in Memphis, at the opposite end of the state from his home, he received more votes than the Middle or West Tennessee Conservatives on the judicial ticket.[15]

This judicial election victory was the last for the Tennessee Radicals. The steady pressure of Conservatives, both in open condemnation of Radicalism and in the many manifestations of Kukluxism, was one factor in the dissolution of Brownlow's party. Secondly, the desertion of Radical supporters continued persistently to reduce the white Radical ranks as one after another refused to support further Radical measures or considered the time ripe for relaxation of existing proscriptions. The enthusiasm of the Negroes not otherwise deflected by Kukluxism grew less as they witnessed their continued exclusion from officeholding and their poor returns in the way of public education. Furthermore, fatal dissensions and animosities were developing among the Radical factions. The collapse of Radicalism was greatly hastened by a state supreme court decision two days after the judicial elections in which Brownlow's actions in nullifying various county registrations were declared unconstitutional. The effect of this decision was to restore the privilege of voting to many thousands who would certainly vote with the Conservatives. Therefore, when the Radical party convention split over the nomination of a gubernatorial candidate, the Conservatives were elated.[16]

---

[12] Printed with Nelson's card announcing his candidacy, in Nelson Papers under date of April 27, 1869. Also published in Knoxville *Whig*, May 5, 1869.

[13] *Idem.*

[14] *Idem.*

[15] Memphis returns sent by Landon C. Haynes to Nelson, June 1, 1869, in Nelson Papers.

[16] Alexander, *Political Reconstruction in Tennessee*, 199-214.

Governor Senter, himself seeking re-election but opposed by another Radical Republican, made an enigmatic decision to end voting restrictions and restore universal manhood suffrage. This he could do because the Radical legislation giving the governor complete control of all registration commissioners worked as well in reverse. He removed most of the Radicals from those strategic positions and replaced them with commissioners who would ignore the Radical disfranchising legislation and allow all male adults to register and vote. As a result, the Conservatives hastily put candidates in the field for all offices except the governorship and swept the election, returning Senter to office in the arrangement. While this betrayal by Senter of the Radical regime control of the state could be viewed as an unmitigatedly corrupt bargain, various circumstances suggest that Senter acted from principle, having reached the conclusion that ex-Confederates had been disfranchised long enough and that the state would be safe in the hands of a coalition consisting of both Unionists and ex-Confederate Whigs. There is little doubt that he was courted by leading ex-Confederate Whigs, and it is certain that he never intended to assist the ante-bellum Democrats to get control of the state.[17]

Nelson was urged to become a candidate for the legislature in this unexpected windfall on the grounds that "so much is to be done and undone that a few old heads will be greatly needed to direct control and maybe restrain younger ones." [18] Nelson did not choose to make the race, but talk of a United States Senatorship for him also developed. At this late date the prospects looked excellent that his ambition deferred since 1851 could be gratified; and his friends urged him to consent to a contest before the legislature. However, he had expressed to Andrew Johnson a wish that Johnson might be elected to the Senate and would not consider interposing himself between Johnson and that vindication. Therefore, he refused to be considered.[19]

In the fall of 1869 the Conservative legislature set to work undoing much of the Radical Reconstruction program in Tennessee. A Constitutional Convention was authorized, and its work was approved by the people on March 26, 1870. The new constitution abruptly terminated the tenure of judges elected in the May, 1869, judicial elections by providing for their successors to be chosen in the regular state elections of August, 1870. Nelson was again persuaded to seek one of the six seats on the enlarged state supreme court, and this time was easily elected by the largest vote received by any candidate in the contest for supreme court seats.[20] When the September term of the court opened in Knox-

---

[17] *Ibid.*, 215-25.

[18] John W. Leftwich to Nelson, July 23, 1869, in Nelson Papers.

[19] Temple, *Notable Men of Tennessee*, 439; A. A. Kyle to David T. Patterson (Andrew Johnson's son-in-law), July 20, 1869, Johnson Papers.

[20] Temple, *Notable Men of Tennessee*, 177; Nashville *Republican Banner*, August 26, 1873. This latter reference is an obituary commenting on the size of Nelson's vote in this election.

ville in 1870, Nelson began a new phase of his legal career in familiar surroundings but in the unfamiliar role of judge.

Some of Nelson's acquaintances believed that he was out of his element on the bench and that judicial labors were irksome and uncongenial to him. Others afterward thought that these months were as "pleasing and agreeable to him as they were satisfactory to the profession." [21] Certainly they were busy months, for the dockets were so crowded that in one brief term at Nashville the court disposed of more than seven hundred cases. Six volumes of the court reports were required to contain the opinions written during the fourteen months Nelson was a member, and he delivered the opinion of the court in his full share of the cases. Judging by the multitudinous citing of precedents from English history and law and authorities on international law as well as from American Federal and state courts, it would appear that Judge Nelson had easily transferred to the bench the rule of "abundant caution" which had so long guided Counsellor Nelson at the bar. If he found the work irksome, it was not revealed in an unwonted brevity.[22]

One of the first tasks before the court was to reverse the former Radical judges' opinion that the Confederacy was not a *de facto* government. A great number of cases had arisen as civil suits by individuals against Confederate soldiers for damages they had committed to property. The defense that the acts were done in response to proper orders had been rejected by the Radicals on the grounds that the Confederacy was an illegal rebellion and its orders not legal grounds to justify any individual act. Nelson and other Conservative lawyers had sought repeatedly to have the Confederacy declared a *de facto* government so as to relieve from civil liability the countless thousands of individuals who had taken property under its authority. The Radical courts had not only rejected this attempt but in some cases had declared the rebellion to have been legally a conspiracy in which every participant was civilly responsible for the acts of every other person engaged. Now that the Conservatives were in possession of the courts, no time was lost. In the first term of the new court in September, 1870, at Knoxville, Nelson read the opinion of the court in the case of Smith *versus* Brazleton, declaring the Confederacy to have been a *de facto* government.[23]

Nelson approached the problem from many angles and cited many precedents from international law, domestic law, and known acts of Congress and the President of the United States during various wars. Having satisfied himself that on various grounds the Confederacy was a real government, he wrote with evident satisfaction in vindicating his own course in 1861 and 1862:

[21] Ingersoll, "Biographical Sketch of Thomas A. R. Nelson," *loc. cit.*

[22] Tennessee Supreme Court *Reports*, 1870-71, Volumes I-VI (Heiskell 1-6).

[23] *Ibid.*, I (Heiskell 1), 44-67.

Were it an original question, we would, without hesitation, declare that a government which assumed to form a Constitution, had a President and Cabinet in actual authority, a Congress that enacted laws, on most subjects of national legislation, and published them in due form and enforced them; which was recognized as a belligerent power, by two of the greatest nations on earth; was enabled to issue and keep afloat a currency; set on foot a navy that harassed the commerce of the United States throughout the world; marshalled immense armies; fought great battles, and kept the power of the United States at bay for four years, was, to all intents and purposes, a *de facto* Government; and that it required no recognition on the part of the Government of the United States, to establish a fact well known to millions of people, and which will be transmitted to future ages, in every truthful history, that has been, or may be, written, of the war.[24]

Soon after the delivery of this opinion, Nelson asked a former law partner what the people were saying about the decision. He was not able fully to appreciate the humor of the reply: "They are saying a great deal. Among other things they say that Jeff Davis, after four years of fighting, with all his armies, was unable to establish the Southern Confederacy, but that you with a few bold lines of your pen have succeeded in *setting it up*." [25]

The court never intended, on the other hand, to legalize every private act of theft in which the thief wore a uniform. The case that reached the supreme court on this point related to a soldier of the United States Army. One of the Radical judges of a lower court, intending to protect the soldier from legal claims of ex-Confederates, had ruled that a private soldier could take any property as contraband of war without special orders. Nelson wrote the opinion reversing that ruling and put into the record indignation at the behavior of both armies in East Tennessee:

Such a doctrine, if maintained and enforced, would subject peaceful citizens to the most tyrannical visitations, searches and exactions of the soldiers, and destroy every vestige of private rights and personal security. It would subject the inhabitants to the iron will of armed and lawless power, and confer upon the soldier the unlimited discretion to regard, as contraband of war, every article of property that might please his fancy, or stimulate his avarice. It would make him judge, juror and executioner, according to his own capricious, vindictive and arbitrary will, and bring the people into the most slavish, degrading and intolerable submission. Whatever may have been the practice of the armies in our civil war, such a doctrine is contrary to the spirit of our institutions, and can not, in the view of the law, be tolerated, for one moment, by the slightest sanction or encouragement.[26]

After quoting Halleck's *International Law and Laws of War* in regard to the evils resulting from irregular requisitioning and foraging by an army and citing the Articles of War of the United States, Nelson

---

[24] *Ibid.*, I (Heiskell 1), 66-67.

[25] Temple, *Notable Men of Tennessee*, 178.

[26] Branner *versus* Felkner, Tennessee Supreme Court *Reports*, 1870-71, I (Heiskell 1), 228-35.

showed his aggravation with military activity by the quotation he selected from a parallel Kentucky case:

Neither the right of impressment nor the right to exact military contributions, belongs to every petty military officer, but must come from the commander of a district of country, or a post, or an army, and not from every straggling squad who may be under the command of some inferior officer of low grade.[27]

Another critical problem resulting from the see-sawing of armies across Tennessee was related to Confederate money. After the war many suits were entered to collect damages from those who had forced creditors to take Confederate money in payment for debt—on the common law ground that duress invalidated executed contracts. This was an extremely delicate problem for the courts because there had been some real injustice done. Nelson was assigned the task of marking the tenuous line bordering duress. In Rollings *versus* Cate he held that duress must be real and personal:

. . . we cannot perceive, as a legal question, how the fear of offending the government, which may have been common to all the citizens, can be imputed as duress, in private transactions, where no threats or force were employed.

To hold that every citizen who passed, or received Confederate Treasury notes, under some general or indefinite apprehension that his failure to recognize the currency, would give offense to the Government, or any of its officers, acted under duress, and that his action can now be repudiated and disowned, would open the flood-gates of litigation, and unsettle all dealings and transactions in this State, in which that currency was employed. It would disturb the repose of society, shake the titles to property, and produce evil results, immeasurable and incalculable.[28]

On the other hand, three months later, in Bogle *versus* Hammons *et al*, Nelson clarified a case of true duress:

In that case [Rollings *versus* Cate], there was no proof of beating, imprisonment or threat; no proof of any military order; no other or higher evidence than a vague, indefinite and unsatisfactory statement that there was "a general state of fear among Union men in regard to disobeying rebel rule, or refusing to take their money; and many Union men had been arrested;" which hearsay statement was objected to and held to be inadmissible in evidence.

But there is a marked distinction between that case and the case now under consideration. Here, a stringent military order is established by proof. Here, it is shown that the order was published throughout the country. The order itself contains a threat of fine, imprisonment and confiscation. It was issued by an officer of high rank, and was circulated by soldiers who were in arms. It was not a mere *brutum fulmen*, but was vigorously executed, and created general trepidation and alarm. The defendant, Hammons, himself a soldier, artfully turned the order to his own private and personal advantage. He did not use it in aid of the cause which he had hired himself to support as a sol-

[27] *Ibid.*, 235.
[28] Tennessee Supreme Court *Reports*, 1870-71, I (Heiskell 1), 98-104.

dier, but employed it as a means of coercion, to compel a contract which he could not otherwise have obtained; and, with the view of arousing to the greatest extent the fear of his victim, actually misrepresented it [saying that General Forrest would hang any who refused Confederate money], and theatened, with it and by its assumed operation, the life of the complainant, and not merely his imprisonment or the confiscation of his property.[29]

How to undo the wrong done years before without at the same time doing a second injustice complicated this type of case. In the one mentioned above, Hammons had forced Bogle to sell him his house and farm and had moved in. Nelson's decision for Bogle in the case, noting that Bogle did not account for the Confederate money he had received from Hammons, directed that the market value of that money at the time, however slight because of acute inflation, should be accounted for by Bogle and that Hammons should account for rents and profits of the land while in his possession minus the value of any permanent improvements he had made.[30]

A great variety of cases from lower courts over which Radical judges had presided with considerable bias came to the supreme court on appeal. One of the most remarkable was Gunter *versus* Patton, in which a circuit judge charged a jury that a Unionist unwillingly conscripted into the Confederate forces was honor bound to desert at the first opportunity—and that voluntary continuance with his unit made him civilly liable for damages because of property seized by them. Again drawing on his own experience for sharper delineation, and with obvious self-justification of his course during the war, Nelson argued:

Under the laws of war, as recognized and promulgated by both belligerents in the late civil war, desertion from either army was punishable with death; and the position that a soldier in either army was under a legal obligation to incur this penalty, is simply monstrous. . . .

Viewed in the light of the Constitution and laws of the United States, and considering the Government of the Confederate States as a failure, there can be no question that while said government continued it was a usurpation. But the duties and obligations of citizens residing within its limits were not, and could not from the necessity of the case be, the same in a state of war that they were in time of peace. New, but temporary, duties and obligations arose which, it is impossible for sophistry to ignore. The authority of the rightful Government was displaced by the red hand of war. The allegiance of the citizen was suspended so long as the corresponding duty of protection could not be performed on the part of the Government. But when the Government resumed, and was able to maintain its authority, and to protect the citizens against the power of the usurper, the obligation of allegiance revived. Meanwhile, so long as the usurpation was enabled to maintain its authority, and to compel or permit the citizens to join its armies, . . . a soldier in that service could not take, nor was he required by any law, human or divine, to take upon himself the responsibility of determining, while the war and his relation as a

[29] *Ibid.*, II (Heiskell 2), 136-46.
[30] *Ibid.*, II (Heiskell 2), 145.

A picture of Thomas A. R. Nelson from the *Green Bag*, V (1893), 234.
No source for the picture is given.

soldier continued, when it would be safe for him, by desertion, to brave the
military power that controlled him. If caught in the act of desertion, no fan-
tastic or quixotic notions of sublimated patriotism would save him from the
penalty of an ignominious death, and it is unreasonable to require that he
should incur such hazard.[31]

But it was not only the judge of a lower court who might be responsible for a miscarriage of justice. From 1866 to 1869 jury service had
been denied to ex-Confederates, and Radical juries had handed in some
outrageous verdicts. In reversing one such decision, Nelson's opinion for
the court interpolated: "It was tried, moreover, on the 21st of April,
1868, when the mode of selecting juries, as then established by statute,
was of such a character as to occasion general distrust in regard to the
impartiality of jury trials in this state." [32] In another opinion he remarked that "it is not improbable that, in times of great public or party
excitement . . . gross perversions of the noblest objects of the jury trial
have occurred, in cases of great magnitude, and especially such as involve
the discretionary ascertainment of large damages." [33]

Not every case was without a light side. In one breach of promise
suit love letters in evidence were too personal to be printed in the record.
The forlorn maiden had written at one point: "Rather than have things
take the turn I see they are taking, I would rather live in a log cabin with
a dirt floor and eat hog and hominy. Pride has never been my weak
side." [34] In a slander case in which the plaintiff was suing for damages because her chastity had been publicly denied by the defendant, battery
after battery of witnesses had been called on each side—each to impugn
the character and try to destroy the testimony of the previous group. In
this case Nelson maintained that the defendant should have been permitted to try to prove the unsavory general character of the plaintiff in
order to reduce the amount of damages. He quoted Starkie on the law of
slander to the effect that unless the previous character of the plaintiff
could be shown, the court would be maintaining that a virtuous woman
was entitled to no more damages than a prostitute if her character were
assailed.[35]

Nelson's passionate devotion to personal liberty and his sensitive personality were well illustrated in a dissenting opinion. The majority of the
court upheld the constitutionality of a state law prohibiting the bearing
of arms. Nelson's dissent concluded: "Regretting, as I do, that the nobler
objects of bearing and wearing arms are too often and too horribly per-
verted, I cannot approve legislation which seems to foster and encourage
a craven spirit on the part of those who are disposed to obey the laws,

[31] *Ibid.*, II (Heiskell 2), 254-64.
[32] Witt *versus* Haun, *ibid.*, I (Heiskell 1), 166.
[33] Riles *versus* Bussell, *ibid.*, I (Heiskell 1), 294-99.
[34] Coover *versus* Davenport, *ibid.*, I (Heiskell 1), 368-84.
[35] Hackett *versus* Brown, *ibid.*, II (Heiskell 2), 264-78.

and leaves them to the tender mercies of those who set all law at defiance." [36]

Lawyers were well pleased with Nelson's extended defense of their lien rights against clients who attempted to evade proper fees.[37] And his last opinion, delivered on November 8, 1871, established the rule that was to govern sales of property by chancery decree for the next generation—the rule that an auction sale, although formally concluded, must be reopened if a prospective purchaser appeared and offered as much as ten per cent more than the closing bid.[38]

During these fourteen months Nelson's opinions were the equivalent of a full volume of six hundred pages of the Tennessee Supreme Court *Reports*. And although some division of labor along lines of special interest or experience was possible, each judge had to bear his responsibility in the decision of cases involving criminal and commercial law, equity and real estate, torts and contracts, corporate and administrative law, and constitutional and international law.[39]

During this period of judgeship, Nelson was attacked by the Radicals through the Federal courts in an attempt to unseat him and other members of the court because of disqualification under the Fourteenth Amendment.[40] Nelson's reaction was electric. He proposed to challenge the constitutionality of the ratification of the Fourteenth Amendment and to cite the instigators of the unseating movement for contempt of court. His colleagues and partner had to urge restraint upon him in the matter.[41] The Federal grand jury in Knoxville examined witnesses concerning Nelson's public letter advising support of the Confederacy which he had issued after seeing the Emancipation Proclamation in October, 1862. Evidently an attempt was being made to indict him for holding office contrary to the Fourteenth Amendment, but nothing came of this proceeding.[42]

Nelson's career as a judge ended unexpectedly and unhappily. About supper time on the evening of September 27, 1871, as he sat reading in his home on West Cumberland Street in Knoxville, his twenty-six-year-old son, David, burst through the door. David told his father that he had just shot and killed James H. Clanton, a former Confederate general from Alabama, who was in Knoxville on legal business. He called it self-defense and a duel; but the origin of the matter was obscure, and he was planning to flee Knoxville. Nelson tried to dissuade his son from leaving

---

[36] Ingersoll, "Biographical Sketch of Thomas A. R. Nelson," *loc. cit.*

[37] Hunt *versus* McClanahan, Tennessee Supreme Court *Reports*, 1870-71, I (Heiskell 1), 504-10.

[38] Ingersoll, "Biographical Sketch of Thomas A. R. Nelson," *loc. cit.*

[39] *Idem.*

[40] John Baxter to Nelson, February 13, 1871; A. O. P. Nicholson to Nelson, August, 1871, in Nelson Papers.

[41] John Baxter to Nelson, February 16, 1871, in Nelson Papers.

[42] A. O. P. Nicholson to Nelson, August 12, 1871, in Nelson Papers.

and urged him to submit to the authorities and take the consequences of his conduct rather than become a fugitive. But David was hysterically excited and left the room. After about fifteen minutes of stunned waiting for David to calm himself, Nelson went to talk further with him but could not find him. David had slipped out of his father's house, borrowed a horse from a friend without telling him why he needed a mount, and fled the city. The sheriff was soon along looking for David; and, according to the newspaper reports, the seriously ill friend who provided the horse died of shock when he learned the reason for David's request. Nelson sent another of his sons with the sheriff to seek David and try to persuade him to return. The following day the newspaper reports were extremely unfavorable to David, indicating that he had shot Clanton in a drunken rage before Clanton could draw his own gun.[43] Nelson's next few days and nights were filled with deep sorrow and apprehension.

As other information came to light, David's case began to seem more favorable.[44] David returned voluntarily the second day after the shooting and was released on twenty-five thousand dollars bond. A large number of Nelson's friends would have been honored to sign the bond; indeed, all of the needed signatures could have been procured in an hour in Knoxville. But Nelson, in his sadness, felt the need to call on old friends. He telegraphed Brownlow, then in the United States Senate as a Radical, asking him to sign; and Brownlow, sympathizing as only one who had known the same anguish could, rushed from the Senate floor to make the arrangements.[45]

The details of the Clanton affair remained shrouded in alcoholic fog and rationalization, but the general picture came into focus.[46] Clanton, a very prominent Alabama lawyer, who was at the time chairman of the Alabama State Democratic Committee, was in Knoxville as an attorney for the State of Alabama in a dispute with regard to the Alabama and Chattanooga Railroad. Clanton had been a Whig and a member of the American party, and in 1860 he had supported John Bell for the presidency, but he abandoned the Union when he considered that the North was attempting to coerce the South. He became a major general in the Confederate army and gained a reputation as being rash, impetuous, and given to violence although never mean or scheming. As a prominent Conservative during the postwar years, Clanton had, in blind rage, attacked the Radical lieutenant-governor of Alabama on the street in Montgomery. And he had also been involved in violence since his con-

---

[43] Knoxville *Chronicle*, September 28, 1871; Nashville *Republican Banner*, September 29 and 30, 1871.

[44] W. R. Sevier to Nelson, October 9, 1871, in Nelson Papers.

[45] Temple, *Notable Men of Tennessee*, 179-80.

[46] Allen J. Going, "A Shooting Affray in Knoxville with Interstate Repercussions: The Killing of James H. Clanton by David M. Nelson, 1871," in East Tennessee Historical Society's *Publications*, No. 27 (1955), 39-48.

nection with the railroad suit, brandishing a gun in Montgomery and employing force against a crowd of abusive observers. He seemed to feel that his opponents in the raliroad case were plotting to assassinate him or provoke him into a duel in the hope of having him killed. Furthermore, fellow travelers with Clanton on the train to Knoxville overheard him drunkenly bragging about what he would do to the East Tennessee Unionists when he got to their territory.

After the case in which Clanton was counsel was under way in Knoxville, on September 27, 1871, following the adjournment of the Wednesday afternoon session of Federal court, Clanton and a group of men interested in the trial were walking toward the center of town. Tomlinson Fort, an attorney for the opposing faction but friendly to Clanton, introduced him to David Nelson, who had become a practicing lawyer at Cleveland, Tennessee, not far from Chattanooga, after he left the Federal army. The Knoxville *Press and Herald* of September 29, 1871, published an account of the ensuing exchange of words based on interviews with witnesses:

Clanton . . . remarked that he "had now got through his law business and was ready to see the town." Nelson said: "I can take you where there is something very nice if you are not afraid." Clanton said pleasantly: "Do I look as if I were afraid?" Nelson replied: "I do not know whether you are or not." General Clanton replied: "I am not afraid of anything or any man." Nelson again repeated: "I do not know whether you are or not," in a manner which Clanton seemed to think insulting, and he retorted: "If you think I am, try me; name your friend, time and place, any time or any place." Nelson very excitedly said: "This time and place is as good as any. Take your stand."

Clanton, who habitually carried a gun, stepped into the street and asked Fort to step off the distance for a duel. Fort declined, protesting that David Nelson was obviously drunk and should be ignored. Nelson, meanwhile, rushed into the St. Nicholas saloon and, throwing off attempted restraints, seized a double-barreled shotgun from an adjoining store. When he emerged, he fired the two barrels in quick succession, and Clanton fired one pistol shot which struck the curb. Clanton sank into the street, dying.

According to one version, Nelson, partly hidden by some beer barrels as he came out of the saloon, rested his gun against an awning post and struck Clanton with his first blast. Clanton was unable to raise his gun high enough to hit Nelson when he fired, and then Nelson discharged the second barrel. However, Nelson claimed that as he ran from the saloon the first barrel went off accidentally and aimlessly and that he killed Clanton with the second barrel only an instant before Clanton would have had good aim.

David was indicted on a charge of first degree murder by the grand jury which had heard testimony by Tomlinson Fort and by Judge C. F. Trigg who had observed the shooting from his hotel room. Newspaper editorials expressed sympathy with Clanton's family and chagrin that he should have been killed while a guest in Knoxville. Even the state legislature adopted a resolution of sympathy and regret in the name of the people of Tennessee and sent it to Mrs. Clanton and her large family. The resolution specifically expressed no opinion as to the guilt or innocence of David Nelson. However, one of Nelson's colleagues on the supreme bench, Peter Turney, wrote him ten days after the affair that Clanton "was a bully and a brute and . . . pursued his enemies with the venom of a blood hound and with cruelty without measure." The evidence, taken altogether, suggests that Clanton was expecting to be drawn into a fight and mistook David's alcoholic blundering and pridefulness as a deliberate trap. He may have seized the initiative by baiting the much younger man into a duel and unexpectedly got the worst of it. In any case, David's liberty and perhaps his life were in danger unless successfully defended in the trial set for January, 1872, only three months away.

Nelson resolved to let nothing interfere with his son's defense and, after the Knoxville term of the court ended, sent a letter of resignation to the governor of Tennessee. Governor John C. Brown, a former Confederate general, refused to take any action on Nelson's resignation until he could attempt to persuade him to withdraw it. "I am very much grieved that you should resign, and earnestly hope that you will yet reconsider the question. . . . I sincerely hope that you will find it compatible with your sense of duty to remain on the Bench." [47] When Nelson declined to withdraw his resignation, Governor Brown replied: "It gives me much pain to have you retire from a position, that you have filled with so much credit to yourself, and universal satisfaction to the profession, and to the country." [48]

Chief Justice A. O. P. Nicholson was deeply upset by Nelson's resignation. He had written Nelson in the summer about boarding in Knoxville during the fall term of the court: "You must get me a place near you. I have been close to you for so long [less than a year] that I have a fancy for keeping up the association." [49] Upon being shown Nelson's resignation by Governor Brown, Nicholson hastened to write of his disappointment. "From the time we met at Knoxville until we closed our late term I found my heart all the time warming towards you, on account of the many noble traits of character which I saw constantly developing during our intimate association. . . ." Of the court term after David's killing of General Clanton, Nicholson said: "I knew that your feelings were lacerated by the deep family affliction under which you were suffering and against which I saw that you were struggling with a degree of forti-

---

[47] John C. Brown to Nelson, November 22, 1871, in Nelson Papers. Nelson's letter of resignation is not in Governor John C. Brown Papers in the Tennessee State Library, Nashville.

[48] *Id.* to *id.*, November 28, 1871, in Nelson Papers.

[49] Nicholson to Nelson, August 12, 1871, in Nelson Papers.

tude which was more than human. . . . In parting with you as an associate judge I wish to assure you that I deeply lament the occurrences which have resulted in what I regard as a public calamity. But I most sincerely hope that your own personal interest & happiness may be promoted by your return to the bar." [50]

Another of the supreme court judges, Peter Turney, wrote Nelson that he deeply regretted his resignation. "I had hoped that while I was a ('so called') judge I might always have you with me at our hearings and deliberations. To me, our association has been uninterruptedly pleasant increasing as we passed along together." [51] The supreme court clerk wrote that he missed Nelson very much and that "many regrets are expressed at your retirement, and many compliments and expressions of regard are uttered with all of which I heartily sympathize." [52] The bar at Nashville passed highly complimentary resolutions on Nelson—the usually empty nature of which being denied by one friend's private letter commenting: "I think [the resolutions] were an honest tribute and truthful expression of feeling and opinion. Several leading members have expressed to me privately, similar sentiments." [53]

Nelson's departure from his brother judges was clouded by more than his family burden. He was too accustomed to the sometimes fierce encounter of the legal arena to handle his judicial duties with never failing dispassionateness. In connection with one case, Nelson and another of the judges had an unpleasant disagreement that was not soothed at the time of Nelson's resignation. But perhaps the most distressing problem arose between Nelson and Nicholson. In one case Nelson had pressed his objection to Nicholson's opinion to the point that Nicholson flared up. Later, when a case was decided in which Nelson had disqualified himself because he had been counsel and about which he had much anxiety, Nelson jumped to the conclusion that Nicholson decided against him because of a grudge surviving from the previous clash. In the letter of resignation to Governor Brown, Nelson made reference to the matter.

Nicholson, who saw the resignation, responded in the same letter in which he lamented Nelson's retirement. He was mortified that Nelson should think such a trifling thing could "for an instant interfere with those warm personal feelings of attachment for you which I then cherised [sic] and never ceased to cherish." "If I had ever suspected," he declared, "when the Swan case was decided, that you supposed me capable of being in any degree influenced by the trifling occurrence in the Rogers' case, I would have resigned my seat at once, sooner than have subjected myself to such a suspicion from one who had so entirely my

[50] *Id.* to *id.*, November 30, 1871, in Nelson Papers.
[51] Turney to Nelson, December 5, 1871, in Nelson Papers.
[52] J. B. Heiskell to Nelson, December 11, 1871, in Nelson Papers.
[53] James W. Deaderick to Nelson, December 11, 1871, in Nelson Papers.

personal regard." Saying that it was the most painful act of his judicial experience to decide the case against Nelson, he reported that the other judges were unanmious in their concurrence.[54] Nicholson displayed no anger or resentment toward Nelson, only surprise and pain; and their friendship continued. Undoubtedly the obviously unnerving strain in regard to David was properly estimated by Nicholson as the cause of this temporary unreasonableness.

As his sixtieth birthday approached, Nelson was again devoting his energy to his profession—with a lucrative and challenging practice. On March 15, 1872, he recorded that he had collected during the preceding two and one-half months three thousand dollars on his judge's salary from the preceding year and more than six thousand dollars from fees.[55]

Tennessee was back on even keel from the viewpoint of the Conservatives; but Radical Reconstruction was raging in most of the South, and President Grant was seeking his second term. Nelson would find it difficult indeed to remain inactive while the Conservatives sought desperately to halt the Radical juggernaut.

---

[54] Nicholson to Nelson, November 30, 1871, in Nelson Papers.
[55] Nelson's notation is found in the Nelson Papers under date of March 15, 1872.

CHAPTER XIV

Justly Honorable

T HE FINAL EPISODE of Nelson's public career was conditioned by the persistence of Whiggery in Tennessee and other states. Leading members of the Whig party were reluctant to concede that it was dead and rarely ceased to seek some reincarnation of its much vaunted "conservative principles." In February, 1872, John Baxter, a former Whig and leading Conservative at Knoxville, asked Nelson to sign jointly with him a circular letter proposing a state convention of Conservatives as opposed to either Republicans or Democrats. Nelson had planned to take no active part in the 1872 presidential election because David's case, postponed by the January session of the court, was not settled; and he had rejected repeated invitations to run for Congress after his resignation from the court. Nevertheless, he gave Baxter's letter careful consideration and decided to sign it.[1] Reactions to this letter catapulted him into the thick of his last political encounter.

The background of the letter was the continuing strength of Whig sentiment in Tennessee after the collapse of its party organization. The John Bell campaign of 1860 had been, as far as Tennessee was concerned, simply a continuation of the Whig party under a new name. And Reconstruction in Tennessee was largely carried out by former Whigs because the Democrats had generally accepted the Confederacy and were disfranchised by the Brownlow regime.[2] The convention in January, 1865, which took the first steps in restoring civil government in Tennessee was dominated by Whigs. Of the ninety-five members whose ante-bellum political affiliations have been identified, eighty-four had been Whigs.[3] When the first legislature was elected, its overwhelming majority were old-line Whigs—a fact Brownlow commented upon triumphantly in his paper, which was still called the *Whig*.[4] In the first congressional election after the war, in 1865, none but ex-Whigs came even close to victory, and only one Democrat has been identified among the candidates.

---

[1] C. M. McGhee to Nelson, December 4, 1871; *id.* to *id.*, December 9, 1871, in Nelson Papers, reveals Nelson's refusal to run for Congress. Nelson's own explanation of the signing of the letter was published in the Nashville *Republican Banner*, February 23, 1872.

[2] Alexander, "Whiggery and Reconstruction in Tennessee," *loc. cit., passim.*

[3] *Ibid.*, 293.

[4] Knoxville *Whig*, April 19, 1865.

During 1865 some of the Tennessee Conservative Whigs were in contact with Northern Whig leaders concerning a plan to revive the Whig party nationally by re-establishing it in the South with a short platform of conservative principles which would draw the conservative-minded men of the North from both Republican and Democratic parties. Thaddeus Stevens and other congressional Radicals almost certainly knew of these plans, and this knowledge may partially account for their determination to keep the South so well suppressed that no serious third-party movement could get under way. Their "bloody shirt" propaganda served to discredit prospective Southern leadership in the eyes of Northern conservatives.[5]

Although the national party revival failed in 1865, former Whigs continued to dominate Tennessee politics. In the 1867 election all of those prominently mentioned for the governorship had been Whigs, as had been all eight of the Radical and at least six of the Conservative party congressional candidates. The only known Democrat in the contest suffered the worst defeat.[6]

By 1869 Brownlow's radical course had driven most of the former Whigs from his party, and Governor Senter's enigmatic decision to connive with Conservatives to evade the franchise laws and re-establish *de facto* universal manhood suffrage probably had strong Whig overtones. He may well have been approached by Whigs in the Conservative party with a proposition contemplating the restoration of the Whig party in the state. When Senter returned to Nashville after his re-election, he was greeted by a mass meeting which heard former Whig Governor Neill S. Brown praise him as the savior of the state. At this very time Senter privately commented to a colleague: ". . . the views you express in relation to the formation of a new party coincide fully with my own feelings & desires & permit me to assure you if such a thing be necessary between us that I never will agree to affiliate in any degree with the defunct progressive States rights Democracy in any shape whatever."[7]

Both before and after this 1869 election in Tennessee, many of the Conservative papers in the state urged avoidance of the name "Democratic" and adoption of the name "Liberal." In the 1870's the terms "Liberal" and "Conservative" were considered compatible. Men calling themselves by either term were in general agreement on supporting constitutional government against the inroads of radicalism, ending Radical party misrule in the South by returning the privilege of voting to ex-Confederates, and cleaning up the corruption in the Federal government. Some former Whigs suggested "Liberal Conservative" party as a name for the new movement. In 1870 so many former Whigs were still avoid-

[5] Alexander, "Whiggery and Reconstruction in Tennessee," *loc. cit.*, 298.
[6] *Ibid.*, 299-300.
[7] D. C. Senter to L. C. Houk, August 23, 1869, in Leonidas Campbell Houk Papers (McClung Collection, Lawson McGhee Library, Knoxville).

ing the name "Democratic" that Andrew Johnson was urged to be in Knoxville for a meeting because he was needed to indoctrinate the people with the "idea that they must adopt the Democratic name, or become Radicals." [8] Describing the coalition which had elected Senter in 1869, a Nashville newspaper correspondent wrote:

You must know that in Tennessee the proportion of Old Line Whigs is very much larger than in any of the Southern States except Virginia; but unlike the Old Line Whigs of Virginia, who were made good enough Democrats by the process and progress of the war, the Old Line Whigs of Tennessee were never reconciled to the faith of the faithful. . . . Hence the origin of the term "Conservative." It is a compromise intending to cover a great area of material having discordant antecedents, but which is united under the general principle of universal suffrage, hostility to Radical intolerance, and what they call Copperhead Bourbonism.[9]

The Whigs held a decided predominance over former Democrats even in the election of 1869 when all ex-Confederates were allowed to vote. In the state senate all eight of the prominent leaders were Whigs. This absence of Democratic leadership was hardly attributable to coincidence. One old-line Democrat wrote of his county Conservative nominating convention that the "Old Whig spirit" rekindled and a former Whig won the nomination over a candidate sponsored by the Democrats in the group.[10] In the house of representatives of the legislature elected in 1869 the Whigs had a preponderance of two to one among members whose ante-bellum political affiliations have been identified. But the Constitutional Convention of 1870 contained almost half former Democrats, and by the general elections of November, 1870, the party name "Democrat" was employed freely and interchangeably with "Conservative." [11]

Within the defeated Tennessee Radical Republican party, plans were then laid to overcome the Democrats by attracting Whigs back into a Republican party that would actually be the old Whig party of the state. Whigs within the Republican party who hoped for this result were anxious that no drastic steps be taken against the new Democratic state administration such as congressional approval of military intervention, for winning back old-line Whigs involved the necessity of maintaining a conservative policy and hoping for excesses on the part of the Democrats. The Democratic legislature elected in 1870 obligingly committed the hoped-for excesses, such as flagrant gerrymandering of the state against Republicans. But, on the other hand, national Republican leadership was plunging deeper into extreme Reconstruction measures and providing no enticement for Tennessee Whigs.[12]

---

[8] John Williams to Johnson, July 2, 1870, in Johnson Papers.
[9] Memphis *Avalanche*, August 19, 1869.
[10] Alexander, "Whiggery and Reconstruction in Tennessee," *loc. cit.*, 302.
[11] *Idem.*
[12] *Ibid.*, 302–03. See also Verton M. Queener, "A Decade of East Tennessee Republicanism, 1867-1876," in East Tennessee Historical Society's *Publications*, No. 14 (1942), 59-85.

With this state of affairs existing as the elections of 1872 approached, many Tennessee Whigs abhorred Republican radicalism but doubted that the Democratic party could provide either a suitable or a successful vehicle for opposition to the Republicans. Seymour's defeat by Grant in 1868 had impressed them greatly, and they doubted that the Democratic party would nominate a man who could do any better against Grant's bid for a second term. When a split in the Republican ranks was precipitated by the Liberal Republican movement, many Whigs were encouraged to think that their long-deferred hope for a rejuvenation of "conservative principles" was at hand. It was to these hopeful former Whigs that John Baxter addressed his circular letter in February, 1872, which Nelson, after careful deliberation, chose to support with the prestige of his name.

Nelson did not intend this letter for publication, but it immediately found its way into print in Knoxville, Nashville, Memphis, and other places in the state.[13] It deplored the corruption in the Federal administration that had allegedly become so common as to elicit little notice and charged that both the Democratic and Republican parties were so extreme in their "principles and prejudices" that neither was capable of "restoring tranquility." Neither party had shown itself disposed to wield power judiciously or constitutionally, and the history of neither entitled it to public confidence. The Liberal Republican Convention called to meet in Cincinnati was described as the result of a call by alarmed, distinguished men of both parties to "patriotic men of all parties to meet them in convention." Nelson's name was appended directly after the following paragraph:

A disorganization of the Democratic party is essential to the defeat of the Radicals. Democracy, for some years, has simply served, in a national point of view, to keep the Radicals united. Let us, therefore, like sensible men, take a new departure, and if we cannot get all we want, secure the next best thing attainable. If you concur get all the signatures you can in the next ten days and return. The call can then be published, naming the time and place for holding the convention.[14]

The strictly Democratic party press of the state bristled at this suggestion of disintegration of their party and said that Nelson's friends would be "amazed" at such "madness." Nelson's response was immediately published in the Knoxville Press and Herald and copied by other sympathetic papers. He began by explaining that he had not intended to participate actively in the presidential canvass for private reasons. "Had it been otherwise, I would not have hesitated to address the people, as I have often addressed them, either in public assembly, or through the press or by means of a circular." Then followed his explanation that the letter sent was a private one not intended for publication, but that he

---

[13] Nashville Republican Banner, February 20, 1872.
[14] Idem.

had signed it and accepted full responsibility for its contents. Turning then to the reasons for his action, he explained:

The idea of "disintegrating" the Democratic party is not of very recent origin. It prevailed so extensively in 1866 that one of the ablest bodies of men ever assembled in the United States convened in Philadelphia and virtually gave expression to it in recommending the formation of a National Conservative party. That Convention was composed of those who had been Democrats, Whigs, Republicans and rebels. I may be mistaken in the opinion, but have ever since believed that, if its actions had been cordially adopted and followed, a Conservative would have been elected President in 1868. But the Northern Democracy refused to wheel into line and were worse beaten, in the State elections that soon followed, than they ever were before or since, except in the memorable contest of 1840.

In a free government, like ours, it is scarcely possible for any man who is accustomed to think and act for himself, to find any party with whose doctrines and practices he agrees in every particular. No one man can control public opinion. Political platforms, as well as political parties, are the result of compromise and concession on the part of individuals who compose the respective parties. As it seemed impossible to get the democratic party to give up its organization and as there was no other organization opposed to Radicalism, it became necessary for those who were opposed to the Radical party to act, if they acted at all, with the democracy. The old issues which divided the democratic and old Whig parties before the war—bank, tariff, internal improvements by the general Government, and distribution of the proceeds of the public land—seemed to have been swallowed up in the vortex of revolution, and the most absorbing questions that agitated the public mind grew out of the Reconstruction policy of Congress.

Such of the old Whigs who were opposed to that policy, had no other choice than to join the Democracy in giving effect to their opposition.[15]

Nelson then turned to the subject of Andrew Johnson, maintaining that he could have been elected in 1868 had the Democrats nominated him, and criticizing sharply those Tennesseans who had refused to elect Johnson Senator after 1868. He returned to the forthcoming election with the opinion that the Republican party could not possibly be defeated without the votes of some who had acted with that party in the past but that the old-line Whigs who opposed the Radical programs had too long been trained to "hate the very name of Democracy." "Many of them are deterred from acting with that party by their ancient political antagonisms and prejudices. If a new party were formed, with a new name and a new platform, such as was contemplated by the Philadelphia Convention [of 1866], then all the friends of the Constitution and of an honest and economical administration of the government . . . would rally around its standard without feeling that they could be charged with changing their principles or going over to the camp of their political adversaries." He denied that he was trying to dictate to anyone—a charge leveled at his position—and pointed out that the letter was solely

---

[15] *Ibid.*, February 23, 1872.

to discover whether a large number concurred in the general idea to try to call a state convention. "It may be that my views are erroneous," he concluded, "and others have as much right to criticise as I have to express them. I am reluctant to believe, however, that they will fill my friends with 'amazement,' or that sensible men of any party can regard that as 'madness' which, more than five years ago, received the sanction of so august a body as the Philadelphia Convention." [16]

The editor of the Nashville *Republican Banner* discussed Nelson's card in a two-column editorial in which he disagreed completely about Andrew Johnson's chances of election and the propriety of sending him back to the Senate, even maintaining that the South made a dreadful blunder when it "arrayed itself on the side of Andrew Johnson in that suicidal fight with Congress." But differing however extensively with Nelson's views and his course in defending Johnson, the editor said of Nelson:

No citizen of the State, in the private walks of life, or who may have attained official positions of eminence by the suffrages of his fellow-citizens, enjoys a more spotless reputation, or can boast a more unimpeachable political record. A profound thinker, a sincere patriot, an honest man—eminent in the law, a jurist of acknowledged capabilities, a statesman in the truest sense, his views upon political affairs affecting the interests of his fellow-citizens, are entitled to respectful consideration and will receive it, despite unfriendly partisan criticisms, cavalierly expressed and unworthily conceived. Here is a man who expresses his views with the frank fearlessness of a statesman—not in the hesitating, calculating, uncertain and stilted sentences of the professional politician who would accompany every bold, manly brave, independent thought, with an apology for its utterance. . . . Judge Nelson need be under no apprehension, that in the estimation of genuine patriots, his circular is likely to be considered as actuated by a spirit of dictation. The people of Tennessee are far more likely to applaud the courage of a citizen of prominence and influence, who dares to speak his mind undismayed by possibilities of party ostracism or executive committee excommunication.[17]

The Chattanooga *Times* charged: "Mr. Nelson belongs to that class of old line Whigs of which the Nashville *Banner* is the favorite representative, who are moved to phrenzy by the name of democracy, like a mad bull at the matador's flag, or a turkey gobbler by a red bandana handkerchief." [18] This was a remarkable description to apply to the chairman of the Tennessee delegation to the last Democratic National Convention, who had nominated Andrew Johnson for the presidency.

It is true that some Tennessee Whigs became Radicals rather than be called Democrats—in the words of one observer, "men of some ability who forgot to be patriots to remember they were Whigs." [19] Others became firm Democrats—forgetting to be conservatives to remember they

[16] *Idem.*
[17] *Idem.*
[18] Quoted in the Nashville *Republican Banner*, February 27, 1872.
[19] Alvan C. Gillem to Andrew Johnson, September 30, 1866, in Johnson Papers.

had been Confederates. Nelson's attitude might well have been expressed
as a paraphrase of Lincoln's famous letter to Horace Greeley on slavery
and the Union: If there be those who would not oppose radicalism unless
they could at the same time save the Democratic party, I do not agree
with them. If there be those who would not oppose radicalism unless
they could at the same time destroy the Democratic party, I do not
agree with them. If I can defeat Radicalism by co-operating with Democrats, I will do it; if I can defeat it by opposing Democrats, I will do it;
and if I can defeat it by sometimes opposing and sometimes supporting
Democrats, I will also do that. What I do about parties, I do because I
believe it will help save the nation from radicalism.

A Tennessee delegation was sent to the Cincinnati convention of the
Liberal Republicans, but Nelson would not be a member of the delegation. He also refused overtures that he run as an independent candidate
for the governorship against the Democratic nominee. Partly because of
Nelson's reluctance, the Tennessee Conservative movement leaders decided not to contest the state elections but concentrate on the national
movement.[20] The Cincinnati convention named Horace Greeley, whom
Nelson and the Tennessee delegation had opposed; but it adopted a platform arraigning Grant's administration for corruption and "bloody shirt
waving" and demanding the immediate and complete elimination of
Radical Reconstruction in the South.

The Tennessee partisans of the Liberal Republican movement held a
state convention in Nashville on May 20, 1872. Nelson had been approached as to his willingness to be nominated as elector-at-large on the
Greeley ticket if not expected to canvass and had written a letter declining to be considered.[21] However, on the meeting day of the convention,
Nelson received a telegram from Nashville notifying him that he had
been nominated for the position. His letter had been read to the convention, and the fact that his private and business affairs would prevent
a speaking tour had been made known, "but the sentiment universally
prevailed that the liberty taken with your name was absolutely indispensable to the very life of the movement." "The moral force of your
name," continued the telegram, "in connection with a popular movement against aggressive and arrogant partizan dictation was necessary
to shield the cause locally from partizan ridicule. . . . Your declination
would not only embarrass but it would sadly discourage many of us of
the younger generation of liberals from the late rebel ranks, who yearn

---

[20] A. S. Colyar to Nelson, March 6, 1872; *id.* to *id.*, April 21, 1872; Albert Roberts
to *id.*, March 25, 1872, in Nelson Papers. See also Clyde L. Ball, "The Public Career
of Colonel A. S. Colyar, 1870-1877," in *Tennessee Historical Quarterly*, XII (1953),
23–47, 106–28, and 213–38. Pages 217–22 of this latter reference discuss the third party
movement and Colyar's support of Greeley.

[21] Albert Roberts to Nelson, May 11, 1872, in Nelson Papers.

for leaders of heroic mold and moral courage instead of the small intriguers and demagogues of the hour." [22]

Emerson Etheridge, West Tennessee Whig and gubernatorial candidate of the Conservative party against Brownlow in 1867, was named as the other elector-at-large with Nelson. From his nomination by the Liberal Republican faction in Nashville on May 20 until the meeting of the Democratic National Convention in July, Nelson took no action. On July 10 the Democrats swallowed their pride and also nominated Greeley, the man who had said: "I do not say that all Democrats are rascals, but it is undeniably true that all rascals are Democrats." [23] The next day Nelson wrote his letter of resignation as electoral candidate, saying that he had been very reluctant for private reasons to canvass and would have resigned earlier but for the fear that the Democratic Convention would not accept Greeley. If Grant, Greeley, and a third candidate nominated by the Democrats had been in the contest, Nelson felt that he would have been compelled to campaign for Greeley in Tennessee.[24] He expressed pleasure at the action of the Democrats and saw no further need for a Tennessee Greeley electoral ticket other than the one the Democrats would put in the field. He made an address at a Knoxville ratification meeting for Greeley, saying that Greeley was not his first choice personally or politically but that in politics there must be concession. He was pleased that Greeley was a life-long Whig and that his running mate was a life-long Democrat, making it a truly bipartisan ticket. He condemned the Grant administration extensively and gave his full support to Greeley.

Nelson's private reasons for not desiring to canvass included the fact that David's murder trial was still not settled, having been postponed again on July 9, 1872, because of the absence of Judge Trigg, a material witness.[25]

The last requests that Nelson received for his political support were in behalf of Andrew Johnson. Johnson had entered a state-wide contest for congressman-at-large as an independent against Republican Horace Maynard and Democrat Frank Cheatham, a former Confederate general. Nelson was urged to come to Middle Tennessee to help in Johnson's campaign; and when Johnson was unable to attend a rally in his behalf at Nashville, Nelson was implored to speak in his place because "we look upon you as being his closest and most intimate friend. . . ." [26] With the

---

[22] *Id.* to *id.* (telegram), May 20, 1872, in Nelson Papers.

[23] Stryker, *Andrew Johnson*, 800.

[24] Nelson's letter of resignation was published in the Nashville *Republican Banner*, July 13, 1872.

[25] Going, "A Shooting Affray in Knoxville with Interstate Repercussions: The Killing of James H. Clanton by David M. Nelson, 1871," *loc. cit.*

[26] A. S. Colyar to Nelson, October 13, 1872; *id.* to *id.*, October 24, 1872, in Nelson Papers.

Democrats divided, Maynard won the election; however, Johnson had been given an opportunity to defend his record in all parts of the state.

The political kettle continued to boil as 1873 opened, and on February 5 Nelson received an ardent political letter inquiring, "Can we not unite in the next canvass, the Union Johnson Democrats, the old line Union Whigs, like yourself and the Republicans and forever control the state?" [27] Certainly there was work to be done in the political arena—a nation to be rescued from radicalism; and Nelson might well have expected to render important service toward that end. But, for him, there would be no "next" canvass.

David Nelson's trial finally began on May 27, 1873, although Judge Trigg was still not present. The defense pleaded self-defense against a reckless, violent, and dangerous man. Thomas H. Caldwell, a witness called by the prosecution, admitted under cross-examination that Clanton was in a very belligerent mood and was evidently expecting to be challenged to a duel. Caldwell also believed that when Nelson came out of the saloon, Clanton said something like "I am ready for you." A saloon keeper testified that he thought Nelson's first shot an accidental one and his second shot a reply to Clanton's. Other witnesses were examined on the point that Clanton was a dangerous, fighting man when intoxicated. The trial was concluded on May 30 when the jury deliberated only five minutes before acquitting Nelson. Reactions in Alabama were unfavorable—the Montgomery *Advertiser* calling the trial a farce. But the matter was legally finished.[28]

Nelson continued to teach his large Sunday School class of adults and young people at the Second Presbyterian Church of Knoxville during the hot summer weeks of 1873. He had also accepted another civic responsibility as president of the Knoxville Library and Reading Room Association.[29] Late in August he delivered a lecture on the Bible before his church congregation.[30] Cholera was epidemic in East Tennessee that summer, but Nelson was in excellent health and was very careful to take the customary precautions against the disease. Despite such efforts, however, on Wednesday, August 20, he began to feel ill. He kept at his legal work until Friday, then he went to bed and had a physician called. Friday night and Saturday, although very ill, he was not thought to be in an alarming condition. Dr. Sevier of Jonesboro, a relative of Nelson's,

---

[27] W. J. Hill to Nelson, February 5, 1873, in Nelson Papers.
[28] Going, "A Shooting Affray in Knoxville with Interstate Repercussions: The Killing of James H. Clanton by David M. Nelson, 1871," *loc cit.*
[29] Notice of election is in the Nelson Papers under date of March 26, 1873.
[30] Temple, *Notable Men of Tennessee*, 180-81.

was sent for on Saturday and arrived on the midnight train to find him suddenly sinking into a coma. He was roused once with stimulants but slipped into semi-consciousness.[31] He probably realized his condition because snatches of his favorite hymn could be made out by his family at the bedside:

> Yet a little while we linger,
> Ere we reach our journey's end;
> Yet a little while to labor,
> Ere the evening shades descend;
>
> On the banks beyond the river,
> We shall meet no more to sever;
> In the bright, the bright forever
> In the summer-land of song.[32]

At 6:30 on Sunday morning, August 24, 1873, death came. Nelson's body was interred at dusk the same day in Gray Cemetery in the presence of a grieving throng who had not even known of his illness. As his casket was carried to the grave, one hand supporting it was that of Horace Maynard, who had voted to impeach Andrew Johnson and was still a Radical Republican. Another was that of John Baxter, who had sought election to the Congress of the Confederate States of America. A third was that of Oliver P. Temple, who opposed Nelson politically from 1864 until his death but would write of him: "There was in him a combination of high qualities such as is seldom seen united in any single individual. . . . Even his political enemies, in times of high excitement, never doubted his honesty and good faith. . . . [They] would have entrusted their lives—their all—to his honor and his keeping." [33]

After an extended obituary the Knoxville *Chronicle*, which had supported Grant while Nelson denounced him less than a year before, concluded:

His temperament was such that he was likely to be most favorably known by those most intimate with him. Those who saw only the stern, unrelenting champion at war with oppression, injustice, and all manner of wrong, would hardly suspect a heart as gentle as mercy, and a charity as open as the light to every appeal of suffering and want. The Roman solidarity of his character gave way at times to an almost boyish and frolicsome playfulness. This phase of his nature flashed out in the short intervals of consciousness during the dreadful hours of his last night. When . . . he was roused for a few moments from the fatal lethargy that was stealing over him, he recognized his old friend, Dr. Sevier, and addressed him pleasantly, *Quid agis*—(what are you doing,) and used other similar expressions habitual to him when in a lively mood. And so he passed away into the Unknown, and we all feel that a great light has gone out.[34]

---

[31] Obituary in Knoxville *Chronicle*, August 27, 1873.
[32] *Idem.*
[33] Temple, *Notable Men of Tennessee*, 167 and 180.
[34] Knoxville *Chronicle*, August 27, 1873.

Nelson's young friend, the editor of the Nashville *Republican Banner* who yearned "for leaders of heroic mold," wrote that to attempt to sketch the life of such a man would be to essay a political history of Tennessee for at least a quarter of a century. And this was written about a man who was briefly a prosecuting attorney, fourteen months a judge, and once a congressman. But perhaps another of the editor's comments would have pleased Nelson most: "Truly has the archer struck a shining mark. For in the long roll of victims to the pitiless scourge . . . there will be found no more honored and *justly honorable* name than that of Judge Thomas A. R. Nelson . . . a man of large heart and large brain; a conscientious Christian; a sternly honest man—one of the noblest Romans of them all." [35]

If Nelson had had an opportunity to pass his life in review, surely he would have found himself in agreement with Cyrano de Bergerac that a man should not, "like the obscure creeper clasping a tree-trunk, and licking the bark of that which props it up, attain to height by craft instead of strength," but rather "scorning to be the parasite, the creeper, if even failing to be the oak, rise, not perchance to a great height . . . but rise alone!"

---

[35] Nashville *Republican Banner*, August 26, 1873.

An Appraisal

THIS, THEN, IS THE PORTRAIT of a leader called Conservative. A host of East Tennesseans recognized him as one of their own and were gratified by his love of their "secluded land." Admiration of his sheer ability at the bar and on the stump was heightened by esteem for his high sense of mission as a lawyer and by his clients' confidence in his utter devotion to their interests. His audiences took delight in his love of combat in law or politics, together with his sense of fair play in either arena, and they commended his sensitiveness in matters of personal honor and his gentlemanly treatment of worthy adversaries. Almost all who knew him revered his rigid integrity and sincerely appreciated the caution with which he reached conclusions. The lucid, confident, and informed presentation of his views generally made deep impressions on his hearers. But perhaps the tap root of his leadership was planted firmly in the general recognition by his constituents of his boundless efforts to serve them through school and church, law and politics.

His conservatism was displayed in many ways. He abhorred extreme departures from established norms—such as secession and "higher law" doctrines, polygamy and floods of non-English immigrants, vindictiveness and political proscription. He believed strongly in the institution of the family, carefully-considered marriages, and the fostering of family interests even at the expense of career. His sense of continuity, which is the hallmark of conservatism, was revealed not only in his devotion to family but also in the careful conservation of his personal papers. And he always sought to defend those things which he held to be essential bulwarks against radical alteration of the culture he so highly valued. Among those bulwarks he included political democracy in the only setting he deemed practicable, united under the Constitution; freedom for the individual and its implementing agency, the bench and bar; Anglo-American predominance in the population; and Protestant Christian ascendancy within the framework of separation of church and state.

His perspective may not always have been the broadest, and he was harshly denounced for inconsistency by some—including even his own son. But alike in the trackless expanse of the calm and in the swirling currents of the vortex he resolutely plotted the conservative course, willingly risking ridicule and party excommunication, loss of property and liberty, and once even life itself.

Critical Essay on Authorities

Manuscripts

The Thomas A. R. Nelson Papers are in the McClung Collection of the Lawson McGhee Library, Knoxville, Tennessee. These papers consist of a voluminous collection of letters received, letters sent and recovered, copies of letters sent, manuscript speeches, professional papers, and clippings and broadsides. Nelson kept scrapbooks in very orderly form and amassed nineteen scrapbooks pertaining to the years from 1839 to 1872. In these scrapbooks he pasted newspaper clippings and other printed materials from a wide range of sources; and he hand indexed each volume to use as a ready reference in his public addresses. The unfortunate thing about the collection from the viewpoint of the biographer is that it has been stripped of all personal correspondence between members of the Nelson immediate family. Not a single letter remains between Nelson and either of his wives, and only two from any of his nine children, which escaped the notice of the person stripping family letters because they were signed Ecila Noslen [Alice Nelson]. One copy of a letter to a daughter from Nelson is in the collection. There is no evidence that the bulk of the family personal letters is extant.

Important letters from Nelson or bearing directly on his life are located in the John Bell Papers (Library of Congress), the David Campbell Collection (Duke University Library), the Andrew Johnson Papers (Library of Congress), and the Oliver P. Temple Papers (University of Tennessee Library). A few items of value were located in the Papers of Abraham Lincoln (Library of Congress), the Joseph Smith Fowler Papers (Library of Congress), and the Leonidas Campbell Houk Papers (McClung Collection, Lawson McGhee Library, Knoxville). An item of value for one phase of the study was a typescript entitled The Southern Unionist and written by Samuel M. Arnell, Jr. This is based on an original manuscript by Arnell, Sr., written as a participant in Tennessee Reconstruction. The original Arnell manuscript is not available; the one by his son is in the possession of Professor Stanley J. Folmsbee of the University of Tennessee. A diary of great value for its hostile view of Nelson's Civil War course is the diary of William G. McAdoo, Sr., 1857-1868, owned by Mr. Brice McAdoo Clagett and deposited with Mrs. Clayton Platt of Ambler, Pennsylvania. A copy of entries pertinent to East Tennessee was loaned to the writer by Professor Stanley J. Folmsbee.

Of great value for direct information on Nelson as well as for community background data were the unpublished, original returns of the assistant marshals for the Seventh Census of the United States (1850) and the Eighth Census of the United States (1860) taken in Carter and Washington counties. These original returns for Schedule IV are deposited in the Duke University Library, presumably because at the time of their distribution to the states by the Census Bureau the Tennessee authorities did not request them.

Published Writings of Thomas A. R. Nelson

Although Nelson was not a professional writer he did write a great quantity of material for publication in one form or another. His close personal friendship with William G. Brownlow opened the columns of Brownlow's Whig (published at Jonesboro and later at Knoxville) to Nelson's many letters to the public and political addresses. Many of these newspaper pieces were actually long pamphlets, filling many columns of very fine print; and they throw valuable light on Nelson's thinking because he was very much in the habit of going before the public in writing on any suitable occasion. They take on additional value from the well-documented tendency of Nelson to glory in perfectly candid or even painfully frank explanations. Some of the more important of these public letters or speeches, published usually in more than one paper, may be found in one form in each of the following: Jonesboro *Whig*, April 28 and May 12, 1841; Knoxville *Whig*, November 29 and December 20, 1851, June 7, 1856, May 31, 1859, June 8 and August 24, 1861, May 27, 1868; Nashville *Republican Banner*, June 28, 1861; Knoxville *Press and Herald*, February 21, 1872.

During his one term in Congress Nelson made one short and two long addresses, found in the *Congressional Globe*, 36 Cong., 1 Sess., 46-48 and 50-52; *ibid.*, Appendix, 190-95; and *ibid.*, 36 Cong., 2 Sess., Appendix, 106-11. During his service as counsel to Andrew Johnson in the impeachment trial he made many brief appearances and delivered an extended closing address found in *Trial of Andrew Johnson*, 3 vols. (Washington, 1868), II, 118-87.

Nelson's thinking during the crucial year, 1863, would remain unknown if it were not for the valuable poems and extended notes which he published anonymously in 1864: [Thomas Amis Rogers Nelson], *Secession; or, Prose in Rhyme, and East Tennessee, a Poem* (Philadelphia, 1864).

His opinions written as judge of the Tennessee Supreme Court fill the equivalent of about six hundred pages and are found scattered through the *Reports* of that court for 1870-71 which appeared in six volumes (Heiskell 1 through 6). These opinions not only reveal the quality of Nelson's legal powers but also contain numerous revealing passages relating to events through which he had lived.

Biographies, Biographical Sketches, and Reminiscences

There is no biography of Nelson, but two biographical sketches by contemporaries furnish an intimate picture of the man nowhere else found: Henry M. Ingersoll, "Biographical Sketch of Thomas A. R. Nelson," in Bar Association of Tennessee *Proceedings* (Nashville), Twelfth Annual Meeting (1893), 152-66; and Oliver P. Temple, *Notable Men of Tennessee from 1833 to 1875* (New York, 1912), 166-81. The latter reference also contains sketches of most of Nelson's more prominent East Tennessee contemporaries and is of basic value to this study. Temple was an active participant in many of the important struggles of Nelson's career, sometimes as supporter of Nelson and sometimes as opponent. Two other very short sketches are: Joshua W. Caldwell, *Sketches of the Bench and Bar of Tennessee* (Knoxville, 1898), 282-86; and John W. Green, *Lives of the Judges of the Supreme Court of Tennessee, 1796-1947* (Knoxville, 1947), 150-54. Many valuable references to Nelson appear also in Oliver P. Temple, *East Tennessee and the Civil War* (Cincinnati, 1899). Genealogical information on the Nelson family may be found in a scrapbook of clippings from the Knoxville *Sentinel* of articles by one of Nelson's sons, Selden Nelson. The scrapbook is entitled East Tennessee: History and Genealogy, and is located in the McClung Collection of the Lawson McGhee Library, Knoxville.

Studies of Nelson's contemporaries found most useful were: E. Merton Coulter, *William G. Brownlow, Fighting Parson of the Southern Highlands* (Chapel Hill, 1937); James W. Bellamy, "The Political Career of Landon Carter Haynes" (M. A. thesis at the University of Tennessee, 1952); George Fort Milton, *The Age of Hate: Andrew Johnson and the Radicals* (New York, 1930); Lloyd P. Stryker, *Andrew Johnson: A Study in Courage* (New York, 1936); and Joseph Howard Parks, *John Bell of Tennessee* (Baton Rouge, 1950). Other biographical studies employed were: Albert V. Goodpasture, "John Bell's Political Revolt and His Vauxhall Garden Speech," in *Tennessee Historical Magazine*, II (1916), 254-63; Robert Cassell, "Public Career of Newton Cannon" (M. A. thesis at Vanderbilt University, 1930); Clyde L. Ball, "The Public Career of Colonel A. S. Colyar, 1870-1877," in *Tennessee Historical Quarterly*, XII (1953), 23-47, 106-28, and 213-38; George Fort Milton, *Eve of Conflict; Stephen A. Douglas and the Needless War* (New York, 1934); Arda S. Walker, "John Henry Eaton, Apostate," in East Tennessee Historical Society's *Publications*, No. 24 (1952), 26-43; Gregg Phifer, "Andrew Johnson Versus the Press in 1866," in East Tennessee Historical Society's *Publications*, No. 25 (1953); *id.*, "Andrew Johnson Takes a Trip," in *Tennessee Historical Quarterly*, XI (1952), 3-22; *id.*, "Andrew Johnson Argues a Case," in *ibid.*, 148-70; *id.*, "Andrew Johnson Delivers His Argument," in *ibid.*, 212-34; *id.*, "Andrew Johnson Loses His Battle," *ibid.*, 291-328; Ray Gregg Osborn, "Political Career of James Chamberlain Jones, 1840-1857," in *Tennessee Historical Quarterly*, VII (1948), 195-228 and 322-34; James G. Randall, *Lincoln the President: Springfield to Gettysburg*, 2 vols. (New York, 1945); Carl Sandburg, *Abraham Lincoln: The War Years*, 4 vols. (New York, 1939); E. I. McCormac, *James K. Polk, A Political Biography* (Berkeley, 1922); Powell Moore, "James K. Polk and Tennessee Politics, 1839-1841," in East Tennessee Historical Society's *Publications*, No. 9 (1937), 33-39; L. Paul Gresham, "The Public Career of Hugh Lawson White," in *Tennessee Historical Quarterly*, III (1944), 291-318; and *Biographical Directory of the American Congress, 1774-1927* (Washington, 1928).

Histories, Monographs, and Collections

Two general histories of Tennessee furnish ready background and continuity: Philip M. Hamer, *Tennessee: A History, 1673-1932*, 4 vols. (New York, 1933); and John Trotwood Moore and Austin P. Foster, *Tennessee, The Volunteer State*, 4 vols. (Nashville, 1923). These volumes also contain considerable biographical material about Tennessee individuals. Very useful information in studying political geography of Tennessee is found in Austin P. Foster, *Counties of Tennessee* (n.p., 1923). County by county election returns are compiled in *The Tribune Almanac . . . 1838 to 1868* (New York, 1868).

Of great importance in an understanding of Nelson's childhood and early years are: Stanley J. Folmsbee, "Blount College and East Tennessee College, 1794-1840," in East Tennessee Historical Society's *Publications*, No. 17 (1945), 22-50; *id.*, "The Laws of East Tennessee College, 1821," *ibid.*, No. 16 (1944), 97-108; Laura E. Luttrell, "One Hundred Years of a Female Academy: The Knoxville Female Academy, 1811-1846; The Tennessee Female Institute, 1846-1911," *ibid.*, No. 17 (1945), 71-83; Frank Merritt, *Early History of Carter*

County, 1760-1861 (Knoxville, 1950); and Paul M. Fink, "Methodism in Jonesboro, Tennessee," in East Tennessee Historical Society's *Publications,* No. 22 (1950), 45-59.

Nelson's role in the origins of the Whig party in Tennessee and the issues developed during the life of the Whig party involved extensive use of the following: Thomas P. Abernethy, *From Frontier to Plantation in Tennessee* (Chapel Hill, 1932); *id.,* "The Origin of the Whig Party in Tennessee," in *Mississippi Valley Historical Review,* XII (1925-26), 504-22; Thomas B. Alexander, "The Presidential Campaign of 1840 in Tennessee," in *Tennessee Historical Quarterly,* I (1942), 21-43; E. Malcolm Carroll, *Origins of the Whig Party* (Durham, 1925); Arthur C. Cole, *The Whig Party in the South* (Washington, 1913); Stanley J. Folmsbee, *Sectionalism and Internal Improvements in Tennessee* (Knoxville, 1939); James W. Holland, "The Building of the East Tennessee and Virginia Railroad," in East Tennessee Historical Society's *Publications,* No. 4 (1932), 83-101; Powell Moore, "The Political Background of the Revolt Against Jackson in Tennessee," in *ibid.,* No. 4 (1932), 45-66; *id.,* "The Revolt Against Jackson in Tennessee, 1835-1836," in *Journal of Southern History,* II (1936), 335-59; Ulrich B. Phillips, "The Southern Whigs, 1834-1854," in *Turner Essays in American History* (New York, 1910); Charles Grier Sellers, Jr., "Who Were the Southern Whigs?" *American Historical Review,* LIX (1953-54), 335-46.

Indispensable to an understanding of the American party in Tennessee during the 1850's, as a background for Nelson's participation, were: Ray Allen Billington, *The Protestant Crusade, 1800-1860* (New York, 1938); Sister Mary de Lourdes Gohmann, *Political Nativism in Tennessee to 1860* (Washington, 1938); Murry Bryant Measamer, "A History of the Know-Nothing Party in Tennessee" (M. A. thesis at the University of Tennessee, 1931); and W. Darrell Overdike, *The Know-Nothing Party in the South* (Baton Rouge, 1950).

The literature of sectional controversy is almost boundless. Those studies found of direct value for Nelson's biography were: Mary R. Campbell, "The Significance of the Unionist Victory in the Election of February 9, 1861, in Tennessee," in East Tennessee Historical Society's *Publications,* No. 14 (1942), 11-30; Avery O. Craven, *The Growth of Southern Nationalism, 1848-1861* (Baton Rouge, 1953); Margaret B. Hamer, "The Presidential Campaign of 1860 in Tennessee," in East Tennessee Historical Society's *Publications,* No. 3 (1931), 3-22; Joseph H. Parks, "The Tennessee Whigs and the Kansas-Nebraska Bill," in *Journal of Southern History,* X (1944), 308-30; and Kenneth M. Stampp, *And the War Came: The North and the Secession Crisis, 1860-61* (Baton Rouge, 1950).

Nelson's Civil War years were necessarily ones of inaction in most respects, and secondary works were not employed in any specific sense other than background material. With the coming of the Reconstruction Era Nelson resumed his active work, and the following were found most useful: Thomas B. Alexander, *Political Reconstruction in Tennessee* (Nashville, 1950); *id.,* "Whiggery and Reconstruction in Tennessee," in *Journal of Southern History,* XVI (1950), 291-305; Howard K. Beale, *The Critical Year: A Study of Andrew Johnson and Reconstruction* (New York, 1930); Walter L. Fleming, ed., *West Virginia Documents Relating to Reconstruction* (Morgantown, West Virginia, 1904); *id.*, ed., *Documentary History of Reconstruction*, 2 vols. (Cleveland, 1906); "Notes of Colonel W. G. Moore, Private Secretary to President Johnson, 1866-1868," in *American Historical Review*, XIX (1913-14), 98-132; James W. Patton, *Unionism and Reconstruction in Tennessee, 1860-1869* (Chapel Hill, 1934); Verton M. Queener, "The Origin of the Republican Party in East Tennessee," in East Tennessee Historical Society's *Publications*, No. 13 (1941), 66-90; *id.*, "A Decade of East Tennessee Republicanism, 1867-1876," in *ibid.*, No. 14 (1942), 59-85. Of great value with regard to a matter of deep personal alarm to Nelson in his last years was Allen J. Going, "A Shooting Affray in Knoxville with Interstate Repercussions: The Killing of James H. Clanton by David M. Nelson, 1871," in East Tennessee Historical Society's *Publications*, No. 27 (1955), 39-48.

Contemporary Newspapers

Of value beyond measure to the student of Nelson's career was his relation to William G. Brownlow. Brownlow was a life-long personal friend of Nelson's and a political supporter until 1862. Brownlow's paper, the *Whig*, was edited in Nelson's home town of Jonesboro from 1844 to 1849 and in Knoxville from 1849 to 1869 with the exception of suspension during the Civil War. Brownlow published news stories, editorials, and proceedings relating to Nelson on every possible suitable occasion. Furthermore, Nelson's proclivity to explain his position or his actions in detailed letters to the public found a ready outlet in the *Whig*. More than one issue of that paper had its front page covered almost completely with an address or a public letter by Nelson. The public career of Nelson to 1862 could almost be written from the files of the *Whig*. In the Library of Congress is deposited the editor's own file of the *Whig*, unbroken and replete with marginal comments written in by the editor's son, John Bell Brownlow. Another paper of importance was the Nashville *Republican Banner* (1837-1875), Whig party paper in the ante-bellum period and a Conservative party organ during Reconstruction. In this latter period Nelson found a friendly outlet in the *Republican Banner* after the Knoxville *Whig* had ceased publication upon the departure of its editor to the United States Senate.

Other newspapers with the periods used were: Jonesboro (Tennessee) *Express* (1861); Knoxville *Chronicle* (1873); Knoxville *Commercial* (1866); Knoxville *Register* (1862); Louisville *Courier* (1859); Memphis *Appeal* (1861); Memphis *Avalanche* (1869); Nashville *American* (1851); Nashville *Banner* (1836); Nashville *Daily Press* (1865); Nashville *Dispatch* (1865); Nashville *True Whig* (1851); Nashville *Whig* (1840); Nashville *Union* (1836-65); New York *Herald* (1868); New York *Times* (1868); Philadelphia *Press* (1868); Richmond *Enquirer* (1861); Richmond *Whig* (1861); Washington *National Intelligencer* (1868); Washington *Star* (1859, 1868). The major files have been searched for all Tennessee contemporary papers and for national papers at times of Nelson's emergence upon the national scene. The above dates indicate only those dates under which material was located that proved directly useful.

Published Government Documents

Material important for concrete background delineation was taken from the *Sixth*, *Seventh*, and *Eighth* censuses of the United States, and also from the Tennessee State Planning Commission, Preliminary Population Report (Nashville, 1935), a mimeographed, bound volume. Items of value were taken from the Tennessee *House Journal*, 1865-66, and from the *Acts of Tennessee*, 1843-44 and 1865-66. And many valuable references to Nelson were found in the *War of the Rebellion: A Compilation of the Official Records of the Union and Confederate Armies*, 128 vols. (Washington, 1880-1901).

Nelson's own speeches and judicial opinions are found in the *Congressional Globe*, 36 Cong.; in the *Trial of Andrew Johnson*, 3 vols. (Washington, 1868); and in the Tennessee Supreme Court *Reports* for 1870-71, 6 vols. (Heiskell 1-6).

Index